Taming the Electoral College

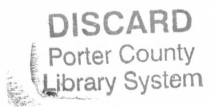

Taming the
Electoral College

ROBERT W. BENNETT

STANFORD LAW AND POLITICS

An imprint of Stanford University Press · Stanford, California 2006

Stanford University Press
Stanford, California
© 2006 by the Board of Trustees of the
Leland Stanford Junior University

Library of Congress Cataloging-in-Publication Data

Bennett, Robert W. (Robert William)
    Taming the electoral college / Robert W. Bennett.
        p. cm.
    Includes bibliographical references and index.
    ISBN 0-8047-5409-8 (cloth : alk. paper) —
    ISBN 0-8047-5410-1 (pbk. : alk. paper)
    1. Electoral college—United States. 2. Presidents—United States—
Election. 3. Election law—United States. I. Title.
KF4911.B46 2006
324.6'3—dc22

                                                              2005027481

Printed in the United States of America on acid-free, archival-quality paper

Original Printing 2006
Last figure below indicates year of this printing:
15   14   13   12   11   10   09   08   07   06

Typeset at Stanford University Press in 10/14.5 Minion

For Harriet and Ariana

Contents

Preface   ix

1. Introduction   1

2. A Critical Short History of the Electoral College, Part I: From the Constitutional Convention Through the Twelfth Amendment   12

3. A Critical Short History of the Electoral College, Part II: Operating Under the Twelfth Amendment   27

4. Evaluating the Electoral College: The Nationwide Popular Vote Alternative   46

5. The Contingent Procedure for Selection of the President by the House of Representatives   74

6. The Case of Two Candidates Ending Up in an Electoral College Tie   86

7. The Problem of Faithless Electors   95

8. Electoral Votes for Third-Party (or Independent) Candidates   122

9. Miscellaneous Pitfalls in the Electoral College Process   144

10. Popular Election of the President Without a Constitutional Amendment   161

11. Conclusion   179

Notes   191

Index   259

Preface

I was primed to delve into electoral college problems when controversy started to swirl around the 2000 presidential election. Like many Americans I follow the world of political practice with substantial interest. No doubt in part because of that, my scholarly energies had migrated over the years from constitutional law and theory to the larger democratic setting of which constitutional law is a part. This had led to a book project in which I advanced an explanatory framework for understanding a number of "puzzles" of American democracy. That project was winding down as the election controversy was heating up. The electoral college played no particular role in that earlier scholarly effort, but the more public face of presidential "elections" did. As the election drama unfolded, it quickly became apparent that a host of electoral college issues were hiding in the shadows of the developing controversy, and that political insiders were paying attention to those issues, while most of the rest of us were not. I was ready for a new challenge, and the election seemed to serve one up that was at once close to my scholarly interests and brand new.

Actually more than one. Like many constitutional scholars, I was drawn as well to the role that the U.S. Supreme Court assumed in the 2000 election and began work on the possibility that the Supreme Court had gravitated to a new conception of its role in American government. I may well return to that effort one day. But it became increasingly apparent that the electoral college issues were fully as important and engaging as the role the Court had played, but considerably less attended to. This relative neglect of the electoral college is actually widespread and longstanding. Certainly in America's law schools, judicial review takes center stage, while the electoral college barely surfaces. My hunch is that students in most constitutional law courses never even hear the phrase "electoral college" uttered.

And once my attention was directed there, I found there was fertile ground for creative thinking, no doubt in good part because of the prior neglect. Jim Speta of the Northwestern Law School faculty came up with a suggestion for an academic conference on the election, and I eagerly joined with Jim and others on a planning committee, taking special interest in the electoral college. The conference was held at various locations at Northwestern University's two campuses in January of 2001. Attention had been lavished on the fact that the "winner" of the nationwide popular vote had lost the election. In thinking about this, I formulated an idea for instituting a popular election for president without going through the difficult process of constitutional amendment to abolish the electoral college. I presented this novel (as far as I can tell) idea as part of a panel on the electoral college chaired by Patricia Conley of the Northwestern political science department, and consisting of electoral college scholars David Abbott, Judith Best, and Nelson Polsby. Anyone who knows that group will not be surprised that I had my idea sorely tested. I later published two articles about the idea, hopefully refined because of the conference discussions. And since that time, there have seemingly been few waking moments when I haven't been thinking—and learning—about the electoral college.

My interest has certainly been fed by the fact that electoral college mysteries are so neglected. The field is not entirely unplowed, of course, but given the relative importance of the subject, the existing literature is astoundingly sparse. I found ample room for creativity. Thus the election's close electoral college tally suggested the possibility of a tie vote, given that there is an even number of electors. The preexisting literature had basically ignored that possibility, and I published an article, and a subsequent oped piece, on the tie possibility—including a rather simple solution. In the several electoral college articles I published I presented nonconstitutional solutions to the problems I identified, and I found myself increasingly intrigued by the importance in the electoral college context of finessing the process of constitutional amendment. The possibilities in that realm had also been essentially ignored in the preexisting literature. Once I was thinking in that vein, yet other ideas for important reforms with nonconstitutional solutions occurred to me, and I easily concluded that there was a book to be written with nonconstitutional electoral college reform as its organizing theme.

Portions of this book have appeared (or will have appeared) in earlier articles, three in The Green Bag, 2d series (*Popular Election of the President Without
a Constitutional Amendment*, 4 The Green Bag, 2d ser. 241 [2001]; *State Coordination in Popular Election of the President Without a Constitutional Amendment*,
5 The Green Bag, 2d ser. 141 [2002]; and *The Peril that Lurks in Even Numbers:
Selecting the President*, 7 The Green Bag 2d ser. 113 [2004]), and one in the
Northwestern Law Review (tentatively titled "The Problem of the Faithless Elector: Trouble Aplenty Brewing Just Below the Surface in Choosing the President," which will be part of a 100th anniversary volume of the *Review*, coming
out in late 2005 or early 2006). I am grateful to those publications for permis-
sion to adapt the content of those earlier articles.

Among the useful conversations (including by email) I have had on the elec-
toral college with friends and colleagues at Northwestern, at Brooklyn Law
School, where I spent the 2004–5 academic year as a visiting professor, and on
the fly, I think particularly of those with Ronen Avraham, Steve Calabresi, Greg
Caldeira, Bob Chira, Neil Cohen, Charlotte Crane, Shari Diamond, Paul Edelman, Dan Farber, Ken Manaster, Janice Nadler, Mike Paulsen, Rick Pildes, John
McGinnis, Michel Rosenfeld, Stephen Siegel, Paul Sracic, Emerson Tiller, and
Gordon Wood. In addition, I presented workshops on various aspects of the
project at several law schools: Northwestern, Brooklyn, NYU, and Hofstra. The
discussions at those events were uniformly stimulating and informative. My
thanks also go to Jim McMaster of the Northwestern Law School Library staff
who was very helpful in corralling obscurities for me. Student research assis-
tants at Northwestern (the law school and the college) and Brooklyn have also
been of great assistance. These include Ben Aderson, Tara Croft, Dylan Hen-
dricks, Joo Hui Kim, Dietrich Knabe, Riya Angela Kuo, Stephanie Lackey, Erica
Razook, Joe Russell, Jim Stein, and David Winters.

This is, in short, anything but a one-man effort. Still, the usual caveat about
remaining errors being mine is especially required. I was initially surprised at
the number of rather basic errors about the electoral college that appear in the
existing literature, and I have pointed many of them out in the text and notes.
As the project progressed, however, I became increasingly understanding of
how those errors might have come about. The ins and outs of the electoral college are exceedingly complex. Obviously I have tried to avoid basic errors as I
have probed more subtle dimensions of the college. But I do appreciate that op-
portunities for error abound.

Finally, my very great thanks go out to Brooklyn Law School, for the support given during my visit there, and to the Northwestern University School of Law and its Julius Rosenthal Fund. Northwestern has been my academic home not only during the years of this project, but for more than thirty-five years now. This effort is in a real sense the product of lessons learned over that entire span of time.

Taming the Electoral College

CHAPTER ONE

Introduction

The 2000 presidential election was among the most tumultuous in American history, arguably rivaled only by a smattering of presidential elections in the Nineteenth Century. Initially the 2004 election seemed to promise more of the same, or even worse. While the most dire predictions about 2004 did not come to pass, in combination these first two elections of the Twenty-First Century[1] provide ample reason for soul searching about American elections, including the most unusual way in which we choose the president and vice president in the United States. The American way of selecting our highest executive officials, and what might feasibly be done to make it better, are the subject of this book.

The president and vice president are formally chosen by a vote of "electors" making up what has now long been known as the "electoral college." At the present time there are 538 of these electors allocated among the states (and the District of Columbia). They never meet as a body,[2] but rather vote separately for the two offices in mid-December meetings held in the electors' respective jurisdictions. The votes of these state-by-state groups of electors are then aggregated in a counting session held by a joint meeting of the two houses of Congress in early January. If all authorized electors have voted, and all their votes pass muster, a vote of 270 electors—a majority of the 538—is required to choose the presidential and vice presidential winners.

No doubt because of the difficulties that surfaced in 2000, American news media seemed to lavish attention on the electoral college in the runup to the 2004 election. Despite this attention, in all likelihood most American voters remained then, and still remain, oblivious to the role of the electoral college, supposing instead that the president and his vice presidential "running mate" are jointly voted into office by a process of popular voting held not in December but in early November.[3] Those who pay a bit of attention may appreciate that the final accounting to declare a winner takes place on a state-by-state basis, leading to what I will call the "contemporary understanding of the presidential election process." Pursuant to this understanding, political parties nominate candidates for president and vice president, and each state—including for this purpose the District of Columbia—then holds a November popular election to determine how its allotted electoral votes will be cast for the two offices, taken as a paired duo. At least in the typical case where there are only two sets of candidates who garner electoral votes, the winners can usually be determined on that November election night, or perhaps the next morning, by toting up the electoral votes after the state-by-state popular vote counts are in.

The populace can be forgiven for a set of "misimpressions" that leaves this contemporary understanding in the public consciousness, for the system regularly provides the electorate with signs of just such a popular voting process at work. To start with, the presidential electors are themselves all chosen by popular election in November on what is routinely called "election day."[4] In most states, moreover, the popular electorate indicates its presidential and vice-presidential preferences as a tied pair on "short ballots"[5] on which the names of the electors nowhere appear. The typical voter thus signals a preference not for a group of electors as such but for a set of candidates for president and vice president. That designation is transformed into a vote for electors by virtue of fine print, perhaps appearing on the ballot, but often only to be found—should anyone really undertake to look—tucked away in the statutory tomes of the state.[6] Even in those few states where the names of electors are still found on the ballot, those of the presidential and vice-presidential candidates are typically given considerably greater prominence.

This voting for electors takes place on a state-by-state basis, and the mass media report the results from one state at a time, though they also routinely and with great fanfare announce nationwide vote totals. Election "results" are then usually available on the night of election day, weeks before the presidential electors meet and cast their votes, and weeks more before those electoral votes are officially counted in the congressional joint meeting.[7] Those latter two events are scarcely reported on at all. With rare exceptions, moreover, the electors vote in accordance with commitments they have publicly assumed beforehand—to the very candidates for whom the majority of voters in each state have signaled a preference.

The electoral college's choices for president and vice president also usually coincide with the winners of the nationwide popular vote. In the Twentieth Century, "[n]o American President . . . [was] chosen by the electoral college after a definitive defeat in the [nationwide] popular vote."[8] The first election of the Twenty-First Century was remarkable in good part because it was not true to that pattern. The 2000 electoral college winner received more than half a million fewer popular votes than did his principal rival, producing what is sometimes called a "wrong winner" in the literature critical of the electoral college.[9] But then the 2004 election returned to the prevalent pattern, with the electoral college winner capturing the nationwide popular vote as well, by more than three million votes.

In this way, both the electoral college process and the electoral college results are usually suggestive of presidential selection through one form or another of popular vote, and it is perfectly understandable that the electoral college fades into the deep background of the nation's political consciousness. In fact the electoral college vote and its later official counting have largely become a formality, and it may not even be fair to say that the electorate fails to appreciate what is *really* at work. As the late Chief Justice William Rehnquist stated in his recent book on the contentious election of 1876, "in normal presidential elections, the voting of the electors is a formality, predetermined by the popular vote cast in each state on [election day]."[10]

At the same time, there is peril in ignoring the ins and outs of the electoral college. For one thing, "usually" is not always, as the 2000 election brought home. But more than that, those intimately involved in presidential election campaigns must keep their eyes on the formalities. At least those who manage presidential campaigns for major party candidates must appreciate that it is the electoral college vote that is ultimately decisive, that it is possible to win the presidency without winning the nationwide popular vote. Their business is that of winning elections, and since it is the electoral college count that secures that end, successful campaigns for the presidency are waged with an "electoral college strategy." Those campaigns are plotted on a state-by-state basis, and some states loom large in campaign efforts of candidates—in a two candidate race, it is typically the same states for both of them—while others can safely be ig-

nored. And if political insiders necessarily pay attention to the details of the
electoral college, the rest of us seeking to evaluate, and perhaps improve, the
process would also do well to pay attention.

Over the years, some presidential elections have highlighted the peculiarities
of the electoral college, for those obliged or simply inclined to pay attention. In
1888, for instance, Grover Cleveland won the nationwide popular vote for president, but lost the election because Benjamin Harrison received a majority of
the electoral votes. More recently, while Bill Clinton handily won both the popular and electoral college tallies in 1992, before election day the vigorous independent candidacy of H. Ross Perot had created a good deal of uncertainty
about the electoral college outcome in a number of states. That state-by-state
pre-election uncertainty left the final result of the presidential race also in
doubt. Even if not professional political operatives, those who followed those
campaigns with some care were inevitably alerted both to the role of the electoral college and to some of its intricacies.

And some elections highlight troubles in the process in a way that stimulates
attention to the possibilities for electoral college reform. In 1800 an electoral
college tie necessitated recourse in early 1801 to a contingent procedure in
which the president was selected by the House of Representatives. It took
thirty-six ballots in the House to choose Thomas Jefferson over Aaron Burr.
This led directly to adoption of the Twelfth Amendment to the Constitution,
which for the first time separated the electoral college balloting for president
and vice president. The 1876 election, about which Justice Rehnquist wrote,
provides a second example. A specially appointed commission resolved disputes in several states when rival slates laid claim to having won the statewide
popular election for electors. The controversy that swirled around both the
process and the outcome led directly to Congress's adoption of the Electoral
Count Act a number of years later. That statute still governs the counting of
electoral votes in the joint meeting of the two houses of the Congress, centrally
including how many sorts of disputes over the *bona fides* of individual electors,
or of entire slates, are to be resolved.[11]

The 2000 election seemed from the start to be cut from this latter cloth. It
was not simply that the winner of the nationwide popular vote lost the electoral
college count. The election highlighted vulnerabilities in the electoral college
process at almost every turn. Thus the Twelfth Amendment had continued the

limitation in the original constitutional provisions that electors could not cast both of their two votes for "inhabitants" of their own state. In the 2000 election this raised questions about the votes of Texas electors for the Republican ticket that was the odds-on favorite in the state, because both George Bush and Dick Cheney, the Republican nominees for president and vice president respectively, had called Texas home in the years immediately preceding their nominations.[12] Had the Texas votes for one or the other been disqualified, there would have been no decisive electoral college choice for that office, and a troublesome constitutional backup procedure for that office would have come into play. It was even possible in that event that we would have ended up with a president and vice president of different political parties.

Then there were the extraordinarily close and controversial results in the state of Florida, leading to the unparalleled heavy hand of the U.S. Supreme Court in the process. And had it not been for the attention paid to Florida, the contests for presidential electors in Texas—and in some other states as well—might well have commanded more attention and controversy. The close race in Florida was of interest, of course, because the electoral college count seemed to be extremely close, closer in fact than in any election since 1876. Finally, if anticlimactically, one of the 538 electors decided to abstain, rather than cast the vote that those who voted for her had fully expected. Each of these features of the 2000 election was suggestive of problems in the electoral college mechanism for choosing the nation's two principal executive officers.

Despite this litany of danger signs, there was remarkably little push for electoral college reform in the wake of the 2000 election. This neglect was probably a product of various forces. Perhaps most important in turning the nation's gaze away from the electoral college was the terrorist attacks on the United States in September of 2001. These diverted attention from the way in which the commander-in-chief is chosen to what he does in the office once there.

But there were also other electoral problems that made demands on a limited store of attention. Some of those problems have simply been more visible than the electoral college, and others more readily susceptible to reform. In the realm of visibility, scholarly attention has been lavished on the unprecedented involvement of the courts—and particularly the U.S. Supreme Court—in the selection of the president. In the past, state courts have occasionally played important roles in reviewing claims of election fraud or miscounting of votes, even in federal elections.[13] On rare occasions, federal courts have even invoked federal constitutional law in reviewing claimed instances of egregious electoral unfairness.[14] But in the 2000 presidential election the Supreme Court found that the fact that different standards applied in different localities of a state in the official recounting of votes violated the norm of equality of treatment embodied in the Fourteenth Amendment's Equal Protection Clause.[15] There was no precedent for this focus on intrastate variation *simpliciter*, or for the involvement of the U.S. Supreme Court, in a presidential election. Moreover the Court called a halt to the recounting process, leaving the initial vote tabulation in place, despite the virtual certainty that an evenhanded recount would have produced a different vote tabulation.[16] Since the initial count was so close, it is entirely possible that a full and fair recount would have produced a different outcome in Florida and hence in the nation.

This jarring action was in large part because a presidential election operates under stringent time pressures. The more typical elections for members of legislative bodies present the luxury that the operation of government can proceed even if the identities of one or a few members of the legislature remain in doubt for some significant period of time. For the American president in contrast, the pressure is great to produce a new holder of the office before the old one departs.

Whatever the justification for the Court's action, when difficulties arose in earlier presidential elections the country worked through them without the intervention of the federal courts.[17] Much of the academic world in general, and the law professoriate in particular, is preoccupied by the role of the courts in American governance, and particularly with that of the U.S. Supreme Court. The result has been that the Court's involvement had a ready-made set of observers with articulate commentary as its standard *modus operandi*.[18]

Another concern that attracted significant attention was the disenfranchisement of ex-felons in the Florida balloting. In the original constitutional scheme, eligibility to vote in federal congressional elections was left to state law.[19] This state discretion is now very substantially hemmed in by constitutional amendments (amplified by some court decisions and federal statutes) that forbid discrimination in voting on various grounds.[20] The Constitution has little to say about qualifications to vote for presidential electors, because the states remain largely free to designate how those electors will be chosen. Despite this possible opening for a different set of qualifications to vote in presidential elections, in recent years states have uniformly extended the right to vote for presidential electors to the same electorate that votes in other federal and state elections.[21] And a number of states have used the residual discretion they retain over voting qualifications to exclude felons from voting.[22] Some, including Florida, also exclude ex-felons from the franchise, and indeed Florida (along with Alabama) leads the nation in the disenfranchisement of black men on account of the felon and ex-felon population that is not permitted to vote.[23] This ex-felon disenfranchisement may well have changed the 2000 election outcome in Florida, and that brought the problem of felon qualification laws a large degree of media, public, and political attention. As a result, in the wake of the 2000 election a few states—not including Florida—reexamined the electoral treatment of felons and ex-felons.[24]

Problematic aspects of the 2000 voting process itself became visible almost immediately and were probably especially important in diverting attention from the electoral college.[25] Surely foremost among them was that of ballot design. In part the intrastate disparities with which the Supreme Court grappled were the product of disparate ballot design.[26] Popular attention was especially fixated on these problems in the early phases of the Florida controversy, and this easily blended into problems of local discretion in deciphering votes on those ballots of imperfect design. After the selection of George Bush as president was an accomplished fact in the 2000 election, the Congress passed a statute that makes funding available to states that invest in improved voting processes.[27] Making use of the federal funds, a number of states have now enacted significant reforms.[28]

A final possible reason for neglect of electoral college reform in the wake of the 2000 election is the decidedly uphill battle that such reform appears to face. For obvious reasons, it was the fact of a "wrong winner" in the 2000 election that commanded most of the electoral college concern, and the alternative of a nationwide popular vote that seemed the obviously responsive reform.[29] In virtually all other elections in the United States, the votes for the various candidates are cumulated, and the candidate with a plurality, or perhaps a majority, of the total is declared the winner. As mentioned, many American voters may well assume that we choose the president through an integrated nationwide vote that follows this pattern. It is thus not surprising that the most vocal advo-

cates of electoral college reform after the 2000 election joined generations of reformers before them in advocating that we replace the electoral college with a
nationwide popular vote for president (and vice president).[30]

At the same time, it is regularly assumed that a constitutional amendment
would be required to institute a nationwide popular vote for president. In
Chapter Ten I will raise questions about that assumption, but as long as the assumption holds sway it stands as a very substantial obstacle to change. There
would be groups of winners and losers in instituting a nationwide popular vote,
and the calculus of just where the populations of particular states fall in that accounting is not at all clear. We will also return to that set of questions in Chapter Ten. But in part because of the uncertainty, in a large number of states political elites and ordinary citizens alike might fear loss of influence. Yet
constitutional amendment requires the assent of three-fourths of the states, in
addition to two-thirds of each House of Congress.[31] Constitutional amendment, in other words, would require agreement by a large number of actors
likely to worry that the move to a nationwide popular vote would disserve their
interests, or those of their constituents.[32] In 1970, an amendment that would
have instituted a nationwide popular vote for president actually received the required two-thirds vote in the House of Representatives, but then never got a
vote in the Senate because of a filibuster. Even had the Senate hurdle been overcome, however, the required three-fourths of the states would have remained as
a very formidable obstacle.[33]

In winning reelection in 2004 George Bush captured majorities of both the
electoral college and the nationwide popular vote. Had he instead won the popular vote but lost in the electoral college, then each of the two parties would
have been "burned" by a "wrong winner" in successive elections. That scenario
would have been unprecedented and might conceivably have provided a favorable political climate for a move to direct popular election of the president.
Without that prod to action, however, there is likely to be little traction in any
move to a nationwide popular vote through a constitutional amendment.[34]

There is, however, an alternative way to think about electoral college reform.
Instead of concentrating on one big change in moving to a nationwide popular
vote, we might focus instead on a series of smaller ones that might be accomplished without constitutional amendment. And there is much to be said for
this alternative agenda. For if the "wrong winner" was the most visible electoral

college quirk that the 2000 election brought into focus, it was not, as we saw earlier, the only one. Nor in my view was it the most perilous. Even among those with no direct interest in the outcome, a move to a nationwide popular vote would be controversial. We will delve more fully into that controversy in Chapter Four. But unless and until a nationwide vote is put in place, there are more serious problems to be avoided by a more finely grained approach to reform that can be pursued without constitutional amendment.

That, at least, is the working premise of this book. My aim is to explore how we might avoid the worst problems presented by the electoral college processes without doing so through constitutional amendment, at least directly and in the short term. I turn in Chapters Two and Three to a short critical history of the electoral college, highlighting the important ways in which the institution has changed over the years. This will yield a picture of the present operation of the institution and lay the groundwork for discussion of possibilities for reform. We will see that many of the difficulties brought to the surface by the 2000 and 2004 elections are the product of a formal structure laid down in the Constitution that is poorly adapted to political developments since that time. In any event, we will require the perspective of where the electoral college has been to help work our way to a more congenial future for it. Chapter Four is then devoted to explanation and evaluation of the large-scale reform proposals advanced over the years. With the difficulties posed by constitutional amendment in mind, I will then turn in Chapters Five through Ten to discussion of a variety of problems, along with suggestions of how at least some of them might be addressed without resorting to amendment.

I will first concentrate on some particularly awkward and potentially quite mischievous features of the electoral college mechanism for choosing the nation's two senior executive officers. Chapter Five deals with the backup procedures for selection of the president (and vice president) if the electoral college processes prove unavailing. The backup procedures—in the House of Representatives and the Senate, for president and vice president respectively—are constitutionally required whenever no candidate commands a majority of the electoral college. That may come about for a variety of reasons, and Chapter Six concentrates on one of them, an electoral college tie between just two candidates.

Chapter Seven deals with another possibility for relegating selection to the backup proceedings—elector discretion, which surfaces in the votes of what are called "faithless electors." Aside from calling the House and Senate contingent procedures into play, moreover, faithless electors can bedevil the process in other ways. Apart from problems in accurately tabulating the popular vote, the contingent procedures to select the president (and vice president) and the possibility of faithless electors are the two aspects of American electoral process that are potentially most subversive of the orderly and wholesome choice of a president. Neither of these played a decisive role in the 2000 or 2004 election, but each was just below the surface, poised to cause trouble. And each can be made less potentially mischievous by early attention that need not involve the difficult process of constitutional amendment.

Chapter Eight deals with the problem of a third (and additional) political party, electoral votes for the candidates of which can also throw the electoral college process into disarray in several ways, including sending the executive office sweepstakes into the backup procedures. The role of minor parties in American politics is, however, a large and difficult subject. Minor parties can, for instance, change the dynamics of presidential politics in decisive ways, even though they never threaten to capture any electoral votes. Arguably that is what happened in the 2000 presidential election. But there is likely no effective way to exorcise this possibility without interfering with the operation of minor parties in American politics in a wholesale way. For the present I want to steer clear of that complexity. If we focus more narrowly on the possibility that minor parties may confound the process by capturing electoral votes, there may be progress that can be achieved without undue risk of ripple effects that might bring harm. Chapter Eight explores that possibility through use of a contingent selection procedure for electors that states could implement.

With these discussions of "mid-size" problems in hand, I then comment in Chapter Nine on a miscellany of other—"smaller"—problems that may call electoral votes into question. I will offer solutions to most of these problems, but they are partial solutions at best, and in some cases may be almost as impractical as constitutional amendment. I will try to be clear-eyed about the possibilities, but it may turn out that sweeping constitutional amendment retains some allure. If that is the case, I also think that a bit of indirection may hold some promise in charting a route to constitutional change. Chapter Ten is devoted to the possibility of popular election of the president without a constitutional amendment. The mechanism of pulling off that change is closely related to the suggested way of dealing with the possibility that minor political parties may capture electoral votes. As a permanent means to a popularly elected president, it leaves much to be desired, because it skirts as many problems as it confronts. But it may have a great deal to recommend it as an interim step that would give the constitutional amendment possibility more visibility and impetus on the nation's agenda.

Finally, I will try to put the lessons of the book into perspective in a concluding Chapter Eleven. Presidential elections come every four years, and any given one of them is likely to serve the major purposes of elections well, engaging large segments of the populace, identifying with decisiveness those who will hold the nation's elected executive offices for the ensuing four years, and bestowing legitimacy on those selections. But the 2000 election in particular taught us that we should be alert to possibilities that all will not go so smoothly. Close examination of the electoral college drives home a certain urgency to that lesson. Simple odds may give us the time to respond to challenges that the electoral college poses, but we would do well not to prolong for too long the period of taking chances.

CHAPTER TWO

A Critical Short History of the
Electoral College, Part I

From the Constitutional Convention
Through the Twelfth Amendment

The constitutional convention of 1787 entertained a number of different possibilities for selecting an executive under the new constitutional structure. Both the Virginia plan advanced by that state's delegation to the convention and the competing small states' New Jersey plan assumed that the task should fall to the new national legislature. But that hardly led to immediate agreement, as the two plans had very different conceptions for constituting that legislature, with voting power proportionate to state population in the Virginia plan and equal state representation in the New Jersey plan. In addition, choice by the legislature was resisted by those who wanted an independent and energetic executive, particularly if service by the executive for a second term was possible. The fear was that the executive would be subservient to the legislature if he was chosen initially by it and was dependent on its approval to succeed himself.

A nationwide popular vote had some influential early backing, but it was haunted from the start both by the varying qualifications to vote imposed by the states, and by southern states' insistence on a weighted say in the choice of the executive on account of their slave populations. (Needless to say, there was no thought given to the possibility that slaves would be allowed to vote.) The popular vote possibility was also resisted by representatives of the less populous states, who feared that a choice determined by a nationwide vote would inevitably result in a president from a center of greater population.[1] And finally, there was some sentiment that by giving the executive a nationwide popular mandate, popular election might make him too powerful.[2] The tensions over state prerogatives and slavery, and between more and less populous states were, of course, also present in the composition of the new national legislature. They were resolved in that latter context by the "Great Compromise" that gave us our national bicameral legislature, with representation apportioned in one house— the Senate—equally among the states and in the other—the House of Representatives—by state population, counting slaves in the latter case at three-fifths of a person.[3] This compromise on the nature of the legislature laid the groundwork for accommodations that would then be incorporated into the electoral college.

Pennsylvania's James Wilson had earlier introduced the possibility of geographically delineated districts in which "electors" would be chosen through popular election. Those electors would in turn choose the executive. This idea of an intermediate group which would do the selecting then resurfaced as a device to distance the selection of the executive from the legislature itself, while making use of the national legislative apportionment scheme as the basis for allocating voting power. The device of an intermediate body of electors likely also had some appeal to allay a common concern that parochialism might dominate the selection process. The states necessarily loomed large in any conception of how the new nation would be organized. They were, after all, entities with functioning governmental structures and identities stretching back through colonial history. But if selection of the national executive was delegated to the states acting separately—and presumably through their legislatures—each state might simply opt for a "local boy." A smaller and select group that would actually make the choice commended itself as likely to enlarge beyond each state's borders the field of people who would be given serious consideration for the office.[4]

In the scheme that was eventually incorporated into the Constitution's executive branch Article II, each state was assigned a number of electors equal to its total representation in the House and Senate. The "manner" of choosing these electors was left to each state's legislature.[5] The Congress could determine the date on which they would vote—it was required to be the "same throughout the United States"—and also when the electors would be chosen.[6] In 1792 it chose the beginning of December for the elector voting, and allowed the states to choose electors anytime in the preceding thirty-four days.[7] Once chosen, the electors would select a president and, incidentally, a vice president. The inclusion of a vice president seems almost to have been an "afterthought,"[8] and the Constitution assigns no duties to the office, save that the vice president serves as president of the Senate[9]—a provision found in the legislative Article I, rather than in the executive Article II—and succeeds to the presidency in case of the removal from office of the president, or his death, resignation, or inability for some other reason to serve.[10]

In a provision that, as we shall see, proved to be short-lived, the electors were to cast two votes for two different persons they judged qualified to be president. Those two votes were to be undifferentiated between president and vice president.[11] Only one of an elector's votes could be cast for an "inhabitant" of his own state, and a majority of the whole number of appointed electors was necessary to prevail in this electoral college vote. The runner-up would become vice president, regardless of whether he too had a majority. And then, once the electors had made their choices, they would go out of business. A fresh process for choosing electors would be set in motion every four years, as the nation faced anew the choice of a president and vice president.

The electors were to be independent decision makers, "men," in Alexander Hamilton's words, "most capable of analyzing the qualities adapted to the station and acting under circumstances favorable to deliberation, and to a judicious combination of all the reasons and inducements which were proper to govern their choice."[12] They were to deliberate and then exercise choice to come up with the best person(s) for the job of president. With only the one job assigned to them as electors, it appears to have been assumed that they would operate with a large measure of independence from their respective state legislatures, even if they had been chosen directly by those legislatures. And then, to ensure the independence of the electors from federal officialdom as well, the Constitution provides that "no Senator or Representative, or person holding an office of trust or profit under the United States" can serve as an elector.[13] If it all worked, highly distinguished electors would be able to operate largely free not only of legislative interference or fealty on both the state and the federal level, but of interest group pressure. The electors would exorcize political haggling from a task that should have none of it. As an 1874 Senate Report put it:

The theory of the electoral college was that a body of men should be chosen . . . who would be distinguished by their eminent ability and wisdom, who would be independent of popular passion, who would not be influenced by tumult, cabal, or intrigue, and that in the choice of the President they would be left perfectly free to exercise their judgment in the selection of the proper person.[14]

We should digress to note that this reading of history—that the electors were meant basically to be independent decision makers rising above political considerations in a search for the best available executive for the nation—has been challenged on occasion over the years. A recent example is provided by an Internet piece by Walter Dellinger, writing in 2004. Dellinger insists that it is "a myth that the Framers designed an 'electoral college' with the idea that an elite set of men would gather to choose the person they thought should be president."[15] Like Dellinger, the commentators who have taken this position have tended to be defenders of today's electoral college and may somehow have thought it important to rebut a claim that the contemporary operation of the college has strayed from the original design. Thus Dellinger says that "[t]he Electoral College system works today essentially as the Framers of the Constitution intended."[16]

Quite apart from whether contemporary acceptability of the electoral college need be tied to its original design, it is entirely unclear what the "essence" is that Dellinger—and like-minded others—might have in mind. These commentators have had little to say about what the electors *were* to do. All they may mean is that electors would not be casting their votes in a vacuum where they would remain entirely unaware of, and uninfluenced by, the sentiments of other political actors, including the populace at large. But in that form the claim is not terribly interesting, for once past infancy each of us brings socially influenced views and attitudes to any task we undertake. If these commentators really mean to assert that electors were originally intended not to exercise independent choice, but rather to parrot choices previously made by the electorate in the fashion that electors most typically do today, the basis for any such claim is hard to fathom.

To the extent that evidence is cited, it consists largely of the fact that a nationwide popular vote for president had been the "first choice" in particular of three influential delegates to the Constitutional Convention, James Madison,

James Wilson, and Gouvernor Morris.[17] Then, in defending the Constitution as ratification was being debated, the three used rhetoric of attachment of the presidential selection process to the "people." For several reasons this is a very fragile basis on which to deny that electors were to exercise genuine choice and discretion in choosing the president.

First, mention of "the people" in this context is likely misleading in parsing the way the system was presumed to operate, even by those who used the expression. Reference to the "people" was frequently employed at the time not to characterize direct popular choice—or even indirect—but rather for all manner of decision-making outlets in the new system, where ultimate sovereignty was presumed to reside with the "people," in contrast to the "sovereignty" of the English monarch. Thus Hamilton's famous defense of judicial review in Federalist 78 insists that it brings no implication that the judiciary is superior to the legislature, but only that "the power of the people [as expressed in the Constitution] is superior to both."[18] In postconvention debates and discussion, moreover, these constitutional convention luminaries often described involvement of the "people" with basic accuracy (at least if one equates the "people" and the electorate), but without denying elector discretion. Thus Wilson told the Pennsylvania ratifying convention that "the people may elect with only one remove."[19] And in Federalist 39, Madison said that "[t]he president is indirectly derived from the choice of the people." Madison also spoke in this postconvention period—with equal accuracy—of the electoral college as a device for selection of the president by "the states."[20]

Second, no matter how distinguished, the vocal champions of a nationwide popular vote were only a small minority of the delegates to the convention. A number of the other delegates were, in fact, dead set against popular election.[21] In a direct vote on the question, a popular vote for president was defeated, nine states to two.[22] And the system that was chosen might have but did not require popular election even for the choice of electors.

The most fundamental problem with this view that electors were "intended" to be dependent recorders of decisions made by the electorate—if this is the "essence" that Dellinger and others have in mind—is that it makes nonsense of the office of elector. For with that conception of the office, it simply served no purpose. We will return in Chapter Seven to the problem of ascribing an "intention" or "purpose" to words that are enacted in a formal way by a process that involves a large number of individuals, but in this historical treatment it should suffice simply to note the improbability that *any* of the actors involved would have thought that the elaborate electoral college process was erected simply to record decisions made elsewhere. Thus it is hardly surprising that a broad range of the most respected commentators over the years has insisted that independence and discretion of the electors was central to the original conception of their role.[23]

While they quickly came collectively to be called an "electoral college," the Constitution does not use that term, and, as we have seen, the electors were never officially to meet as a single body. Rather they would "meet in their respective states," on a day that Congress could determine and that, as mentioned, was to be "the same throughout the United States."[24] Each set of electors was to send a signed and sealed certification of its vote to the president of the Senate,[25] who of necessity would be the outgoing vice president of the United States, the new holder of that office not having yet been chosen. Before a joint meeting of the Senate and House, the president of the Senate was to open the electors' certificates, and in a peculiar passive construction, the Constitution provides that "the votes shall then be counted."[26]

The seemingly awkward choice of separate state meetings for the electors may have been borne of practical concerns in a day of primitive travel,[27] but it may also have had some theoretical appeal. To appreciate this point, let us step back for a moment to examine an almost palpable ambivalence among the constitutional framers about a well-functioning representative legislature. Madison had famously argued in Federalist 10 that while the tendency to factional self-dealing is "sown in the nature of man," an extended republic such as that contemplated in the Constitution would multiply factions which would often battle each other to a standstill, or at least to relative impotence, limiting the damage to the public weal that they otherwise might do. Representative democracy could allow a public-regarding search for answers above this battle of interests by assigning decision making to a select "small number of citizens. . . . whose wisdom may best discern the true interest of their country."[28] This is a "trustee" or "republican" conception of a well-functioning legislature. But others saw the legislature as a vehicle for expressing and then compromising among private interests, rather than as a body that might transcend them. For those who shared this "agency" or "liberal" vision, the legislature was not a vehicle for distancing politics from constituencies, but rather the only efficient way in a mass society to carry on compromise and then governance in the direct service of those interests.[29]

For the legislature there was no real resolution of this tension, as there is not to this day. Many among the constitutional framers may not have confronted, or perhaps even appreciated, the tension. But for those thinking about the executive, and especially for those concerned about an energetic one, there was really no choice. It was taken for granted that an effective executive could not be a body of people who would haggle and compromise. It thus could not embody within itself a large variety of private interests that were each to be given their individual due. The executive must instead be above factional strife.[30] With this as the ideal, the method of choosing the executive should involve not a bargain among private regarding factions—not even if conceived as "constituencies"— but rather a search for that unusual individual who would rise above the battle of interests. Separate meetings of each state's electors might then be seen as a device for ensuring that bargaining would not insinuate itself into the process. The "detached and divided situation" of the electors, as Alexander Hamilton put it in Federalist 68, would expose them much less to "heats and ferments." With no knowledge of the deliberations of the other electoral college delegations, each group of electors could ask and answer for itself the question of just who in the country would best answer the call of being an executive for the entire nation.[31]

Attractive as this picture might have seemed, however, it immediately posed its own problems. A series of simultaneous disparate meetings might result in votes for a whole variety of candidates, even with two votes per elector and the limitation that only one of those two votes could be cast for an inhabitant of the elector's state. It was widely taken as given that George Washington would be the first president. He was a national hero seen as above factionalism and easily able to stand up to the legislature. But it was less clear that after Washington had served as president disparate electoral college meetings would readily coalesce on any single person as just right for the office. A candidate who commanded a mere plurality of the electors' votes would have no mandate behind him, and might be doomed to function in the shadow of the legislature. To allay this concern the Constitution required that the electoral college choice would be determinative only if it commanded a majority of the "whole number of electors appointed."[32]

This in turn required a fallback procedure, for the electoral college vote might be indecisive. In addition, because electors cast two votes, it was possible for two candidates, or actually even three, to garner a majority of the appointed electors,[33] so the fallback provision dealt as well with the possibility of a tie among candidates with a majority. In the case either of such a tie, or of failure of any candidate to obtain a majority, the choice of president was relegated to the House of Representatives. The choice was to be from among those with the five highest number of electoral votes in the case where no candidate commanded a majority of the electors. And a majority of the state delegations was necessary for any candidate to prevail in the House.[34]

Initially the Senate—the members of which in the original constitutional scheme were to be chosen by the state legislatures—was advanced for this contingent procedure,[35] but in a peculiar compromise, the House was substituted, with each state delegation in the House given one vote and a majority of the delegations necessary for the choice.[36] Substitution of the House for the Senate with each state entitled to one vote seems peculiar, because it mixes use of one house with the equal state weighting of votes of the other. Indeed, a fallback procedure that employs the national legislature at all is in some tension with the concern otherwise evident that the executive not be beholden to the legislature. This concern was softened in the procedure chosen, because the House choice was to be among a limited set of possibilities passed onto it. And House selection, by providing the stamp of approval of the chamber selected by the "people," may have been thought to provide something of a substitute mandate when no candidate had secured a majority in the electoral college.[37] In any event, once the House had chosen, the candidate with the next highest number of electoral college votes would become the vice president.[38] Note that if the contingent House procedure for selection of the president was required because no candidate had commanded a majority in the electoral college, the vice president chosen in this way may have had more electoral votes than the president. If there initially had been a tie in the electoral votes for this vice-presidential slot, however, the choice of vice president was relegated to the Senate. Nothing was said explicitly about the voting procedure in the Senate, but presumably each senator was to have one vote.[39]

There seems to have been a difference of opinion about the frequency with which the House fallback procedure for the choice of a president would be necessary. Some convention delegates, like Pennsylvania's Wilson, thought that "Continental Characters . . . [like Washington would] multiply as we more & more coalesce, so as to enable the electors in every part of the Union to know & judge of them."[40] The House contingent procedure might then seldom be necessary. Others, in stark contrast, seem to have thought that recourse to the House would be common, that usually the electors would effectively nominate a variety of candidates and that the House of Representatives would then choose the president.[41]

In retrospect it is astounding how quickly many of the assumptions that informed this entire electoral college scheme proved to be false. One enthusiast for the electoral college insists that the electoral college apparatus was "a carefully considered and thought-out solution to the problem" of choosing an executive.[42] It seems more likely, however, that delegates with a lot on their minds devoted less careful attention to the mechanism for selecting the president because they were confident that Washington would be the initial choice in any event.[43] But whether or not the electoral college provisions were "carefully considered" at the outset, they were certainly not far-sighted.[44]

Even while many clung to a view of politics as rising above factions in the search for the common good, it turned out that ferocious differences surfaced about just what the "true interest" of the new republic was, and that the multiplicity of interests and sentiments coalesced around two large-scale groupings characterized by a great deal of mutual distrust. Political parties, nowhere mentioned in the Constitution, quickly became the organizing media of politics, and almost immediately reached not only into the legislature but into the electoral college mechanism for selecting the president as well.[45] Electors increasingly came to think of themselves as agents of political parties rather than as engaged in deliberation about who in the nation might best serve as a wise president above factional politics. And with political parties as instruments of political coordination and communication, cooperation among the various state electoral college delegations could proceed before the simultaneous far flung meetings of those delegations.

Alexander Hamilton presciently perceived one potentially serious problem with the presidential selection process as the nation was gearing up for the very first use of it. Washington was the overwhelming favorite for the presidency, and John Adams emerged as a strong candidate for vice president, in part because of the geographical balance he could bring to a first administration. Hamilton became concerned, however, that a great many electors might cast their two ballots for Washington and Adams. If this produced a tie, the process gave the electors no way to signal that Washington was their choice for president, and the determination would be thrown into the House of Representatives.[46] While that would be unseemly, the House would surely vote for Washington in that first election. But Hamilton feared a more momentous misstep as well. Some single elector might vote for Adams but not Washington, and Adams would then become president. To forestall this possibility, Hamilton urged a number of electors in Connecticut, New Jersey, and Pennsylvania to vote for Washington, but not Adams. Adams took umbrage at Hamilton's machinations, and the incident poisoned the relations between the two.[47]

In any event, the larger trends were clearly evident as early as the third presidential election in 1796. Washington had received one of the votes of every elector in each of the first two elections and could likely have been elected again. But he shunned a third term. With Washington headed for retirement, the nascent Federalist and Jeffersonian[48] political parties that had emerged were emboldened and were given rough national shape by congressional caucuses. The two caucuses each produced a slate of a presidential and a vice-presidential candidate. The spirit of party was sufficiently strong to guarantee that no candidate would achieve Washingtonian unanimity in the electoral college balloting, but party discipline was not yet sufficient to rigidify the electoral balloting. By one account almost "40 percent of the electors [still] cast a ballot for someone not nominated by their party's congressional caucus."[49] The result—not quite the factionless deliberation envisaged by the craftsmen of the Constitution's electoral college process, nor yet modern party politics—was the choice of the Federalist John Adams as president and the "Jeffersonian" Thomas Jefferson as vice president. Adams received votes from a majority of the electors.

Jefferson, while close behind, fell short of a majority, but as we have noted, the runner-up did not require a majority vote of the electors to become vice president under the Article II provisions in place at the time. As the Federalist and Jeffersonian parties further coalesced in the following years, the 1796 choice of executive officers divided between parties came to be seen as a failure of party discipline, and this conception led directly to the fateful drama of the 1800 election.

In 1800 Adams and Jefferson were the presidential choices of their respective congressional caucuses, as they had been four years earlier. Political parties had sufficiently gelled at the state level that most electors considered themselves to be party loyalists. The Jeffersonians' choice for vice president was Aaron Burr, and, haunted by what had happened in 1796, all the Jeffersonian electors cast their two votes in those far-flung meetings for Jefferson and Burr.[50] In a variation of what Hamilton had feared in 1789, each achieved the required majority, but they had the same majority.[51] There was an electoral college tie. The Federalists, in contrast, had dealt with the tie possibility, one Rhode Island Federalist elector having cast his "second" vote for John Jay instead of Adams's "running-mate" Charles Cotesworth Pinckney. In marked contrast to four year earlier, the Rhode Islander was the only elector to break party ranks in 1800.[52] But the Federalists lost, and over on the side of the victorious Jeffersonians, Burr did not gracefully step aside. The choice of president was thrown into the House of Representatives.

We have seen that in the case of a tie between two candidates, each of whom commanded an electoral college majority, the choice fell to the outgoing House. There were sixteen states at the time, so that the required majority was nine states. While the Federalists easily commanded a majority of the House as a whole (64-42), the Republicans actually controlled eight of the delegations. The Federalists either controlled the others or could cause a standoff in them.[53] The Federalists struggled on behalf of Burr, whom many considered likely to be more accommodating than Jefferson. They held firm through thirty-five ballots to deny the ninth state that Jefferson required.[54] This was true despite the fact that Alexander Hamilton, not a member of the legislature but one of the Federalist's most prominent national figures, argued behind the scenes for Jefferson whom he disliked over his fellow New Yorker Burr with whom he professed personally to be on cordial terms, but thought quite "unfit" to be president.[55]

Eventually the deadlock was resolved through the brokerage of Delaware's lone congressman, the Federalist James Bayard. Bayard had played an important role throughout the House phase of the drama, reportedly having earlier claimed authorization from Burr in offering a Maryland congressman the post of secretary of the navy in return for a vote for Burr.[56] At the outset the Federalists had accepted a procedure that foreclosed other House business until the presidential selection was settled. This kept the pressure on, and eventually Bayard arranged a reasonably graceful bow to the selection of Jefferson. Federalist representatives from the deadlocked Vermont and Maryland delegations absented themselves, thus allowing their delegations to vote for Jefferson. Bayard himself abstained, so Delaware did not vote at all in the final tally. The Federalist South Carolina delegation also abstained, with the result that Jefferson won on the thirty-sixth ballot, with ten delegations in his camp. Four diehard Federalist delegations remained steadfast for Burr. Bayard claimed that at least one reason he eventually relented was that he had secured Jefferson's agreement on several matters. The agreement, if secured at all, was indirect, and Jefferson later denied that he had authorized any concessions.[57]

The Twelfth Amendment was adopted in 1804 in direct response to the difficulties of 1800 and 1801.[58] The amendment separated the elector balloting for president and vice president. Each elector was to cast one vote for each office. This eliminated the possibility of a tie between two candidates, each of whom had a majority of the electors, but recourse to the House was retained if no person obtained a majority of the electors in the vote for president. The House would then choose from among the three presidential candidates with the highest number of electoral votes. In the case of the vice presidency, the requirement of a majority of the electors was inserted, and the Senate would choose from the two highest vote-getters if no candidate commanded a majority. The total numbers of candidates for the two offices in these contingent procedures was probably derived from the five from whom the House was to choose the president in the original scheme.[59]

The Twelfth Amendment is perhaps most remarkable for what it did not change.[60] Most fundamentally, the office of elector was retained. By that time it was clear that electors were at least often casting their votes pursuant to prior commitment, rather than exercising any real discretion informed by discussion among electors.[61] The state legislatures had been employing a variety of selection mechanisms for choosing electors, including naming them outright and conducting popular elections, sometimes at large from the state as a whole (a so-called "general ticket"), and sometimes from geographic districts within the state. But selection of party loyalists had become the pattern, even in the case of popular elections, where party identification was trumpeted as voters made their choices. This might have suggested direct votes on candidates, either by legislatures or (at the discretion of legislatures) by the voters, but no such move was given serious consideration. The Twelfth Amendment reads as if it is fully as innocent of the involvement of political parties as had been the electoral college provisions it replaced.[62]

Separating the votes for president and vice president may even have exacerbated the "problem"—if one viewed it that way—of elector attachment to political parties. Under the original scheme electors were to vote for two persons, each of whom they judged to be qualified to be president. Given the uncertainties about what was happening in other states, electors had an incentive to vote for two qualified presidential candidates, even if one was clearly the party-designated candidate—or their own personal favorite—for the office. With the votes separated, on the other hand, the focus of the vice-presidential selection process would be on that office rather than on a potential president. As we have noted, the vice president's formal duties were—and are—modest in the extreme, so that statesmanship, or the ability to rise above faction, or talent along some other "presidential" dimension, could be deemphasized, and other things, like party loyalty or geographic balance with the presidential candidate, could be emphasized instead. The point should not be taken too far. The vice president, after all, remained next in line for the presidency, and that possibility could not sensibly be ignored.[63] But segregating the vice-presidential vote made it no longer a second vote for somebody who might immediately occupy the office of president of the United States.[64]

The focus on the vice president, moreover, might have suggested the awkwardness of having that officer preside at the joint meeting of the two houses of Congress at which the electoral votes were to be counted. The constitutional framers likely assumed that the counting process would be straightforward, so that it would not much matter who presided. But at a minimum it had become painfully clear that the sitting vice president would often be a candidate for the presidency. Vice President Adams had presided at the counting in 1797 when he was elected president, and Vice President Jefferson had similarly presided at the 1801 counting, starting a process through which Jefferson would eventually be selected president as well. These elections should have alerted the country to the possible conflict of interest that inhered in having the vice president preside. Yet that provision too was left undisturbed.[65]

The House (and Senate) contingent selection procedures were also retained, including the provisions that a majority of states was necessary in the House to choose the president and that each state had one vote in the selection. The 1800 election had provided ample evidence of the perils that lay in those provisions. To be sure, the possibility of recourse to the House on account of a tie vote between two—or three—candidates, each of whom had votes of a majority of electors, had been eliminated, but there was no gainsaying that recourse to the House might occasionally still be necessary—after all, the contingent procedure was explicitly retained—and no reason to imagine that the problems of deadlock and partisanship encountered in 1801 would be any less severe in subsequent instances where the choice fell to the House. Indeed, a moment's thought would suggest that it might prove more difficult to find a majority of states able to make a choice among three candidates than between the two that had presented the then recent problem.[66] It does seem likely that the less populous states would have dug in their heels had there been a move to substitute a new contingent selection procedure for president or to change the presidential voting rule in the House. But there is scant evidence that these possibilities were even considered.

And finally, even though the two votes were separated, the provision that only one of an elector's votes could be cast for an "inhabitant" of his state was retained. Perhaps it is understandable that local sentiments in the choice of the national executive remained a matter of concern after 1800. Nonetheless, even after Washington's departure from the scene, nationally known candidates were certainly in view. And the pattern that seemed to be developing was one where political parties tried to provide geographic balance in their tickets, rather than gravitating toward candidates in a single region of the country. Geographic balance, for instance, was no doubt an important consideration in the choice of New York's Burr as the 1800 running mate of Virginia's Jefferson's, as well as in the choice of South Carolina's Charles Cotesworth Pinckney as the New Englander Adams's Federalist running mate in that election.[67] To be sure, the search for geographic balance itself is suggestive of sentiments tied to locality, but not of a process where one need be concerned about elector geographic parochialism in both his choices.

The Twelfth Amendment did smooth the way for the political party slating of paired presidential and vice-presidential candidates that characterizes contemporary American politics. Even without the amendment, it might have been possible to have party slates, by having a single elector break ranks by pre-arrangement. But that would have invited a measure of uncertainty and injected additional complications into an electoral college process that had its share of them already. The Twelfth Amendment can thus be counted as genuine reform of the presidential selection process, even as it has played out over time. But the reform worked by the amendment was modest when set against the problems left untouched. In Chapter Three we will turn to both the constitutional and nonconstitutional developments in the electoral college since passage of the Twelfth Amendment. We shall see that the constitutional changes have, as one commentator put it, left the basic formal rules for the electoral college "unchanged," even though "the manner of presidential selection [had] evolved very quickly into a form which would have been unrecognizable to the Framers."[68]

CHAPTER THREE

A Critical Short History of the
Electoral College, Part II
Operating Under the Twelfth Amendment

By separating the electoral college voting for president and vice president, the Twelfth Amendment eliminated the most immediate problem that had confounded the process for the election of 1800. But the amendment stopped well short of grappling with a variety of additional problems with the electoral college mechanism that were already visible at the time. As we saw in Chapter Two, despite the troubled balloting required in 1801 in the House of Representatives, the Twelfth Amendment left in place the possibility of House selection of the president if no candidate obtained a majority in the electoral college. It ignored the conflict of interest that a sitting vice president might have if he were a candidate for president and also the presiding officer at the joint meeting where the electoral votes were counted. It took no note of political parties which had already become a veritable centerpiece of American politics, despite the constitutional design to hold them, as best as possible, at bay. And, a corollary point, the amendment did nothing to disavow the pretense that when they voted for president in their far-flung meetings, electors were exercising discretion, were deploying judgment informed by searching discussion and debate. Of course the amendment also ignored problems in the process that have only come into focus with clarity in the years since it was passed.

We will return in Chapter Five to the question of just how concerned we should be about the contingent procedure for choosing the president in the House of Representatives. But one reason for uncertainty is that recourse to the

House procedure has been required only once in the ensuing two centuries, and that was a long time ago, in the election of 1824. With Jefferson, Madison and Monroe each having served two terms, by 1824 the White House had been dominated by Jeffersonians—and Virginians—since the turmoil of 1800 and 1801. The Federalists had gone into steep decline, and no genuine competitor had yet emerged for the Jeffersonians, known by the end of this period under the modern name of "Democratic Party." But intraparty sectional rivalries did develop, and there was no obvious heir apparent to Monroe at the end of his second term. The nominating device of a congressional caucus also came under assault, and a number of state legislatures undertook to nominate candidates. In the end the effective choice came down to John Adams's son, John Quincy Adams of Massachusetts, Kentucky's Henry Clay, Georgia's William Crawford, and Tennessee's Andrew Jackson.[1]

There were twenty-four states at the time. While there had been a discernible movement toward popular election as the states' chosen "manner" for designating electors, a minority of states still determined their electors without directly involving the electorate.[2] In this setting Jackson commanded a plurality of the total popular vote for those states that held popular elections, and he also had a plurality of the electoral vote.[3] But he was far short of the required electoral college majority, and so the House was required to choose among Jackson, Adams, and Crawford, the three candidates with the largest number of electoral votes.

Clay had also won electoral votes, and it is worth noting that the Twelfth Amendment's limitation of the House choice to the three candidates with the highest electoral vote totals (instead of the five originally provided for in Article II) may have determined the outcome of the House procedure. Clay was speaker of the House at the time, and might well have prevailed in that forum had he been included in the group from which the House was to choose.[4] In any event, with his own bid for the presidency ended, Clay threw his support to Adams, who then won on the first House ballot. The charge had been made before the House vote that Adams had offered Clay the position of secretary of state in return for his support. This was denied, but Clay did become secretary of state in the Adams administration, and it was clear that Jackson believed that there had been a deal.[5]

A few additional constitutional provisions have since fleshed out aspects of the presidential selection process. The Constitution expresses the tenure of the president and of members of Congress in fixed durational terms. Senators are to serve for six years, presidents (and vice presidents) for four years, and members of the House for two.[6] In "something of an accident of history. . . . [w]hen the dying Continental Congress under the soon-to-be-defunct Articles of Confederation passed enabling legislation to bring the Federal Government under the new Constitution into being, . . . [it] stated that the new Government was to replace the old . . . on the first Wednesday in March of 1789, which just happened to be [March 4 of 1789]."[7] That date was then taken to be the beginning date for all of those terms of office. Congress is constitutionally empowered to set dates for the selection of the presidential electors and for their meetings,[8] and in those early days of slow communication and slow travel it naturally wanted to have that process completed well before that March date when terms were understood to begin. As we saw in Chapter Two, in 1792 it chose the beginning of December for the uniform date for elector voting, and allowed the states to choose electors anytime in the preceding thirty-four days. The result was a lame duck Congress that would be involved in the selection of the new executive, including the House contingent procedure if that became necessary. And that was exactly what happened in 1801.

The same cycle caused problems with the scheduling of congressional sessions.[9] Dissatisfaction grew over the years on these various fronts, and in response the Twentieth Amendment was adopted in 1933. Among its other provisions, the amendment specifies that the term of the newly elected Congress begins on January 3, and the terms of the newly elected president and vice president—presumably whether or not they have actually been selected—start seventeen days later. By statute the joint meeting of the two houses at which the votes are to be counted is to take place on the January 6 after the meetings of electors.[10] The result of these new constitutional and statutory provisions is that it is now the newly elected Congress, not the outgoing one, that counts the electoral votes and then chooses those who are to lead the executive branch if the count proves inconclusive. But with the vice-presidential vote to be counted at the joint meeting, of necessity it is still the outgoing vice president who presides in his capacity as president of the Senate.[11]

Not surprisingly, the Civil War and the constitutional amendments it fostered also left their marks on the electoral college. The Fourteenth Amendment eliminated the provision that slaves would be counted in the census at three-fifths of a person, an accounting that was used for apportionment of the House of Representatives and then derivatively from the House apportionment for the state electoral college allocations as well. While the amendment avoided mention of race or prior servitude, the clear intent was that the freedmen were thenceforth to be counted as full persons. When earlier counted at the three-fifths "federal ratio," the disenfranchised enslaved population of the South had provided a politically hefty "bonus" to the favored states in both the House and the electoral college. Those extra votes may well have been instrumental in producing Virginia's early string of presidents. But ironically, counting the former slaves as full persons opened up the real possibility—fully realized later in American history—that the freedmen would nonetheless be excluded from the franchise, and that the net result would be yet more political power in the House and in the electoral college for the former slaveholding population in the states that had been in rebellion.

To guard against this, the Fourteenth Amendment also provided that a state's representation in the House of Representatives is to be proportionately reduced to the extent that "the right to vote [in federal or state elections] . . . is denied to ['or in any way abridged' for] any of the male inhabitants of such State, being twenty-one years of age, and citizens of the United States, . . . except for participation in rebellion, or other crime."[12] Explicitly included in the covered elections are those "for the choice of electors for President and Vice President of the United States."[13] This does take constitutional note of the practice that had by then become essentially universal of using popular election to select presidential electors. This Fourteenth Amendment sanction for denying the vote to the freedmen has never been invoked, however, and may have been supplanted by the Fifteenth Amendment, which addresses more directly and explicitly the problem of disenfranchisement of the formerly enslaved population.[14]

The Fourteenth Amendment has served as a vehicle for the courts to use in reviewing both discriminatory treatment of citizens in exercising the right to vote and the fairness of the voting process more generally.[15] This is not limited to voting in the presidential context, but it certainly extends to those elections, as illustrated by the Supreme Court's decision in *Bush v. Gore*, the case that brought the 2000 Florida popular vote recount to a halt.[16] More explicitly, the

Nineteenth, Twenty-Fourth, and Twenty-Sixth Amendments limit state discretion to restrict the franchise. The Nineteenth Amendment does so with regard to gender and extends to all elections, as does the Twenty-Sixth, which forbids withholding the vote from those eighteen years of age or older.[17] The Twenty-Fourth Amendment deals with poll taxes, and limits the states only in federal elections, again making explicit mention of elections "for electors for President or Vice President."[18] Finally, the Twenty-Third Amendment, ratified in 1961, gives the District of Columbia a number of electors equal to that of "the least populous state."[19] Since every state is guaranteed at least one member of the House of Representatives,[20] the minimum number of electors a state can have is three. In theory the smallest state electoral college delegation could be larger than three, but three is in fact the size of the smallest delegations, and hence is the size of the District's delegation as well. These various constitutional changes are important, but they do leave intact the basic constitutional structure of the electoral college as defined in the Twelfth Amendment and surviving provisions of Article II.

Other important developments have been worked by statutes at both the federal and state levels. The election of 1876, surely the most contentious in the nation's history, provided a parade of electoral college nightmares. The country was in a period of post–Civil War "Reconstruction." Federal troops were still in parts of the South, and greatly resented by portions of the white Southern population. The modern day "Republican" Party held the White House in the person of the Civil War hero Ulysses S. Grant. But despite continued strong popular resentment of the Democratic Party harking back to the war, even in the North the Republicans were on the defensive politically, given financial turmoil in 1873 and charges of corruption in high places.[21]

In this setting Samuel Tilden, the Democratic presidential candidate, seems to have won the popular vote in the country as a whole.[22] The electoral college had 369 members at the time, and Tilden also had 184 of those securely in his column—one short of a majority. This was without counting any votes from South Carolina, Louisiana, and Florida, three Southern states where the federal presence was still much in evidence, and where the election gave rise to a swirl of charges and countercharges of bribery, fraud, and intimidation—many on both sides apparently quite well founded. There was little in the way of orderly state process for resolving such charges.[23] The result was rival slates of claimants to the office of elector in all three states.[24]

To complicate matters even further, there was also contention about elector legitimacy in Oregon.[25] Oregon was entitled to three electoral votes, and the Oregon Hayes electors clearly had the three highest popular vote totals. The Tilden first-cut national tally of 184 electoral votes thus included none from Oregon. But one of the initially triumphant Oregon electors was a postmaster, and thus seemingly a person who "held an office of trust or profit under the United States," making him constitutionally ineligible for the post of elector.[26] Before the meeting of electors, the postmaster resigned that post, and his fellow Republican electors then selected him to fill the vacancy originally caused by his own presumed ineligibility. An Oregon statute assigned to the remaining electors the authority to fill vacancies in this way, but it said nothing about whether a vacancy could be filled with the very person whose ineligibility had created it. Having discovered the problem, moreover, Oregon's Democratic governor certified in the stead of the ineligible Republican the Democratic elector who had the next highest number of votes.[27] The result was that there were rival choices for Oregon's third electoral slot. Two different electoral counts were submitted from the state, differing by one vote that could put Tilden over the top in the electoral college tally.[28]

Feelings about the election in general, and about the disputes from those four states in particular, ran very high, and there was even talk of a new civil war.[29] The constitutional provisions could not easily provide closure, because they were decidedly unhelpful about how a choice between rival slates of electors was to be resolved. Simply incorporating the original constitutional provisions, the governing Twelfth Amendment provided only that the "votes shall . . . be counted" after being opened by the president of the Senate "in the presence of the Senate and House of Representatives." Was the president of the Senate to resolve controversies, or the joint meeting? If the latter, by what voting rule, one for each House, one for each member, or even one for each state? These questions might have been made completely "academic" for the 1876 election if a single party had controlled all the levers of authority in the picture. But in fact the Democrats controlled the House of Representatives and the Republicans the Senate.[30] There was a real possibility of competing and plausible claims to the presidency with no obvious way for the dispute to be resolved.

Prior to 1876, questions surrounding electoral votes had been resolved at the joint meeting in a variety of ways, sometimes seemingly almost *ad hoc*. For years a loose approach to the electoral count had been possible because the vote in the electoral college had not been close enough to have the outcome of an election turn on decisions that had to be made at that meeting. In the decade preceding the contentious election, however, the governing approach had been that of the so-called "Twenty-second Joint Rule" of 1865, under which "no [electoral] vote objected to ... [was to] be counted, except by concurrent votes of the two houses."[31] This came in response to the Civil War and was sustained by Reconstruction and congressional wariness of the Southern states as they were reintegrated into the governing structure of the country.[32] By 1876, however, the Senate had unilaterally abandoned the Twenty-second Joint Rule,[33] and there was no clarity about what would take its place. It was in this setting that the meeting faced the disputes from the four contested states, any one of which could provide the margin that Tilden needed for victory. With no real mooring, the joint meeting faced its greatest challenge since the Twelfth Amendment had been added to the Constitution.

No doubt in part because the horror of the Civil War was still fresh in mind, the two sides figuratively dodged a bullet, reaching a procedural accommodation with a law providing for an electoral commission to resolve the rival claims from the four states. The commission was to consist of fifteen members, five from each house of Congress and then five Supreme Court Justices. Four of the justices were named in the legislation, and these four were assumed to have partisan—and balanced—leanings. The four were to appoint the fifth justice. It was broadly assumed that he would be David Davis, a Lincoln Supreme Court appointee who was thought to be politically nonpartisan, and that Davis's vote would dominate the proceedings. Then, in an almost unbelievable twist to this extraordinary drama, the Illinois legislature chose Davis for the U.S. Senate, after the bill providing for the commission was passed but before the selection of the commissioners who were not named in the legislation. Davis declined to serve as a commissioner, and Justice Joseph Bradley was named by his fellow justices in Davis's stead. Wielding the decisive commission vote, Bradley resolved all the disputed electoral votes in Hayes's favor.[34]

The legislation provided that the commission's decisions would govern unless rejected by both houses of Congress. In each case only the Democratic

House voted against the commission, formally leaving the commission's decisions in place. But the entire counting process stretched out over a full month.[35] The Democrats might have thought that an obstructionist approach could force the selection process into the House, where they also controlled a majority of the delegations.[36] But with both whispered—and no doubt real—bargaining all about, the Democrats finally relented, just a day before the scheduled inauguration.[37] Hayes thus became president by one electoral vote, 185-184, the closest electoral college vote in the nation's history, with the exception, of course, of the 1800 tie under a different voting protocol. There is continuing dispute about just what was encompassed in the "Bargain of 1877," and in particular whether the rapid damping down and then end to Reconstruction that followed the election had been part of the bargain.[38] There is, however, little doubt that momentous matters of policy and interest were caught up in the choice of Hayes as the new president.[39]

The draftsmen of the matter-of-fact constitutional language about counting electoral votes seem to have assumed that the task would be routine, that electors would have been chosen with decisiveness, and then have voted in straightforward fashion. The joint meeting would then witness a strictly ceremonial exercise in uncontroversial mathematics.[40] But even before 1876 it was clear that any such expectation was misplaced. There had been earlier incidents of rival state governments.[41] The Civil War multiplied these,[42] and the rivalries had surfaced as disputes about elector legitimacy in Louisiana in 1872.[43] As we have seen, the 1876 election compounded the incidents of rival slates, but it was already painfully apparent not only that rival slates were possible but that all manner of additional questions could be raised about the legitimacy of electoral votes.

Most fundamentally, it had long been recognized that questions could arise about qualifications for office. The Oregon dispute of 1876 illustrated a problem of elector qualification,[44] but the Constitution also imposes qualifications for the officers for whom the electors are voting. A president must be a "person" of at least thirty-five years of age, a resident of the United States for fourteen years, and a "natural born citizen."[45] In the 1872 election, a question about these qualifications arose when Horace Greeley, the Democratic nominee, died between "election day" and the day on which the electors met. Some electors voted for him nonetheless, and the joint meeting was presented with the question of whether a dead man is a constitutional "person" eligible to receive electoral votes. (The joint meeting did not count the Greeley votes.)[46]

Issues had also arisen about just when in the process of attaining statehood a territory was entitled to choose electors and then, with statehood attained, to have those votes counted.[47] There could be questions of the timing and the procedures of meetings of electors. Article II says that a date Congress might choose for the electors to meet and vote "shall be the same throughout the United States,"[48] but in the 1856 election Wisconsin's electors met a day late on account of a blizzard.[49] The Twelfth Amendment says that the electors are to "vote by ballot," and a question might be raised about whether that implies secrecy or anything else about the procedure for voting.[50] The amendment also says that the electors are to "sign and certify" lists they prepare of persons voted for and "of the number of votes for each." They are then to "transmit" those lists "sealed to the seat of the government . . . directed to the President of the Senate." On occasion, fault was claimed on account of the way those directions were carried out.[51]

We have also seen that the electors could only vote for an "inhabitant" of their own state for president or vice president, but not both, so that challenge on that ground was possible.[52] And then, since the expectation of what electors were to do had changed so dramatically, there were questions of what to do with "faithless electors," those who voted contrary to their apparent commitments. The Greeley electors who did not vote for him were, of course, "faithless" in a sense, but one could hardly quarrel with that particular breach of faith. The more serious problem was with electors who felt free to vote faithlessly while the candidate to whom they were pledged was fully eligible—and indeed eager—to receive their votes. In Chapter Seven we will treat the problem of whether such faithless votes must be honored. Suffice it to say for the moment that the election of 1876 put an exclamation point on a proposition that had long been evident that the division of authority on matters of the electoral count between state and federal governments was potentially of very great significance.

The 1876 recourse to a commission had little appeal as a long-term solution. It had been stitched together and had allowed the country to get through a crisis, but with the evident partisanship of its members, the commission had invited almost as much controversy as it had avoided. Still, it was painfully clear that some regularized and institutionalized counting process was required. The result was the Electoral Count Act (ECA) of 1887, which, with only slight amendments, governs congressional counting of electoral votes to this day.[53]

The votes to be counted, of course, come from the states, which, as we have seen, are given the constitutional authority to determine the "manner" of appointing electors. This power would seem comfortably to accommodate the authority to resolve disputes that might arise under state law about just who gets to cast the states' votes. The states generally did have in place statutory procedures to resolve disputes over election of state officials, but they had left questions about presidential electors to common law court proceedings. It was these proceedings that had proved inadequate in 1876, though in the case of presidential elections the state procedures were pinched by congressional decisions.

It was commonly assumed that state law disputes about just who gets to cast a state's electoral votes would have to be completed between election day and the day on which the electors were to meet. With the longstanding early December date for the meetings of electors in place, in 1845 Congress had opted for a uniform date for choosing electors as well, specifying a date in early November, which to this day we think of as "election day."[54] The result was that less than a month was available for states to resolve any disputes, and this was clearly insufficient for the types of factually laden controversies that plagued the 1876 election in the three contested Southern states.[55] The ECA thus moved the day for the meeting of electors to early January, more than doubling the time between election day and the meetings of electors. (After the Twentieth Amendment moved the joint meeting and inauguration day to January, this provision of the ECA was amended, so that the meetings of electors now take place in December, unfortunately shortening this period for comfortably resolving disputes to about forty days.)[56]

While these questions of timing were clearly within congressional authority, the ECA moves well beyond them both in regularizing electoral vote procedures and in allocating authority to resolve disputes at both the state and federal levels.[57] On these various concerns little is made clear by the constitutional text. The Constitution, for instance, treats the determination of elector legitimacy rather casually. All it says besides the provision for counting at the joint meeting is that each state's group of electors is to sign, certify, and send in lists of its votes.[58] An early Congress had elaborated on these procedures a bit and had also directed the governor of each state to certify and deliver to the electors themselves lists of the names of those who had been chosen for the office.[59]

The ECA now draws the governor into the process more extensively. Under Section Six of the ECA, each state's governor is to prepare and authenticate a "certificate of ascertainment" identifying the state's electors and showing the votes that each received, along with similar information on all other candidates for elector. This is to be done "as soon as practicable" after the appointment of the electors, or the conclusion of any controversy about their appointment. The governor is to provide copies of this certificate of ascertainment both to the electors who were chosen and to the archivist of the United States.[60] When nationwide popular vote totals are later compiled, state totals are taken from these certificates.[61] After voting, the electors then prepare and certify a "certificate of vote," showing the votes they cast separately for president and vice president. The electors associate this certificate of vote with the certificate of ascertainment they received from the governor and forward the two together to state and national officials, including to the president of the Senate.[62]

The ECA provisions allocating authority to resolve disputes are found in Section Five and in a long and unwieldy Section Fifteen. Close observers of the 2000 election will recall that the so-called safe harbor provision of the ECA played an important role in the decision of the Supreme Court's majority in *Bush v. Gore*[63] that there was insufficient time to conduct a satisfactory statewide recount of the Florida popular vote. Found in Section Five, the safe harbor provision says that state resolution of "any controversy or contest concerning the appointment of . . . electors" through state "judicial or other" procedures that were embodied in law prior to election day is to "be conclusive, and . . . govern in the counting of electoral votes," if the resolution is final "at least six days before the time fixed for the meeting of the electors."[64] Despite some confusion about this provision during the 2000 election, there should be no negative implication that state resolution of a controversy would have to be ignored if it was not final six days before the meeting of electors.[65] The provision rather represents only a kind of guarantee by Congress that a timely resolution of a controversy covered under the section will be given effect. Even without a leisurely stop in the harbor, in other words, the state can still get its resolution of any contest or controversy into port later, for whatever consideration it might otherwise merit.

The safe harbor guarantee clearly was an attempt to nudge the states to adopt expeditious—but orderly—procedures for resolving controversies about the outcome of elections for electors. In the context of the popular elections for which all states have opted, Section Five's concern with "appointment" of electors is most obviously relevant to determinations of electoral fraud or mistake of some sort in the counting of popular votes. Section Five cannot comfortably be read as having relevance for the qualifications of the persons for whom electors vote, nor for the procedures that they follow in voting, since these cannot generally be known until after the safe harbor time limits have passed. And in enacting the ECA Congress fully intended to reserve to itself the authority to pass on whether the conditions of Section Five were met. That reserved congressional authority means that both houses must concur about satisfaction of Section Five status before harbor safety is attained.[66]

Aside from the nudge of Section Five, the ECA's rules for resolving controversies about electoral votes are contained in the rambling Section Fifteen. Under its provisions, objections to electoral votes in the joint meeting must be in writing and must be joined by at least one member of each house if they are to be considered.[67] The states' votes are taken up in alphabetical order, and each qualified objection is to be resolved before the next state's vote is considered. When an objection is properly lodged, each House considers it separately. If a state's governor has certified a group of electors under Section Six, and there is no competing slate of electors from the state, then the votes of the certified slate are to be counted unless both Houses concur in rejecting them. For governor-certified electors, of course, this reversed the presumption of the Twenty-second Joint Rule that had governed for a decade, under which a vote would not be counted unless both Houses accepted it.

The protection for votes by governor-certified electors extends only to votes which "have been regularly given" by electors whose "appointment has been lawfully certified." While the wording of the long section is tortured, any determination that these qualifications have not been satisfied seems to require a "concurrent" determination of both houses. In any event, while lawful certification presumably refers to elector eligibility, the meaning of "regularly given" is more elusive.[68] A joint meeting challenge on account of irregularity, for instance, was leveled in the 1968 election count at the vote of a single "faithless" North Carolina Republican elector, Lloyd Bailey. Bailey had cast his votes for the American Independent Party presidential candidate George Wallace and Wallace's running mate Curtis LeMay, rather than for Richard Nixon and Spiro Agnew, the Republican candidates who had won the popular vote in the state. Each House rejected the challenge, and Bailey's faithless vote was counted, albeit not in a context where it could have changed the outcome of the election. At the time North Carolina had no specific provision in its election law requiring electors to vote as pledged.[69] The acceptance of Bailey's vote by the joint meeting might thus be a precedent of sorts for the proposition that faithless votes are "regularly given," at least in states that do not explicitly forbid them. But the precedent is hardly a strong one, and more generally questions remain quite open about whether a vote should be considered "regularly given" when it suffers from arguable infirmities other than who won the state's election—matters like the procedures electors followed, or the qualifications of the persons for whom they voted.

The even more difficult set of Section Fifteen problems involves competing slates of electoral votes. If only one of the competitors has obtained a Section Five determination, that will be conclusive in its favor, again with the limitation that the votes must have been "regularly given,"[70] and again with the concurrence of both houses necessary for any conclusion of irregularity. If there are competing slates and also competing affirmative Section Five determinations within a state, however, any decision that one or the other determination was rendered by "the lawful tribunal of such state" requires the concurrence of both Houses, as it had under the Twenty-second Joint Rule.[71] Similarly, if there are competing slates, but no Section Five determination, the concurrence of both Houses is necessary for one of them to be counted.[72] This repeated possibility of seemingly decisive differences between the Houses might seem to invite the kind of stalemate the ECA more generally sought to avoid, but near the end of the complex section, gubernatorial certification is again invoked to break any jam. If the two Houses cannot agree in any of these cases of competing slates and either competing Section Five determinations or no Section Five determination, "the votes of the electors whose appointment shall have been certified by the executive of the State . . . shall be counted."[73]

To be sure, this reliance on gubernatorial certification may not solve all problems. For instance, we will turn shortly to the 1960 election, where there were actually competing governor-certified slates from Hawaii. And in the 2000 election Florida's Governor Jeb Bush arguably sent in a certification that was premature under the ECA.[74] Conceivably a challenge could have been leveled on the ground that the purported certification was not effective. Similarly, the 2000 election is suggestive of the possibility that a governor might certify one slate even though a court has ordered him to certify another, or even to with-hold certification. Issue might well be joined on whether an arguably "illegal" certification is entitled to deference under the ECA.

To date, there have not been any very serious tests of the ECA possibilities for rejecting electoral votes. We earlier took a glimpse at the 1968 challenge to a North Carolina elector's votes. The 2000 election certainly presented possibili-ties for challenges to electoral votes, but the Supreme Court's ruling on the Florida recount seems to have preempted any such effort. For the 2004 election, in contrast, California's Senator Barbara Boxer joined members of the House in challenging the Ohio votes, though the effort was widely viewed from the start as basically symbolic.[75] Besides these, it was only the 1960 contest between John Kennedy and Richard Nixon that flirted with ECA controversies in the joint meeting counting process.

For the 1960 election, the nationwide popular vote was quite close, and in-deed the conventional wisdom of a Kennedy popular vote margin of about 118,000 votes as reported by the national media is doubtful because of uncer-tainty about how to allocate popular votes in Alabama, where voters at the time cast individual votes for electors. Some of the electors on the Democratic slate—the result of a primary electoral process—had run as "unpledged" to any candidate, while others were pledged to Kennedy, the national nominee of the party. The reported margin depended upon an allocation to Kennedy of the largest number of votes cast for any Democratic elector. That elector happened to have been unpledged, but even assignment to Kennedy of the highest num-ber of votes cast for an elector pledged to him would have yielded more na-tionwide popular votes than Nixon received. There is, however, no real doubt that many Alabama voters—indeed in all likelihood most of those who voted for Democratic electors at all—cast votes for both pledged and unpledged elec-tors. If Kennedy were credited only with a fraction of the total representing some genuine attempt at apportionment between pledged and unpledged elec-tors, he would have received fewer popular votes nationwide than Nixon.[76]

Kennedy's electoral college margin, in contrast, eventually turned out to be a comfortable eighty-four votes, 303-219. But there were a large number of controversies over the constituent elements in that count. Nixon won California's thirty-two electoral votes, for instance, only by virtue of the delayed inclusion of absentee ballots. The vote was quite close in a number of other states as well, and recounts were conducted in several. It was only in Hawaii, however, that the recount reversed the state outcome. The initial Hawaii count had given Nixon a 141 popular vote edge. The Democrats demanded a recount, and the state's three electoral votes eventually went for Kennedy on account of a popular vote lead of 115. The time pressure, however, prevented the recount from being conducted within the ECA's safe harbor time frame. Indeed, it was not finished until well after the congressionally prescribed December 19 date for the meetings of electors. The Democratic slate had met on the prescribed date—as had the Republican electors—and thus avoided the possibility of a challenge to its votes on that ground. The result was that Hawaii submitted two different "certificates of ascertainment," each certified by a governor of the state, the first an acting governor and the second the newly elected one.[77] There is no telling what controversy might have erupted in the joint meeting count had those three Hawaii votes held the potential to change the election outcome. As it happened, a Kennedy victory was foreordained by then. As the sitting vice president, Richard Nixon presided over the session, and he asked and received unanimous consent for the acceptance of the votes from Hawaii for his presidential rival.[78]

Despite the potential for contentiousness over issues like what is meant by votes "regularly given," or whether a gubernatorial certification is legitimate, it seems fair to say that the ECA has played a steadying role in electoral college controversies in the years since its passage.[79] In addition, there have been a number of momentous electoral college changes at the state level. The most important of these have been in the method state legislatures have chosen for the selection of electors. Even for the first presidential election, some states had opted for popular election of electors—sometimes as part of a complex elimination process in which legislative choice also played a role.[80] But there was a good deal of change and experimentation—indeed some strategic manipulation—by state legislatures in the first few presidential elections. Sometimes questions of how electors would be chosen became issues of salience in elections for the state legislature.[81] In any event, for the 1800 election there remained a variety of means by which electors were chosen, importantly including direct designation by state legislatures. Rather quickly after that, however, popular election carried the day. With very few exceptions, popular election of electors has been used by every state since the 1830s.[82]

It is not only popular election as such that matters, but the rules of those elections. The original idea was that electors would be chosen as individuals, but we have seen that gradually entire "slates" of electors became associated with political parties and with the presidential and vice-presidential candidates those parties had chosen. At the present time, those party "slates" are formally designated in a variety of ways. A majority of states use party conventions, but in some the party central committee makes the choices. In one state the party's presidential nominee names the party's slate, while in another the party nominees for House and Senate seats designate the candidates for elector.[83] But these formalities are less important than the results. As one commentator puts it, "[p]ersons are usually nominated for elector on the basis of long service to their party, because of financial donations to the party or a candidate, or out of the party's wish to have an ethnically or politically balanced elector slate."[84]

Once a state resolves to select electors through popular election, there remains a variety of ways in which that might be done. Without even treating more exotic possibilities, a state's electoral college delegation might be chosen from single-elector districts within the state, through a statewide election for individual electors, or through a statewide electoral choice from among entire slates. If there were a statewide election in which a voter voted for an entire slate, moreover, the state's delegation might be allocated in proportion to each slate's portion of the statewide vote, or might instead consist of the entire slate that got the most votes. The latter is called a "general ticket," or, more colloquially, "winner-take-all." Of these three possibilities, the proportional approach has never been used. Colorado had a popular initiative on the November 2004 ballot that would have instituted proportional allocation of the state's nine electors, but the initiative went down to defeat.[85]

The issue of the degree of state discretion over these matters was posed by a Michigan statute passed in anticipation of the 1892 election. Republicans had been the dominant party in the state, regularly winning all the state's presidential electors under Michigan's general ticket. The Democrats then gained what seemed likely to be only temporary control of the state legislature and decided to divide the state into districts for choice of presidential electors, in the hopes of depriving the Republicans of at least some of the state's electoral votes. Under the plan adopted by an 1891 statute, one elector would be chosen from each congressional district in the state, and then one each from eastern and western sections of the state as designated in the statute. This was challenged on the ground that each elector represents the entire state and hence must be chosen by some statewide process. The issue reached the U.S. Supreme Court, where the Michigan districting was approved in an opinion that affirmed broad state discretion in the "manner" of choosing electors. Relying in part on the early practice of districting, and mentioning that districting was "largely considered the most equitable," the Court spoke of the legislature's power over the "manner" of selection of electors as "plenary" and "exclusive."[86]

The power of a winner-take-all approach had actually become apparent quite early. James Madison had been instrumental in changing Virginia's choice mechanism for the 1800 election from district elections (which he favored in principle) to a statewide general ticket. Madison's motivation was to secure the entire Virginia delegation for his friend and political ally Thomas Jefferson in what promised to be a close national presidential contest.[87] And the advantages of a general ticket for a dominant party in a state are so clear that few states have opted for any other system since the first half of the Nineteenth Century. Jefferson himself, while also in principle favoring election by districts, wrote that "while 10 states choose either by their legislatures or by general ticket, it is folly and worse than folly for the ... [rest] not to do it."[88]

The 1892 Michigan move away from winner-take-all was unusual, and seemingly resulted from temporary political developments.[89] More generally, stability in political control of a state is likely to lead to use of the general ticket, but so is change, for new political alignments are likely to be taken as the best sign of what the future holds.[90] Not surprisingly then, in the first elections of the Twenty-First Century, the District of Columbia and all states but two awarded their entire allocation of electors to the winner of a statewide popular vote. The two holdouts—Maine (since the 1972 election) and Nebraska (since the 1992 election)—selected one elector from each of their congressional districts and two from the state as a whole.[91]

The motivation in these two deviant states is probably quite wholesome. A winner-take-all approach does mean that a state's electoral vote breakdown bears scant relationship to the breakdown of political sentiment in the state.

Whether the losing slate comes close or not is irrelevant. It commands none of the state's electoral votes. Close is, of course, what happened in Florida in the 2000 election (as well as in other states) where the two presidential candidates—or, more technically, the slates of electors pledged to them—ended in a virtual tie, but all the state's electoral college votes went to the marginal victor. Districting does not ensure that a state's popular and electoral college votes will be perfectly congruent. As a practical matter no system can provide such a guarantee, because fractional electoral votes are not permitted. But districting can be expected on occasion to bring the electoral and popular vote counts into closer alignment, and that probably accounts for some of its continuing appeal in Maine and Nebraska.[92] That is perhaps what the Supreme Court was referring to in the Michigan case when it characterized the districting system as more "equitable." We will return to that subject when we take up proposed reforms in the system in Chapter Four.[93]

The winner-take-all approach arguably affected the outcome in a large number of elections over the years,[94] but the election of 1888 deserves brief mention in this short history, if for no other reason than that it generated such little controversy. Grover Cleveland was the Democratic candidate and Benjamin Harrison the Republican standard bearer. Thanks in part to the winner-take-all provision in a number of large states, Harrison captured the electoral college by sixty-five votes while losing the nationwide popular vote by less than 100,000. Both the Prohibition Party candidate in the 1888 election and a combined assortment of others captured votes that easily exceeded Cleveland's popular vote plurality.[95] This is one of only three or four instances over the years where the popular vote and electoral college "results" diverged,[96] but it is the one clear case where the dissonance seems to have gone down quite easily in the land.[97]

Finally, the development of political parties and the appeal of the general ticket have led to integration of parties into the election processes defined in state legislation. Parties nominate slates of electors, and the names of individual electors on the party slates will quite often not even appear on the ballots that members of the popular electorate cast. Instead the ballot may in fine print say something like "electors pledged to" followed in large print by the name of the party's nominees for president and vice president. Or the ballot may only contain the presidential and vice-presidential candidates' names, with the formality that it is "really" electors being chosen made explicit in state statutes. We will explore these matters of ballot format more fully in Chapter Seven.

The net result of these various developments is to give us a presidential selection system that is quite different from the one envisaged by those who came up with the electoral college in the first place. Instead of being marginalized in the process as the framers had hoped and expected, political parties dominate it.[98] The prevalence of winner-take-all has to some degree deprived the less populous states of the electoral college advantage that was built into the system for them.[99] The fact that electors play a role at all is largely hidden from public view. And, as we saw in Chapter Two, the role they do play could not be more different from that originally imagined. Overwhelmingly electors do not come to their meetings to debate and decide on the best candidates for president and vice president. They come to the process, not only with their "minds made up," but typically with no process of choice even in view. They were selected to cast a predetermined vote, and they routinely do so. As one commentator put it, "[l]ike the British monarch, who reigns but does not rule, the electoral college votes but does not decide."[100] Another says that electors are "mere mandarin toys that nod when they are set in motion."[101] In Chapter Seven we will return to the phenomenon called "faithless electors," but the term itself is ironic in light of this history. What are today called "faithless electors" are those who abstain or vote for a candidate other than the one to whom they were pledged. The "faithlessness" is to their pledges. The irony is that it is only they who are faithful to at least a part of the original conception of how the electors were to decide on the presidency of the United States.

CHAPTER FOUR

Evaluating the Electoral College
The Nationwide Popular Vote Alternative

In arguing for ratification of the Constitution Alexander Hamilton suggested that if the electoral college mechanism was not a "perfect" way to choose the nation's executive, "it is at least excellent."[1] This sounds a bit defensive, perhaps an excess of rhetoric in the service of a good cause. There is, of course, no way to know for sure if the method on which Hamilton opined might have been "excellent," for, as we saw in the last two chapters, the electoral college process quickly turned into something quite different from what those who put it together seem to have had in mind. But that itself says something about their choice. In some ideal world the method might have been splendid, but that splendor could not be realized in the real world of American politics. For that reason alone, if we were searching today for a way to select the president, it is thoroughly unlikely that we would come up with something even remotely like the electoral college.[2]

Still, as shaped by political realities over the years, the presidential selection process has for the most part proceeded smoothly enough, with the modern version of the electoral college usually out of both sight and mind. Only when a presidential election is quite close, as was the 2000 election, or promised to be, as in 2004, have substantial segments of the public taken note of the electoral college, usually with some mixture of puzzlement and concern. The net result is that American democracy maintains an uneasy relationship with the modern embodiment of this peculiar institution. Among knowledgeable commentators the electoral college has an ample share of passionate detractors, but also a complement of quite ardent defenders. Sweeping proposals for reform of the electoral college are frequently advanced and then seldom get very far.[3]

This is, of course, not to say that there has been no change in the electoral college since its early break with the initial conception. In fact, the electoral college seems always to be a work in progress. For the most part, however, change has come either piecemeal and at the state level, or off stage in political developments. The initial changes were in large part due to the emergence of political parties, for instance, and the operation of the process is now suffused with their influence. Those parties are more generally embedded in a system of popular election in the contemporary United States, and popular election has now swept the field in the state-by-state determinations of the "manner" of selecting presidential electors, to the point where, except for seeming crises as in the 2000 setting in Florida, reversion to direct legislative designation of electors, or some other less "democratic" mode of selection, seems unthinkable.

There have also been occasional changes in the law at the national level, with the most significant of those changes coming relatively early and in response to crises. Both the elections of 1800 and of 1876 exposed serious frailties in the process, and each was followed by important reforms, the first worked by the Twelfth Amendment, and the second by the Electoral Count Act. In Chapter Three we discussed a variety of additional constitutional changes over the years. The Fourteenth Amendment in particular came in the wake of a national crisis, but not a crisis that had the electoral college at its core. The others were more low-key events, responding at politically propitious moments to an accumulated sense that relatively modest change was required. Perhaps of most significance, the Twenty-Third Amendment, ratified in 1961, extended electoral college representation to the District of Columbia.

One striking part of the recent picture is the relative inaction at the federal level, despite continuing calls for change. Even ardent defenders of the electoral college have come to agree that parts of the system are seriously flawed. They tend, moreover, to agree on the flaws.[4] And in recent years calls for doing away with the electoral college and substituting a nationwide vote for president, have issued with some regularity, from academic circles, to be sure, but from political ones as well.[5] These sentiments have not, however, gelled into action.

At least one reason for the inaction is that it is usually assumed that any important change at the national level would require constitutional amendment.

There has certainly been no dearth of proposed amendments. "Nearly one-tenth of all constitutional amendments proposed in Congress have sought electoral college reform."[6] This is "more . . . than for any other part of the Constitution."[7] But amending the Constitution in any respect was made quite difficult by design, requiring the concurrence of two-thirds of each house of Congress and three-fourths of the states.[8] And the latter requirement looms particularly large as an obstacle to any amendment that would institute a nationwide vote, because substantial state prerogatives are at stake.[9] The roll call of winners and losers from a move to a nationwide popular vote is more complicated than is often assumed. We will try to parse those effects more closely in Chapter Ten. But in the absence of crisis, uncertainty about the effects of change seems often to work against it.

A principal thesis of this book is that much of the reformist energy has been misdirected, in two different though related senses. Reformers have chosen large targets when greater mischief can often be corralled by paying attention to smaller ones. And with those large targets in view reformers have been misled by the assumption that constitutional amendment is the only way to achieve meaningful change.[10] In fact, there is much to be accomplished without navigating the obstacle course of constitutional amendment.

In this chapter I want to examine the principal proposals that electoral college reformers have advanced, with particular emphasis on a nationwide popular election for president, the proposed reform with the most contemporary support. This will give concrete form to the arguments advanced for and against retention of the electoral college. When overheated rhetoric is put to one side, I think it will become apparent that important aspects of the modern electoral college mechanism are, if not "excellent," at least tolerable. This will lay the basis for exploration of more problematic aspects of the process in subsequent chapters. With the nature and degree of electoral college concerns brought into sharper focus, I will in those later chapters suggest some ways to improve the selection process for president (and vice president) without constitutional amendment, providing a good deal more reformist bang for the reformist buck.

The electoral college reformist zeal seems fixated on the specter of a "wrong winner," the possibility of an electoral college victor who obtains fewer popular votes across the nation than one or more rivals.[11] This is, of course, what happened in the 2000 election, and as we saw in Chapter Three, in two or three other elections over the years.[12] Initially, however, it should be noted that the charge that these elections did in fact produce a "wrong winner" is unfair, even if it is assumed that a nationwide popular vote is the "right" way to choose the president. With the electoral college mechanism in place, candidates campaign to win the electoral college vote, not the popular one.[13] If the rules of engagement in these elections had been different, candidates would have campaigned differently, and there is no way to know who would have won the nationwide popular vote.

Be that as it may, the contemporary operation of the electoral college does not make victory turn on the nationwide vote, at the same time as it makes nationwide vote totals easily calculable and readily available. In that sense it both invites victory by a candidate who would have lost the nationwide vote, and at least appears to tell us whether that has happened. The "wrong winner" possibility is then summarized by electoral college critics with the charge that the electoral college is at odds with "political equality—the bedrock principle that no person's vote should carry more weight than another's—[which] lies at the very heart of American democracy."[14]

We will turn shortly to proposals that would take this bull of a wrong winner "problem" directly by the horns and institute a nationwide popular vote for president. But first we look briefly at less sweeping moves in more or less the same direction. Each of the most prominent reform proposals—aside from a nationwide popular vote—seems to take aim at the wrong winner problem by making it at a minimum more likely that the electoral college awards victory to the same person who would have prevailed in a nationwide popular vote. The three most prominent of these more indirect attacks on the wrong winner problem are (1) requiring that each state's electors be chosen from geographic districts within the state; (2) requiring that each state's electors be apportioned among the presidential candidates according to their popular vote totals; and (3) a "national bonus" plan in which the winner of the nationwide popular vote would be awarded a large electoral vote "bonus" to be added to the state-by-state totals under the present system.

The bonus plan would allow states to retain winner-take-all rules—or, presumably, a wide range of other possibilities—for their allotted electors. The proposed bonus would be so large, however, that it would almost surely overwhelm the state-by-state totals, making victory without winning the nation-wide vote extremely unlikely.[15] Commentators have rightly found the bonus idea rather contrived.[16] One calls it a "Rube Goldberg-like system,"[17] after the concoctions of the inventive cartoonist. The districting and proportionality proposals, in contrast, would more directly rein in state prerogatives about the "manner" of selecting electors. Each of the two would forbid a state to employ winner-take-all and thus would open up the possibility of dividing the electoral college vote in the state. There are variations on the proportionality proposal,[18] but in any of the most prominent variants, division of a state's electoral college vote would be virtually certain in most states.[19] A split vote would not be that certain under a districting requirement—even in a closely divided state the same candidate could win narrowly in each district—but, unlike winner-take-all, districting would at least open up the possibility of a split in a state's electoral college vote.[20]

Two of these three proposals could in theory be accomplished through state-by-state action without a constitutional amendment. This is obviously true of districting. Districting was actually used by some states in the earliest days of the electoral college,[21] and as we have seen, Maine and Nebraska have employed districts to choose some of their presidential electors for a number of years now. Those two states each choose two of their electors through a statewide vote, and the rest through elections in the states' respective congressional districts. That states are free to district in this way—or in any other way consistent with constitutional norms like that of equally distributed population—was made clear by the 1892 Supreme Court decision in *McPherson v. Blacker*.[22]

But if states have the authority to choose electors from districts, they do not have much incentive to do so. We saw in Chapter Three that the dominant political forces in a state have an incentive to adopt winner-take-all elections. But at least the larger states can marshal an argument of "principle" as well. The voters in the least populous states are advantaged by the "two Senator bonus" of electors, which yields a more favorable ratio for those states of electors to population. The more populous states are able to overcome the disadvantagement of their voters by shunning districts in favor of "winner-take-all." We will delve more deeply into those matters in Chapter Ten, but there is simply no reason to expect those more populous states to give up the winner-take-all possibility as long as the small state "bonus" remains in place.[23] Nor is there much reason for less populous states to shun winner take all. If forced to the choice in isolation from other states, winner-take-all—as opposed to districting or proportionality—does incrementally increase the small states' electoral college say as well.

The senatorial bonus is a matter of constitutional mandate,[24] so that any systematic move away from winner-take-all could plausibly be expected only as part of a package of constitutional changes. In addition, while the use of geographic districts for choosing electors has had many ardent proponents over the years, the height of its popularity was in the Nineteenth Century.[25] In recent years, moreover, partisan gerrymandering of legislative districts seems to be an ever more secure fixture of American political life,[26] and that makes electoral college districting both less appealing on the merits and even less likely to overcome partisan contentiousness.[27]

Similarly, there would seem to be no legal obstacle to a state's awarding its electors in proportion to the statewide popular vote for presidential candidates, if the "awards" are rounded off to whole numbers of electors. (Any attempt to award fractional electoral votes would raise constitutional problems.[28]) In the early presidential elections electors were not explicitly associated with presidential candidates. Nominally at least electors were chosen as individuals, and hence there was nothing for them to be proportionate to. As the use of slates of electors associated with political parties and their candidates took hold over the years, so did the appeal of "winner-take-all." The possibility of assigning electors in proportion to the statewide popular votes of their candidates was never taken up.

Commentators, and even a few political figures, did keep the idea alive, however, and in 2004 sufficient signatures were collected in Colorado to put a popular initiative on the November ballot that would have committed the state to proportionality in its allocation of presidential electors.[29] The initiative failed, but if it had passed, it would have posed two questions about its legality. First, the initiative provided that proportionality would apply in the 2004 election,[30] and that might have been challenged as unfairly changing the rules after presidential votes had been cast.[31] In addition, there would have been a question of whether a popular initiative qualifies as action of the state "legislature," which is the body constitutionally empowered to determine the "manner" in which electors are appointed.[32] Only the second of those two questions would presumably have been relevant to the long-term fate of the Colorado move to proportionality.

If proportionality had taken hold in Colorado, it is certainly possible that enthusiasm for the idea would have grown elsewhere. But even that is far from clear. The popular initiative is alive and well in Colorado, but that is not true in a large number of states, where any move to proportionality would certainly require action by the state legislature. We have seen that when a state divides its electoral vote, it loses a measure of its electoral clout.[33] That effect is likely to be much more salient—and alarming—to those in control of state legislatures than to members of the electorate at large. If states without popular initiative as a viable option resist the move to proportionality, moreover, adopting states would be likely to reconsider, precisely because the disadvantagement to which they had subjected themselves would then promise to be permanent. In any event, the Colorado initiative failed, and that certainly does not bode well for any nationwide movement toward proportionality.[34]

The limitation that these three reform proposals work on the wrong winner possibility almost surely explains some of the appeal they hold for reformers, but it is important to appreciate that none of the three eliminates the possibility altogether. The senatorial "bonus" alone could yield a "wrong winner."[35] Beyond this, the potential for a disparity between the nationwide popular vote and electoral college "winners" simply inheres in the state-by-state allocation of electoral votes, at least as long as that state-by-state allocation is not tied quite rigidly to state voting totals. And it is hard to see how the two could be tied with the necessary rigidity, for some states have higher voter turnout than others. It would thus only be state allocation of electors *tied to actual turnout and hence assigned after the vote was taken*, combined, moreover, with fractional electors, that could hope to deal with the feared disparity. But if done with the required thoroughness and precision—combined with elimination of the two senator bonus—the trick would be accomplished only by turning the electoral college vote into a shadow nationwide popular vote. There would seem to be no appeal to going through such contortions rather than directly to a nationwide vote.

Each of the three proposals is thus something of a compromise between the appeal of a nationwide popular vote and a reluctance to jettison the present state-centered system. In all likelihood it is this compromise stance that generates some of the coolness toward each of the proposals. To be sure the nationwide vote possibility, to which we turn shortly, brings problems of its own, but its appeal is not at all shrouded. A nationwide popular vote is simply seen as the "democratic" way to choose a president. The compromise variants, on the other hand, cloud this same appeal behind the cover of the state-centered feature of the present electoral college.

It is hardly surprising that a nationwide popular vote for president has come to dominate the electoral college reform movement. Over the years under our constitutional system, we have seen a steady, if sometimes uneven, movement toward relegating decisions to popular election.[36] By virtue of the Seventeenth Amendment, the U.S. Senate, the members of which were appointed by state legislatures under the original constitutional scheme,[37] is now popularly elected. Many states have put in place one or another form of referendum and initiative, direct lawmaking by the electorate that nudges or entirely bypasses the legislative process. The Colorado initiative mentioned above is just one contemporary example of the use of this popular lawmaking. Political party nominees are now selected largely through a system of primary—popular—elections, rather than through "backroom" negotiations among party insiders that once prevailed. The franchise has, haphazardly but surely, been extended to the point where almost the entire adult citizen population is now entitled to vote. Under prodding of court decisions, that franchise is formally exercised in equal measure by all those casting votes, an approach capsulized by the slogan, "one person, one vote."[38] And, as we have seen, we observe the same movement in the electoral college context itself, where popular election of electors now occupies the field.

Popular election of electors probably reinforces the push for popular election of the president in a subtle way. As we saw in Chapter Three, after each presidential "election," the federal government collects from each state a "certificate of ascertainment," which includes the popular vote totals in the state for slates of electors pledged to each presidential candidate. In all likelihood state-by-state popular vote totals would be collected and reported even without these certificates. Vote totals are calculated and reported in preliminary form after the polls close and long before the certificates of ascertainment are prepared. When grounded in certificates of ascertainment, however, those nationwide vote totals are easily depicted as "official." The result is that simple addition yields popular vote counts for the various presidential contenders. In most elections the candidate with the most popular votes easily prevails in the electoral college, and no particular note is taken in the country at large of any differences between the two "winners." But when the two differ, the certificates of ascertainment and attendant collection of popular vote tallies tell us about the difference loudly, clearly, and, seemingly at least, officially.[39] In this way, the charge of a "wrong winner" is given something of a stamp of authenticity.

Direct popular election of the president was actually considered and rejected by the Constitutional Convention.[40] It surfaced again in the early part of the Nineteenth Century, and many variants have been offered over the years. To help clarify the issues, I will concentrate on a specific version advanced in a 1967 report by a Commission on Electoral College Reform formed by the American Bar Association (ABA).[41] Aside from a nationwide vote, the major elements of the commission approach are that the president and vice president be voted for jointly, that qualifications to vote be set at the state level, "provided that Congress may adopt uniform age and residence requirements," and that a runoff election be held between the top two vote-getters in the event that no candidate receives forty percent of the vote in the initial round.[42] While the commission's report cites a grab bag of reasons for moving to direct nationwide election, the crux of its rationale is simply that it is the democratic way to proceed. As the commission puts it, "[i]n summary, direct election of the President would be in harmony with the prevailing philosophy of one person, one vote. . . . This equality in voting should extend above all to the Presidency."[43]

We will turn shortly to the virtues of the present system suggested by defenders of the electoral college, but initially it is important to appreciate that those defenders deny the premise of the nationwide vote proponents that there is something undemocratic about the contemporary electoral college, at least as it typically operates. Putting aside the problem of accounting for "faithless" electors who refuse to honor their pre-election commitments to particular candidates—a subject with which we will deal in Chapter Seven—electors have achieved their offices through popular elections in the states, in which each vote *has* counted equally. This is true alike in those jurisdictions that use the winner-take-all system and in the two states which elect some of their electors from congressional districts. The possibility that the candidate with the largest number of votes nationwide will have lost when the electoral votes are tallied one

state at a time does not make the system undemocratic, according to these critics. That possibility, they point out, is parallel to what happens in the U.S. Senate, where decisions emerge from a two-step process—state-by-state elections
by the electorate, in which each state gets two senators regardless of state population, and then legislative votes by those senators—in each of which stages,
the votes are given equal weight.[44] But that decidedly does not mean that the
second step decisions can be traced back to popular majorities in the country
as a whole.

There is no decisive answer to this argument. Even putting the Senate aside,
consider the way in which the Supreme Court's one-person one-vote idea plays
out as applied to the House of Representatives. Within each state, the requirement holds, so that representative districts must be equally populated.[45] But apportionment among states requires the allocation of whole numbers of representatives to each state. Quite apart from the fact that representatives can win
in individual districts with large margins or small ones, if the size of the House
of Representatives is kept down, representatives in different states will necessarily have quite different size constituencies. It could only be otherwise (other
than through uncanny accident) if district lines were allowed to cross state borders. The disparities are presumably thought to be permissible (despite the one
person one vote idea) because state-by-state allocation of decision-making
power itself serves some permissible ends, as a part of what we typically call
"federalism." Of course, it will no more do simply to incant the word "federalism" than the word "democracy" to justify a system, as we shall see when we
turn shortly to the positive case advanced for the electoral college. But if American "federalism" does open up space for House of Representatives districts of
unequal populations in different states, then it might similarly open up space
for discrete state inputs into the selection of the president.

Indeed the point could be made even more strongly. The definition of
"democracy" is much contested, but decision making in the American variant
is undeniably much more complicated than some simple tracing of ultimate
decisions to popular majorities. Thus if proponents of a nationwide vote imagine that American democracy turns majority sentiments into public policy decisions in even an approximate way, they are badly mistaken. The very fact of
bicameralism, for instance, clouds any attempt to trace legislative outcomes to
popular vote majorities.[46] Bicameralism was initially embraced by the constitu-

tional framers because it would provide a second obstacle before popular sentiment became law.[47] This was done in full realization that the result would more than occasionally be rejection of the "popular will." In many ways, the presidential veto, judicial review, federalism, and the local prerogatives that remain a very important part of the system, were similarly introduced (or retained) because they would impede the reach of majority sentiment, opening up space for individual prerogatives. Political theorists have long recognized that there is no terribly good "democratic" solution to the problem of turning majority sentiments into law.[48] This is true of a representative system but also of direct democracy where issues must be defined and voted on in discrete bundles. The eventual patterns of decisions will often turn on the contents of the constituent bundles that were subjected to votes, with no "democratic" answer to how to allocate the contents among bundles. In the case of American democracy, however, there is no particular reason to think that the translation that concerns these theorists has even been the system's aim.

The commission's proposal illustrates seemingly arbitrary decisions that must be made in the name of democratic decision making, as well as the role that political subunits like states might play in presidential selection. As mentioned, the ABA commission would have allowed a candidate to prevail with forty percent or more of the popular vote. But a candidate with forty percent of the vote would come to office with sixty percent of the voters in favor of others. There is simply nothing magical about the command of a majority. More than that, given that voting turnout seldom exceeds fifty percent in a modern presidential race, a candidate would require a near unanimous vote to command a majority of the entire electorate. In the final analysis, the commission's willingness to accept a "plurality president" represents a recognition that the nature of the support required for victory in a "democratic" election draws on considerations other than high democratic principle.

The commission also left a measure of discretion with the states to establish qualifications to vote for president. In the original constitutional design, state discretion on voting qualifications was quite extensive,[49] but that discretion has been eroded over the years, as the Constitution and, to a lesser degree, statutes have forbidden states to extract poll taxes, or to discriminate in the franchise on a variety of grounds, including race, gender, and—with limits—age.[50] Nonetheless, the states do retain a measure of residual discretion on qualifications, and a number have exercised that discretion, most prominently to deny the vote to categories of incarcerated felons, and, in the case of some states, to ex-felons as well.[51] The continuing state discretion in the commission's proposal was no doubt included as a nod to the role of states in the American system, but it is in some tension with any assumption that the only "democratic" way to choose a president is through an integrated nationwide vote.

At the same time, selection of the president differs from selection of a legislative assembly in one important respect that bears on at least the perceived legitimacy of the disaggregated way the voting is conducted through the electoral college. The president is a single official (as is the vice president), not like the House and Senate a collection of separately elected individuals who will aggregate their inputs into decisions. This is why it is so easy to spot a "wrong winner" of the presidency, but not of some vote in the Senate or House. If democracy is thought to require that elections for individual officers award the prize to the person who garners the largest total number of popular votes, then selection of the president does not meet the test. But if that is the issue, that does not necessarily make it the answer. There is no settled definition of "democracy" that tells us whether in a well-functioning democracy the president must be chosen by an integrated nationwide vote as opposed to an aggregation of votes that are allocated among states and assigned through state-by-state elections (or for that matter in some other way, as, for instance, in parliamentary systems where the legislature chooses the executive).[52]

In thinking about this choice it is well to keep in mind that the appeal of awarding victory to the nationwide popular vote winner can easily be exaggerated, even if one is drawn to a nationwide vote as the decision-making mechanism. For if the popular vote winner is thought to have stronger "democratic" credentials, the evidence we have is that the magnitude of that "democratic" margin is typically not terribly great.[53] In theory under the present system an electoral college victory can be secured with a popular vote total that is a relatively small fraction of that of a rival. In practice, however, in the time since universal adoption of popular election of electors, there has never been an electoral college winner whose recorded popular vote total trailed that of an opponent by more than Hayes's three percent loss in the popular vote in the 1876 election. Albert Gore lost the presidency while winning the popular vote in the 2000 election by slightly more than half a percent of the total. In an environment where little more than half the eligible voters go to the polls, popular vote losses of this order would not seem to bespeak some serious deficiency in "majoritarian" democratic legitimacy.[54]

If for these reasons there is something terribly simplistic at the core of the argument for a nationwide vote for president, the same can be said of the usual defenses of the electoral college. We will return to more telling arguments in favor of the electoral college, but the arguments pressed most vehemently often seem longer on rhetoric than substance. Electoral college defenders, for instance, tend to characterize the college as simply one piece of an integrated whole, the American "federalist" system of government.[55] This use of the concept of "federalism" is rather awkward, because federalism is usually associated with ample discretion at the state level, and by state-by-state experimentation, providing invigorating examples for others. Electoral college defenders, in contrast, tend to favor state popular election with winner-take-all as the *sole* appropriate method through which electors are chosen—no matter how small the popular vote margin in the state.[56]

Whether or not the label is apt, moreover, the rhetoric of "federalism" leads to flights of fancy that tend more to obscure than to illuminate what is at stake. Among the most passionate of electoral college defenders, for instance, are Judith Best, Robert Hardaway, and, more recently Tara Ross, all of whom are drawn to a metaphor of the "solar system" to capture something important about this American "federalism." Interfere with one aspect of the whole, they warn, and the whole system may change in unpredictable ways, spinning out of control.[57] The solar system idea strikes me as little more than colorful imagery. There seems to be no reason to fear rapid and dizzying change throughout the system if we were to eliminate the electoral college and substitute direct election of the president. The electoral college has changed over the years in ways that are fully as momentous as direct election would be, and far from being brittle, the system has proved remarkably adaptable. This indeed is a point repeatedly cited by defenders of the electoral college.[58] Dire predictions could be—and no doubt were—made when other momentous changes in the American system of government were under consideration. Just a few of the changes that come to mind were the move from state legislative selection of senators to direct popular election; extension of the vote to women and the former slave population; adoption of various mechanisms of direct democratic decision making in a large number of states; widespread use of primary elections for the choice of major party presidential candidates; campaign finance regulation; and the Supreme Court's one-person, one-vote jurisprudence. But we have weathered whatever storms came in the wake of these changes without observing a system that seems in danger of spinning out of control.[59]

Beneath the rhetoric, what this vaunted "federalism" really seems to amount to is simply state-by-state designation of electors. For these defenders of the electoral college, winner-take-all is important to the scheme, because it encourages candidates to concentrate on states as integrated units, rather than simply as convenient vehicles for accumulating votes, vehicles which might otherwise be subordinated when others simply seemed more promising. And the reason this state-by-state decision making seems to be important is that it provides a healthy set of incentives for presidential candidates. Just what that healthy set of incentives is, however, and what contribution the electoral college makes to their health, is not always so clear.

Defenders often claim that the electoral college forces candidates to adopt a national focus rather than more parochial local ones. Judith Best, for instance, warns that a nationwide vote system would allow a candidate to win with a "sectional campaign" or one geared to narrow interest groups of one description or another. In the latter category, she mentions particularly a campaign geared to "white Christians," or one that appeals to "suburbanites" to the exclusion of "urban and rural voters."[60] In contrast, Best suggests that the electoral college encourages candidates who can "build broad political coalitions that are essential for a president to govern." Tara Ross's formulation is that with the electoral college, a president "cannot be elected simply by gaining a majority in a handful of states. . . . [H]e must garner support across the nation to have a reasonable probability of being elected."[61] Robert Hardaway champions the electoral college as "best," not for one minority or another, but "for the entire country, for all the people."[62]

With its emphasis on a national perspective for the nation's executive, this is reminiscent of what constitutional convention delegates seem to have had in mind when they crafted the electoral college. As we saw in Chapter Two, many saw the college as a device for choosing a president of talent and judgment who could rise above faction in the service of the whole nation. And it may be true that presidents tend to view the entire nation as their constituency more than do members of the House and Senate. The Constitution says that the "executive power" is "vested in a President of" the entire country, "the United States of America."[63] To be sure, it also says that the House and Senate are branches of "a Congress *of the United States*,"[64] but the president and vice president are the only constitutionally established officers who cannot trace their "constituency" back to individual states or parts of them. This constituency difference does not, however, depend on the manner of selecting the president, at least not if the choice is between the present electoral college and a nationwide popular vote. If anything, the electoral college introduces a state-centered element in presidential selection, thus arguably compromising the national focus of the presidency. Any tendency of the president to view his job as more "national" might then be accentuated rather than diminished if a nationwide popular vote were substituted for the electoral college. At the very least, the claim to the contrary needs some further justification.

At other times, moreover, electoral college proponents emphasize the inducement to focus on local concerns, rather than on national ones. Among the most eloquent of electoral college proponents was Alexander Bickel, who relied heavily in making the case for the electoral college on "the disproportionate influence in presidential elections of the large, populous, heterogeneous states, and more particularly, of ethnic and racial minorities or other interest groups in these states."[65] And in some tension with her claim that the electoral college induces candidates to "garner support across the nation," Tara Ross champions the appeal the electoral college encourages candidates to make to local minorities, using as examples the Hispanic population in Texas and California, the Jewish presence in New York, and the concentration of farmers in the Midwest.[66]

All this can set one's head spinning. A claim that appeal to "white Christians" or "suburban voters" would be unfortunate, but that one to "ethnic and racial minorities" in "large, populous, heterogeneous states" would be desirable needs some explanation. Bickel did not elaborate, but he may have been influenced by American constitutional jurisprudence in which closer scrutiny is given to laws which disfavor "discrete and insular minorities,"[67] because of a concern that they start out politically disadvantaged. Beyond racial minorities, however, agreement on groups entitled to this special constitutional concern, and what it means in particular contexts, quickly dissipates.[68] And Ross's mention of Midwestern farmers as appropriate for solicitude could seemingly find scant justification in any concern about political disadvantagement.

It is, moreover, hard to see why the electoral college might be thought effective in implementing any solicitude for minorities that was thought desirable, except perhaps by accident. Bickel was writing at a time when the "large, heterogeneous states" were closely divided politically, or so he seemed to assume. If those states are lopsided politically, then minorities in them lose their ability to swing the state and hence lose their political clout under the electoral college. The eight most populous states in 2004 were California, Texas, Florida, New York, Illinois, Pennsylvania, Ohio, and Michigan. Some of these remain politically competitive "swing states"[69]—notably Florida, Ohio, Pennsylvania, and Michigan—but others, including three of the four most populous states—California, Texas, and New York—seem to be securely in the camp of one major party or the other in presidential elections. In this context, a nationwide popular vote might actually cause candidates to pay more attention than does the electoral college to Hispanics in Texas and California and to Jewish voters in New York. This suggests that any benefit for minorities from the electoral college is basically happenstance, a fragile basis at best for retaining the college as an important feature of American politics.

None of this is to suggest that the same incentives operate under the different approaches to presidential selection, or that the differences should be ignored. But they should be realistically evaluated. It is true, as Ross suggests, that a nationwide vote would allow a candidate to win by "gaining a majority in a handful of states." But it is also true that victory in the electoral college can in theory be secured with the electoral votes of just the eleven most populous states. Neither bare fact would seem to have much bearing on the politics of winning, at least in the contemporary United States. If the first two elections of the Twenty-First Century are any indication, we are in an era of closely competitive presidential races. In that environment, truly "broad political coalitions" may be unattainable. The only obvious sense in which the electoral college winner in the 2000 election put together a "broader" coalition than the popular vote winner who lost in the electoral college is that he won the popular vote in more states—and in states that occupy more space on the map—than his principal opponent.[70] But surely space on a map is not what matters. If map space were important, winning in Alaska would provide a very good start toward overwhelming victory. But I cannot recall seeing Alaska depicted on an electoral map at anything approaching its relative size in the territory of the United States. Nor can number of states be of much importance. The present operation of the electoral college does not hint that victory in Wyoming and California are even close to equivalent. And if geographic dispersion is somehow thought important, to my eye the electoral vote loser in both the 2000 and 2004 elections actually had a more geographically scattered group of states than did the winner.[71]

Let us instead take seriously the different incentives of the two systems. Most obviously, the electoral college system encourages the most vigorous campaigning—including making campaign promises—in populous states that are closely divided politically. Conversely the electoral college discourages campaigning, and promising, in states that seem securely in one political camp or another, including the most populous states. Thus in both the 2000 and 2004 elections, Florida received a lot of attention from both major candidates, while neither candidate campaigned much in California, by far the nation's most populous state, but one where it seemed from the outset that the Democratic nominee would carry the state.[72] The implications for appeal to "minorities" are fairly clear. The electoral college encourages appeal to minorities—whether or not politically disadvantaged and hence somehow appropriate for special political solicitude—that are concentrated in politically competitive states, and especially in the large ones. A nationwide popular vote, in contrast, would make geographical concentration of minorities relatively unimportant.[73] What would matter more is how large the minority is in nationwide terms—again without concern for whether or not the minority is independently "deserving."

In all likelihood a nationwide vote would cause neglect of the least populous states. That neglect is also found under the electoral college, but there well might be more of it with a nationwide vote. Those less populous states are geographically dispersed, and precious few of the concerns of their citizens are likely associated with the magnitude of their populations (the most likely exception being the retention of the equal state representation in the U.S. Senate). Indeed, it is not clear that the populous and not so populous states were ever united by anything other than extent of population.[74] In any event, a nationwide vote likely would cause candidates to focus attention on more states and on a larger swath of the population than does the electoral college. And a nationwide vote would encourage candidates to campaign in populous states even when their opponents remained decidedly more popular in those states. It is difficult to see why this array of incentives should be thought to make a case for the electoral college.

This is, of course, a "static" analysis, taking the present partisan leanings in states as providing the best indication of campaign incentives. The mobility of the American population, indeed the history of American politics, certainly teaches that the political leanings of states can change. Conceivably parties and candidates might in the future find issues that would have such differential appeal in different regions that their use in a nationwide vote would lead to the sectional divisiveness about which electoral college proponents sometimes warn. Certainly the Civil War taught us sectional divisiveness might be more troublesome than the more geographically dispersed kind. But the eight most populous states mentioned above are found in the north, south, east, and west of the country, and in the middle. Of the four most populous, the two that share a decided partisan leaning—at least in recent presidential elections—are on opposite sides of the continent. Half of the eight are closely divided politically, but even in the relatively lopsided states a large number of voters sympathetic to the "minority" party can be found. Even in the southern states, which seem to lean decidedly Republican in recent presidential elections, the Democratic vote is substantial.[75] And finally, if extreme sectional divisiveness should somehow emerge, it is by no means clear that it would be stifled by the electoral college. In 1860 Abraham Lincoln won an *electoral college victory* with support confined to the northern states that forbade slavery.[76] In the final analysis, the best we likely can do is leave an unpredictable future of campaign incentives in the environment of a two-party race to take care of itself, with whatever system for selecting the president we have chosen on other grounds.

The incentives would also play out in more complex ways for minor party candidates, depending upon the nature of their appeal. Under the electoral college, third-party candidates with appeal that is quite substantial in one or a few states, but decidedly limited elsewhere, might hope to exert influence by capturing electoral votes and thus depriving either of the major party candidates of the required majority "of electors appointed."[77] With this strategy, they would devote little effort to campaigning beyond the limits of their geographic appeal. Minor party candidates with more dispersed appeal, in contrast, will typically have little hope of capturing electoral votes. Any ambitions they harbor to exert real influence on the election, or on policy positions of the eventual victor, must rely either on an ability to unsettle the contest in closely divided states or to bargain with one of the major party candidates in such states in return for withdrawal and support.[78]

Just this sort of contrast was evident in the 1948 election, when Strom Thurmond and Henry Wallace each mounted a third-party effort and each garnered almost the same total number of popular votes. But Thurmond won thirty-nine electoral votes with his Southern-focused campaign, while Wallace got no electoral votes with his more national appeal.[79] It is possible to pursue both strategies simultaneously, and that is indeed what George Wallace did with some success in the 1968 election.[80] Champions of the electoral college might shed no tears at a loss of influence for minor parties in American politics, but a move to a nationwide vote would deprive the minor party regional strategy of its electoral college leverage and hence dampen the incentive for regional candidacies.[81] In that sense it would foster the sort of more national politics that electoral college proponents favor for the major parties. In Chapter Eight, we will return to the problem of third parties and of the varying strategies they might pursue.

There may be other things at stake in any tradeoff of the electoral college, on the one hand, and a nationwide vote, on the other. Proponents of the electoral college, for instance, sometimes argue that if put in office by a nationwide popular vote, the president "could claim to be the only authentic voice of the people," tipping "the balance of power . . . dangerously to the president and away from Congress." This might make the president a "Caesar."[82] This too strikes me as basically empty, if colorful, imagery. This is not because a powerful president might not pose a danger. Debates about the optimal distribution of power among the branches of the federal government go back to the earliest days of the republic. Whatever one's position on that balance, however, we seem to have cultivated a powerful presidency, at least when the president's party also controls the Congress. And it seems likely that whatever contribution a nationwide vote might make to the president's power is already present when the nationwide vote totals are broadcast far and wide on election night, and most of the nation remains entirely ignorant of the meetings of electors more than a month later.[83] Indeed, electoral college proponents are at pains to insist that the popular vote and electoral college winners are almost always the same person, and indeed that the electoral college usually magnifies the popular vote winner's margin.[84] In that environment, it seems more plausible to argue that it is the electoral college vote that poses the larger danger of a president who claims an exaggerated mandate as the choice of the people.[85] Or perhaps the argument could be made that it is the typical pattern of twin victories for the winner that presents the real danger of a "Caesar."[86]

Another argument of electoral college proponents does give greater pause. They urge that the electoral college concentrates concern about fraud and other defective tabulation of vote counting.[87] In the 2000 election, for instance, the country's attention was fixed on counting controversies in Florida, because its electoral votes seemed to be decisive. Had a nationwide popular vote determined the outcome, on the other hand, counting disputes anywhere in the country might have seemed relevant. The theoretical point seems fair enough. If every vote in the country counts equally, as it would in a nationwide contest for the popular vote, then any dispute that might plausibly contribute to a change in outcome—even if only when cumulated with changes growing out of other disputes—will hold the possibility of payoff and hence might be worth pursuing. If the vote is quite close, the result could be disputes about votes in a great many locations.

I do not entirely discount this argument, but several considerations suggest that the concern may be exaggerated. First, improved procedures for both casting and counting votes would be advisable, with or without a change to a nationwide popular vote. We already calculate the nationwide vote, and we never know for sure where the decisive votes—the next election's Florida or Ohio—will turn out to be. We should put in place procedures that will get the count as right as we reasonably can even if our level of concern remains just where it is. In addition, if we face the prospect of close electoral college races in the future (as I will argue in Chapter Six that we might well), then a variety of states may be the locus of attention in presidential races, even if we retain the electoral college mechanism for choosing the executive. Similarly a large number of states can expect to have close senatorial or other races in the future, and accurate counts will be required for them.[88] In the wake of the 2000 election, the federal government did make money available to the states for improved election machinery. That invitation to balloting reform was taken up to some degree and should be pursued quite vigorously, whether or not we move away from the electoral college as our mechanism of choosing the president.[89]

Second, it is not at all clear that close nationwide popular votes would generate controversy with anything like the same likelihood as close electoral college votes. The eventual popular vote margin for Bush in Florida in 2000 was 537 votes. That is close enough so that Gore could mount a recount effort that held some substantial chance of succeeding. And if it succeeded, it would change the electoral vote outcome, where only four votes out of 538 seemed to separate the two candidates. The nationwide margin for Gore in the same election, in contrast, was over 540,000 votes. It is not obvious that that is close enough to justify any recount effort at all. There could, of course, be much closer nationwide votes, but we should not be terribly surprised about occasional electoral vote controversies when there are such a small number of those votes. The comparatively huge number of popular votes in the country makes a similar incidence of controversies relatively less likely.[90]

Finally, even if there were a multiplicity of sites where counting controversies might be pursued, it is not clear that campaigns would be inclined to undertake the chase. In a decentralized environment a nationally coordinated attempt to inflate the vote of one candidate and deflate the vote of another would be an enormously difficult undertaking. Appreciation of this fact of electoral life would be sobering for a party contemplating an effort to overturn an election result on account of fraud (or other irregularity) that depended upon a net effect in the resolution of a multiplicity of controversies.[91] Moreover, a campaign that spreads charges of fraud and mistake willy-nilly might well find none of them taken seriously. Some tradeoff of costs and benefits would be required. In that tradeoff, controversies with a combination of the strongest odor of error and the most votes in play would likely be pursued, while those with fewer votes and fewer apparent problems would be put to the side.

This is in fact what we seem to observe. Florida was by no means the only state where the popular vote count for electors was close in the 2000 election, nor the only close state where a changed outcome would have resulted in a Gore victory. Bush's margin of victory was about 7,200 in New Hampshire, just under 85,000 in Missouri, about 21,600 in Nevada, a little over 80,000 in Tennessee, and less than 41,000 in West Virginia. Some of these margins are more significant in percentage terms than others, but a successful challenge in any one of them could have reversed the outcome of the 2000 presidential contest. At least the result in New Hampshire might plausibly have been overturned by vigorous pursuit of counting irregularities or fraud. And then, had reversal in a Bush state been pursued and succeeded, reversal in states that went narrowly for Gore might have brought the electoral college tally back to Bush. Perceiving this possibility as the Gore challenges were getting under way, the Bush campaign had an incentive to seek reversals from the start in close Gore states. The Gore popular vote margin in New Mexico, for instance, was just 366 votes.

These possibilities were not pursued, however. The likely reasons are that the other Bush states were considered decided long shots by the Gore campaign. Attention was devoted to Florida, where the single best opportunity seemed to be presented. The Bush campaign also chose to concentrate its energies on that one fight. Indeed, even within Florida in 2000 we saw the same pattern. Trailing by just a small number of votes, Gore did not pursue recount efforts throughout the state, but rather in just a "handful of [the most promising] counties."[92] Bush did not pursue recounts at all. And beyond Florida and the 2000 election, we have had a good deal of experience with popular votes for the executive in populous democracies like France and California, with no recurring, or particularly nagging, problem of disputed vote counts everywhere.[93]

The runoff possibility contemplated by the ABA Commission proposal raises additional problems in any comparison between the electoral college and a nationwide popular vote. The commission would require that a candidate obtain at least a forty percent plurality to prevail, and that a runoff between the top two candidates be conducted where none reaches the forty percent mark. The forty percent requirement was a compromise on account of several concerns. First, the commission thought that a candidate who came to office with less than forty percent of the vote would not have "a sufficient mandate." And if a candidate could be elected with less than forty percent of the vote, there could be a "weakening [of] the two party system by encouraging the formation of splinter parties." This, according to the commission, is for the simple reason that "a figure of less than 40 percent would increase the chances of a minor party candidate being able to become President." In contrast a requirement of forty percent would "render extremely remote the possibility of having to resort to the contingent election procedure."[94]

There is a certain "logic" to the commission's forty percent requirement, but it is rather different from the logic that the commission articulates. Over the years the electoral college system has given us a number of presidents who commanded only a plurality of the popular vote, but only one who failed to achieve the forty percent mark. No obvious jeopardy has attached to presidents who came into office behind a plurality between forty and fifty percent. The American experience may thus provide some support for the commission's use of forty percent as sufficiently ensuring a presidential "mandate," though it should be noted that Abraham Lincoln, the one president who failed to command forty percent of the popular vote, was a rather decisive president, and, while certainly divisive, is usually counted as among the greatest successes of those who have held the office. But more generally the commission's forty percent requirement sensibly recognizes that an absolute majority in the first round will often be elusive, while trying to ensure that a new president comes to office behind a solid show of support. Beyond this, however, upon close examination the commission's seemingly straightforward reasoning appears quite questionable.

The runoff possibility may actually undermine rather than bolster the American two-party system about which the commission is so solicitous. The stability of American democracy is often associated with the two-party system, but such a system does make it more difficult for diverse points of view to find effective outlets for expressing that diversity, at least through the sorts of discrete political parties that have become central actors in American politics. In Chapter Eight we will touch further on tradeoffs in fostering two dominant political parties, but any global assessment of the pros and cons of a two-party system is beyond my present ambitions. For present purposes I will simply indulge in the assumption that is widely shared by prominent commentators in the electoral college debates that a measure of encouragement of the American two-party system is desirable. Whether the commission's forty percent and runoff provisions would provide that encouragement is more controversial than the commission seemed to appreciate. Elimination of the electoral college would take much of the air out of the regionally based minor candidate strategy that we discussed earlier. But with an integrated nationwide vote, a minor party candidate could still bargain in return for withdrawal and support, just as more "national" candidates might under an electoral college system. The runoff possibility, however, introduces yet another possibility for that candidate, associated with incentives for what political scientists refer to as "strategic voting."

A voter who votes strategically in a race with three or more candidates in a single member district will not vote for his preferred candidate if the voter judges that the candidate has no realistic chance of prevailing and if the voter further has a decided secondary preference among the candidates he concludes do have realistic chances. This is sometimes said to be the way a "rational" voter will choose, because a vote for his preferred candidate would be "wasted." If large numbers of voters vote strategically, the result will then be to discourage third-party candidacies from the outset, because of a fear that third-party constituencies will not show their support at the ballot box. Strategic voting—in a context of single member districting—is thus often presented as at least part of the explanation for the staying power of an American system of two—and only two—strong political parties.[95]

If this logic is accepted, however, the forty percent requirement accomplishes less than the commission suggests. If the initial field of candidates finds a multiplicity of them fairly evenly matched, then the most strategically inclined voter has no guidance on a pair of candidates from which to choose. If voters are "forced" to vote sincerely for this reason, the result might well be a close division of the vote among three or more candidates, with none obtaining forty percent. But if the race seems to be one between two strong candidates— as would be expected if the two-party system initially retained its hold on American politics—strategic voting could ensure that the forty percent mark would typically take care of itself, eliminating the need for a runoff. Voters would vote strategically and minor party candidates would seldom pose the sort of threat that would push the eventual victor below the forty percent mark. Undisturbed by a runoff requirement, the two-party system already in place might thus ensure that two, and only two, strong contenders would continue to emerge with great consistency. A nationwide popular vote would effectively make the presidential race a "single district" one in which strategic voting would tend to foster a two-party system.[96]

By changing the "rational" calculus for a partisan of a minor party candidate, moreover, the commission's runoff possibility might actually *increase* the chances that no candidate obtains forty percent of the vote in the initial round.

For if each major party candidate can be held below the forty percent showing that avoids a runoff, then the runoff might enable a minor party loser to bargain with one or another of the major party survivors in exchange for support in the runoff. Understanding this, a partisan of one of those minor party candidates could vote sincerely rather than strategically in the initial round, at least if he judges that the ability of his favored candidate to bargain for something in a runoff would represent a measure of victory for that candidate. By diminishing the incentive to vote strategically, introduction of the runoff possibility may thus encourage minor party candidacies and produce the counterintuitive result of increasing the incidence of elections in which no candidate obtains forty percent of the vote in the initial round.[97]

The commission does not really answer this argument from strategic voting. It dismisses the suggestion that a runoff provision might make voters "more inclined to cast 'protest' votes for minor candidates in the original election on the assumption that they will have another opportunity to make their votes 'count.'" The commission instead asserts a belief that "voters would be more inclined to vote for a candidate with an actual chance of election."[98] It is true that if a voter's choice is to cast a meaningful vote sooner or later, then "rational" calculation might tell us that sooner should win. But if the voter perceives that a vote for his preferred candidate might result in some leverage (and not simply represent a "protest"), then that leverage makes it meaningful in a "rational" assessment, and the runoff encourages that possibility.[99]

The commission's rather dense response aside, it is not clear how much power there is in the "rational choice" theorists' argument about strategic voting. There certainly is evidence of strategic voting in presidential elections by partisans of minor party candidates,[100] but there is also uncertainty about the extent of it. The same "rational choice" tradition in political theory insists that voting itself is irrational in any race with a large electorate because of the exceedingly small chance that any single vote will change the outcome of the election.[101] But this aspect of the rational choice analysis has demonstrably limited real world consequences, since we observe that large numbers of those eligible nonetheless do vote. We should thus recognize the possibility that the theorists similarly exaggerate the extent of strategic voting. Perhaps large numbers of voters vote for "expressive" rather than instrumental purposes, and hence will vote sincerely rather than strategically, even when the sincerely favored candidate has no realistic chance of winning.[102] The seeming puzzle of voting on a large scale is suggestive of just such an expressive motivation for taking the trouble to vote.

In addition, other elements of the system may contribute importantly to the two-party system. Legislative control over district boundaries, campaign finance rules, ballot access restrictions, and sheer inertia are just a few of the other influences that likely sustain the American system of two, and only two, major political parties.[103] Thus we see no substantial emergence of third-party candidates in gubernatorial elections in the United States even though some states are quite populous and none disaggregates its votes for governor in the manner of the electoral college. And it is entirely possible that a nationwide popular election for president would strengthen, rather than weaken, the two-party system in a different way, by energizing the efforts of perennial "second" parties in states long dominated by one or the other of the major parties.[104] All this being said, it seems fair enough to recognize a measure of uncertainty about the long-term effects on the two-party system of a move that would replace the electoral college with a nationwide popular vote. Still, minor parties have crept in and out of American politics over the years, and have actually seemed relatively quiescent in the recent past. Any argument that a nationwide vote would bring minor parties roaring onto the scene does seem rather overblown.[105]

The commission also criticizes the electoral college runoff procedure in the House of Representatives, and it is surely right that a fair comparison of the electoral college and a nationwide vote should take into account the fallback procedure in each setting.[106] The commission's principal criticisms of the House procedure, however, do not seem particularly telling. The commission warns, for instance, that selection of the president by the House could lead to a president who lost the popular vote. That possibility does not seem any more dire a prospect when worked by the House contingent procedure than when worked by the electoral college mechanism itself. Particularly in recent years, only two candidates have garnered electoral votes. In that setting, the House's choice would be between two candidates, each of whom likely commanded a very large popular vote. And if there is a third candidate who obtains electoral votes, so that the House choice is from among three, the candidate with the fewest popular votes would be very unlikely to prevail in the House, given a political system that is so dominated by two political parties.

Finally, the commission points out that separation of the contingent procedures for selection of the president and vice president in the House and Senate respectively could result in those offices being held by members of different political parties. If no presidential candidate had commanded a majority of the electoral college, then in all likelihood no vice presidential candidate would have attained the necessary majority either.[107] But the two houses might have partisan alignments that would lean in different directions in the respective choices with which they are faced. Just how serious a problem this would be is another matter. The vice president's constitutionally assigned duties are limited to presiding over the Senate, and there does not seem much harm in having that presiding officer with a different party affiliation than the president. Even without that possibility, the Senate could easily be controlled by a different political party than the one to which the president asserts allegiance. Beyond that, the new president need not give the vice president anything to do. A vice president without much in the way of official duty would nonetheless have a pulpit and might even provide a healthy voice of dissent on a national stage. But if counted as a squandering of public resources, this particular waste would probably not rise very high on a list of misspent public funds. In addition, if something were to happen to the president and the vice president succeeded him, there would presumably be more of a loss of continuity than if the two had had a political party in common. In general it would certainly seem desirable to avoid such disruption, but discounted by its improbability the problem seems less than dire.[108]

Even if the commission's criticisms of the House contingent procedure seem wide of the mark, that procedure *is* deeply problematic. Indeed the problems with the House contingent procedure in "democratic" terms are much more serious than any with the basic electoral college mechanism. The problems with choice by the House have been largely neglected by electoral college reformers, perhaps because their attention has been so focused on large-scale reform—mostly the nationwide popular vote possibility—that would perforce do away with the House contingent procedure. And over the years the House procedure has been required only twice, the most recent time being more than a century and three-quarters ago. It is easy to ignore the most serious of problems if it seems that the chances of them doing concrete harm is extremely remote. Neglecting the problems with the House contingent procedure, however, seems quite misguided. Not only are the problems with the procedure serious and profound, but the possibility that the procedure will be invoked is considerably greater than it might initially seem. I begin my excursion into realistic approaches to important electoral college reform by assessing the House contingent procedure in the next chapter.

The Contingent Procedure for Selection of the President by the House of Representatives

We saw in Chapter Two that the electoral college process faltered in the 1800 election, when Thomas Jefferson and Aaron Burr each obtained the same number of electoral votes. They had been advanced for president and vice president respectively by their common political party, but at the time presidential electors cast two votes, drawing no distinction between the two offices to be filled. Burr did not gracefully bow out of the presidential race, and the Constitution provided that in case of an electoral college tie, the House of Representatives was required to choose the president. Jefferson eventually emerged victorious, of course, but the searing experience led directly to the Twelfth Amendment, separating the presidential and vice-presidential balloting, and eliminating the possibility that two (or even three) candidates would end up in a tie, with each commanding votes of a majority of the number of members of the electoral college. Still, the possibility remained that no candidate would obtain an electoral college majority at all. Article II had provided for House selection in that case as well, and the Twelfth Amendment explicitly retained provision for resort to the House "if no person have . . . [a] majority ['of the whole number of electors appointed']."[1]

When there is no electoral college majority, under the Twelfth Amendment the House makes the choice of a president from among the three candidates with the highest number of electoral votes (rather than the five highest that had been provided for under Article II).[2] And, just as under Article II, the vote in the House is not by members, but by states, with a majority of states necessary for a selection. Since the Twelfth Amendment was enacted, recourse to the House has been required only once, in 1824, when four candidates received electoral votes. With the Federalists no longer a serious political force, the contest was an intraparty affair for what was by then called by its modern name, the "Democratic Party." The House selection was relatively untroubled, requiring only one ballot to choose John Quincy Adams as president. The fact that the House contingent procedure has not been required for almost two centuries now may make that process seem a quaint anachronism, of no particular relevance for the modern day. Perhaps for this reason, many modern commentators have treated the possibility of House selection of the president with nonchalance.

In contrast, expressions of concern were common in earlier days of our constitutional system. Writing not long before the 1824 election, for instance, Thomas Jefferson said that he had always "considered the constitutional mode of election ultimately by the legislature voting by states as the most dangerous blot in [sic] our Constitution, and one which some unlucky chance will some day hit."[3] Having been burned by the House procedure, Jefferson was perhaps not the most detached commentator, but other knowledgeable observers of American politics have been no less critical.[4] To many over the years the House contingent selection has seemed the most ill-conceived element of the eccentric way in which we choose a president.[5]

For a variety of reasons, I think we should hark to those earlier expressions of concern about selection of the president by the House of Representatives. It is, of course, entirely possible that if no change is made we will avoid the House contingent procedure for the next two centuries, as we have for almost the past two. For any given election, there is certainly no terribly good way to gauge the chances beforehand that the House will have to choose the president. But it is very easy to conjure up ways in which no electoral college majority would coalesce around a single candidate. And the 2000 and 2004 elections suggest that some of those possibilities should not be dismissed as remote. Even if the chances of House selection are small, moreover, the potential costs are sufficiently large that we would do well to consider now if and how they might be avoided. And finally, the very possibility that the House might be called upon to choose could impinge in unhealthy ways on the initial electoral college process, even if a single candidate does eventually secure a majority there. In short, we ignore the possibility of House selection at our peril.

There are basically four reasons why there might be no electoral college ma-jority, so that the House contingent procedure would be required. First, the electoral college contest might be a closely matched two-candidate race in which all electors cast votes, and the result is a tie. The 2000 election came close to producing just such an electoral college tie.[6] Not only were the two major candidates separated by only a few electoral college votes, but as we shall see in Chapter Six it is easy to come up with shifts in just a small number of close states (in popular vote terms) that would have produced an electoral college dead heat. The electoral college results were not as close in the 2004 election as in 2000, but they were again close by historical standards, and again the switch of just a few close states would have produced a tie. In the run-up to the 2004 election, perhaps put on guard by what happened in 2000, many commentators issued warnings, and even predictions, of an electoral college tie.[7]

Another possibility for recourse to the House contingent procedure is that three or more candidates might obtain electoral votes, but none a majority. Or there may have been abstentions in the electoral college balloting that pre-vented any candidate from obtaining the required majority. And finally, there might be no majority because one or more electoral votes was disqualified. In subsequent chapters I will focus more closely on these different reasons, and ex-plore for each whether there are techniques of avoidance that would allow us to hold the House contingent procedure at bay. In this chapter I first explain why avoidance, if possible, is desirable.

First, in theory at least this House procedure is considerably more "democ-ratically" problematic than is choice by the electoral college itself.[8] With fifty states, twenty-six must vote for a candidate, and the twenty-six least populous states will do. Under the electoral college allocation produced by the 1990 cen-sus—the one that governed in the 2000 election—the twenty-six least populous states commanded only twenty-three percent of the electoral votes, and had a scant sixteen and a half percent of the nation's population. Under the 2000 cen-sus that will hold sway until the 2012 election, the twenty-six least populous states that could produce a president in the House had—at census time—about eighteen percent of the population of the country and about twenty-four per-cent of the electoral votes. These states were Alaska, Arkansas, Connecticut, Delaware, Hawaii, Idaho, Iowa, Kansas, Kentucky, Maine, Mississippi, Montana, Nebraska, Nevada, New Hampshire, New Mexico, North Dakota, Oklahoma,

Oregon, Rhode Island, South Carolina, South Dakota, Utah, Vermont, West Virginia, and Wyoming.

The House could thus choose a president with considerably less popular support than would be at all likely under the electoral college. Nor should this possibility be particularly surprising, since there was no assumption at the time the presidential selection process was originally crafted that the choice was to be made by popular election, or somehow be traceable to a popular majority. Recall that some of the delegates to the Constitutional Convention assumed that use of the House procedure would be routine.[9] But they also assumed that genuine deliberation about the "best" candidate would take place both in the electoral college and, when necessary, presumably in the House as well. With the advent of political parties and of the use of popular election in the presidential selection process, the applicable norms that naturally come to mind in evaluating the process have shifted dramatically. Not surprisingly many evaluate the electoral college against a contemporary norm of "majoritarian democracy,"[10] and by that standard the House procedure could result in a decidedly "undemocratic" choice.

Even if "majoritarian democracy" is thought to be the appropriate norm, however, this problem is decidedly more theoretical than real. In recent elections, only two candidates have obtained electoral votes. If the House were choosing from two candidates who had tied in the electoral college, then each of the two would almost surely have demonstrated substantial popular support. The House choice would thus not in practice be much more "democratically" problematic than would an electoral college choice. The same would likely be true if the failure of an electoral college majority was due to a smattering of votes for a third-party candidate. Assuming that the House continued to be dominated by the two major political parties—and that party affiliation loomed large in its decision-making process—the real world choice would very likely come down to two candidates, each of whom had shown substantial electoral college—and popular—support.[11] In short, unless and until the political complexion of the United States undergoes fairly radical change, the House choice under any realistic scenario would not raise any problem of "democratic" *bona fides* very different from that posed by an electoral college choice. To be sure, the winner might not have prevailed in the popular vote count, and some degree of resentment is likely to attend any electoral college victory by a "wrong winner."[12] But no serious social discontent—nor any large-scale de-grading of the "democratic" credentials of the winner—seems likely to follow from the choice of one candidate by the House over another where the two were close competitors in the nationwide popular and electoral college votes.[13]

A second problem with the House contingent procedure is exclusion of the District of Columbia from the process. By virtue of the Twenty-Third Amend-ment, the District has representation in the electoral college equal to that of the "least populous state." But the District has no voting representation in the House and hence no say if the contingent procedure is called into action. This might be written off as part of the aberrational treatment of the District more generally. Originally conceived as a sparsely populated seat of government, the denizens of which would have a say in the governance of a state, today's popu-lous District is spurned by Maryland and Virginia from which it was originally drawn, and has no voting members of its own in either house of Congress. In Chapter Six we will catch a glimpse of a recent proposal that would provide District representation in the House. But at the present time that proposal re-mains a distant hope. Until that step is taken, inclusion of the District in the electoral college but its exclusion from the House contingent procedure is at best an anomaly in the presidential selection process that history has be-queathed us. At the same time, if the felt injustice of the District's treatment is associated with the fact that its inhabitants are for the most part citizens of the United States, they are not the only citizens disfavored in the presidential selec-tion process. Indeed the other neglected citizens—in foreign territories or re-siding in foreign countries—do not even have electoral college representation. We will return in Chapter Ten to the general problem of defining the appropri-ate electorate for selection of the president.

A potentially quite serious concern is that the House itself might, at least temporarily, be stalemated in its own choice. For no matter what the cause of an indecisive electoral college outcome, tie votes might bedevil the backup process of selection by the House of Representatives. There are, of course, fifty states—an even number—and that poses the possibility of a tie. But probably more troublesome is the problem posed by House state delegations with even numbers of members. In the Congress sitting as this is written—the 108th—there are seventeen states with an even number of representatives. That num-ber could, however, easily be larger. Writing in 1968, Albert Rosenthal reported that twenty-nine of the fifty states had an even number of congressmen.[14] A state with an evenly divided delegation would cast no vote and jeopardize the possibility of either candidate commanding the necessary twenty-six states. The most obvious possibility for a deadlocked delegation is when it is evenly divided between the major political parties. At the time I am writing this (but with no guarantee it will still be true when you are reading it), four states have House delegations made up of half Democrats and half Republicans.

If the choice of the president hung in the balance, the pressure for party fidelity would surely be great. Still, there would be other pressures. Representatives might feel—or be made to feel—some obligation to vote for the popular vote winner in their state or district. Conceivably some might be inclined to vote for the winner of the nationwide popular vote.[15] One commentator writes of a House member "express[ing] independence or maverick tendencies" or seeking "publicity."[16] The various possibilities might actually introduce a healthy dose of fluidity into the picture, making an extended deadlock less likely. This being said, the real possibility of partisan standoff in delegations could spell trouble. The effective abstention of just a few states due to tie votes in their delegations would substantially increase the possibility that the House might not be able to muster the majority required for a choice.

If the question were to come before the House sitting as this is written, deadlock in the choice of president would be unlikely. After conviction of manslaughter, South Dakota's sole member of the House of Representatives, Republican William Janklow, resigned in January of 2004. He was replaced by a Democrat in a special election, but that still left the Republicans in control of a comfortable majority of delegations. But no choice of president will be made by the House sitting as the 108th Congress. If the House had been called into the process as a result of the 2004 election, it would have been the House of the 109th Congress that would have made the choice. And of course, future elections where the electoral college is unable to decide will engage future iterations of the House of Representatives. For a variety of reasons there is no reason to expect that one party or the other will routinely and easily command the state-by-state majority in the House necessary to prevail in the selection of the president.[17]

One reason is that the House itself is quite closely divided at the present time, and competitive politics can be expected to lead to that result with at least some regularity. But beyond that, a single party's control, or even decisive dominance, of the House by no means assures control of a majority of state delegations. After the 1800 electoral college tie, for instance, the lame duck Federalists had a decisive 64-42 margin in the House,[18] but nonetheless the Jeffersonians controlled eight of the sixteen House delegations. The "dominant" Federalists controlled only six delegations outright, and two were tied between the parties.[19] Close examination of the makeup of the House of Representatives over the years would probably show some correlation between party control of the House and party control of a majority of the delegations. But there is no mystery about why the connection is not a necessary one and is often not found. If one party controls some large state delegations by substantial margins, its total membership mounts up with scant effect on control of state delegations. California's total of fifty-three representatives in the 108th Congress, for instance, easily exceeded the total for the delegations of the twenty least populous states. California's delegation was heavily weighted with Democrats at the time, and that left plenty of room for Republican control of significant numbers of delegations from less populous states, while the overall balance in the House remained close to even.

As a result, both the dynamics and the outcome of the House contingent procedure can be importantly influenced by quite small shifts in the overall political party makeup of the body. Republican control of a majority of state delegations in the 108th Congress, for instance, was fragile. The Republican margin was just one vote in thirteen of the delegations the party controlled. That means that just a few Democratic gains of the "right" House seats could threaten a standoff in the House if choice of a president fell to that body.[20]

If there is a deadlock in the House that extends to January 20, the constitutionally established day for the new president to take office, under the Twentieth Amendment the vice president is to "act as President."[21] The electors would also have voted for a vice president, and since the Twelfth Amendment, the two votes are distinct. We saw in Chapter Two that under the original constitutional provisions for the electoral college, the vice president did not require a majority to prevail. But that was changed when the two votes were separated. With candidates for the two offices, as well as the electors, linked by political party, and the vice president now requiring a majority, an indecisive electoral college vote in the presidential balloting would in all likelihood have been accompanied by an indecisive vice presidential vote as well.[22] In the vice presidential case, the choice is sent to the Senate, where each senator is presumably to have one vote.[23] There being an even number of senators, there could be a tie—and hence a deadlock—in that choice, but the chance is not nearly as great as in the House. For while a majority of senators is necessary for the choice,[24] just as a majority of states is necessary for the presidential selection, no senator faces the problem of internal deadlock that a state with an even number of representatives might face. Still, as we saw in Chapter Four, the separation of the votes, and the different contingent procedures, does raise the specter of a divided administration, where the president and vice president come from different parties.

Another possible, if unlikely, scenario is that neither a new president nor a new vice president would have been chosen by January 20. Should that happen, under authority derived from the Twentieth Amendment[25] Congress has provided a line of succession for "acting presidents."[26] In the unlikely event it did occur, this contingency might well spell trouble, because the legislation turns first to the speaker of the House and then to the president pro tempore of the Senate. In each case, however, resignation from the legislature is statutorily required, no doubt because of the constitutional prohibition on being a "member of either house" while "holding any [other] office under the United States."[27] There might be great reluctance on the part of these officers to resign when it would only bring a temporary post as "acting" president, and indeed great doubt about how long the tenure might last. The legislation does then turn to a succession of cabinet officers,[28] but these officers would be associated with the outgoing administration. At best they would operate as "lame ducks" with no electoral backing whatsoever, and at worst as mischief makers in a process they might like to see prolonged.

If the House was deadlocked, but the Senate had been able to select a vice president, the office of (acting) president could be occupied by an elected official. Whether and how this "temporary" solution would affect the House balloting for the presidency is, however, hardly clear. Some representatives might find the acting president entirely congenial, and for that reason an inducement not to bring the stalemate to an end, but rather to extend it.[29] But with or without a shadow cast by the selection of a vice president, it is the House process itself that provides the most basis for concern.

In the 1800 House choice between Jefferson and Burr, it took thirty-six ballots over six days, but the standoff was finally resolved in Jefferson's favor. The
competition there, however, was between two candidates from the same political party. The candidate of the other major party, the Federalists, had been
eliminated before the matter reached the House.[30] In a contemporary electoral
college stalemate, on the other hand, there would presumably be candidates
from competing political parties, and that would likely make resolution even
harder to achieve. Still, while nothing is certain in this untested world—which
is a large part of the problem—the deadlock would likely be broken, sooner or
later. The peril in a deadlock is, however, by no means confined to the possibility that no decision will ever be forthcoming.

Most unsettling, if the partisan state-by-state breakdown of House delegations were close—and especially if there was no clear majority—the smell of
corruption (what an 1874 Senate Report called "corruption, cabal, and intrigue")—would almost surely attend the choice of president.[31] The presidency
is a sufficiently large prize that a process of bargaining over a great many matters would accompany the voting where the outcome was in any real doubt.
There were allegations that Jefferson made important concessions to break the
1800 deadlock—and similarly that Adams did so in the 1824 election[32]—but for
this purpose the election of 1876 provides the more apt object lesson.

As we saw in Chapter Three, federal troops were still in the South in 1876
when the electoral college outcome was put in doubt by disputes in four different states, three of them in the Reconstruction South. The possibility of a tie
and of recourse to the House contingent procedure did not loom large, because
there was an odd number of electors, and only the two major candidates. The
disputes had to be resolved, however, and the Constitution is decidedly obscure
on how that is to be done. State electors are to send their votes to the president
of the Senate (the vice president of the United States), who is to open them "in
the presence of the Senate and the House of Representatives." Without saying
who is to do it, the Constitution commands that "the votes shall then be
counted."[33] In Chapter Three we got a glimpse of the contemporary governing
norms for this constitutional obscurity, but in 1876 the interpretational precedents were few and inconclusive. Moreover, as we also saw in Chapter Three,
the vice president was a Republican, while the two Houses of Congress were
controlled by different parties. Improvisation was required. A commission was

appointed pursuant to (hard won) legislation. The commission resolved all the disputes in favor of the Republican candidate, Rutherford B. Hayes, leading to a one-vote margin for Hayes in the electoral college. The Democrats could have continued to cause trouble, but relented instead. Hayes became president, and Reconstruction was ended.

The election of 1876 involved neither an indecisive electoral college outcome nor recourse to the House. But it did involve a razor-thin electoral college margin and required the votes and acquiescence of a variety of actors to bring a tense drama to a (relatively) calm conclusion. In such a setting it is hardly surprising that bargaining was commonplace. As we also saw in Chapter Three there is ongoing continuing dispute about just what was encompassed in the "Bargain of 1877," but little doubt that both bargaining and rumors about it were the order of the day.[34]

Who is to say what might be thrown into a bargain to resolve a stalemate in the House of Representatives today? Bargaining is an enduring part of politics, and indeed welcome in its most typical contexts. Ordinary legislative bargaining is a part of an ongoing process, however, with voting rules that will persist the day after the bargain, just as they did the day before. There is a durable, and presumably acceptable, distribution of bargaining chips and a likelihood that a loser in one transaction will gain something back in another. The parties are therefore likely to reason through what is at stake, and there is likely to be a degree of predictability to the process. In selection of the president by the House of Representatives, in contrast, the matter is *sui generis*, and the voting rules are foreign to other business of the body. Even more troubling, the weighty chips that are held by some members of Congress are the product of almost pure chance—or worse. Single member House delegations, members of delegations in partisan standoff, and members whose switch could "swing" a delegation would likely be the most tempting offerees in any bargaining process. The latter two are largely fortuitous, and the first, at least by the measure of population of their states, would seem to have the least at stake.[35] And the payoff in the presidency is so enormous that judgment is likely to be unsettled, and the bargain eventually struck likely to be salutary only by accident.

Precisely because these problems can be foreseen, moreover, bargaining might well have entered the process before it reached the House. The electors are chosen on election day, but they do not meet to vote until about forty days later. One of the unsettled questions to which we will return in Chapter Seven is the legitimacy of "faithless" electoral votes, the extent to which electors have discretion to break ranks with the popular vote that put them in office. I will argue in Chapter Seven that the discretion of electors can and should be corralled. But until that is done broadly and with some decisiveness, the possibility of elector discretion could present even more tempting targets for unseemly bargaining than would members of the House of Representatives if the selection reaches that body.[36]

This is so for several reasons beyond the fortuitous distribution of bargaining chips that would be common to an electoral college facing the prospect of deadlock and to the House procedure. The voting of electors takes place in fifty-one state (and District of Columbia) gatherings. In at least some of those states the votes are held by secret ballot,[37] and at least in the states with larger delegations, it might be difficult for the public to determine which elector(s) had broken faith with the results of the popular election in his or her state.[38] In addition, the office of elector is put constitutionally out of bounds to a U.S. "Senator or Representative, or person holding an office of trust or profit under the United States."[39] As a result, electors will often not be public officials at all. If they do hold public office, it will be at the state or local level. And most fundamentally electors are chosen for all manner of reasons that have to do with service of one sort or another to a political party. Those reasons need have little to do with skill in political negotiation, or with bargaining in the shadow of public scrutiny. No such skill is normally demanded of electors, for no such skill is normally required in their routine task. The simple fact is that electors can be expected to have considerably less experience to provide some compass in any bargaining that might take place. Again there is no reason to welcome any such bargaining that might sway the outcome of the electoral college vote.

If the question does reach a closely divided House and is decided there one way or another, an unseemly bargain might not be inevitable, but suspicion of it almost surely would be. In the environment of mistrust likely to prevail, it would be difficult for a new administration to govern, perhaps even in the most basic ways. I was at pains to emphasize at the outset of this chapter that the most serious problem with the House procedure is not the democratic credentials of the eventual choice. But the theoretical questions that might be raised about those credentials would be likely to haunt the process more than they should. For once the motives of democratic actors are called into question, their claim to legitimacy is likely to come under scrutiny from multiple directions. And under that kind of microscope the House contingent procedure has little to sustain it in the modern day. Under the House procedure the choice of a president is a function neither of the popular vote nor of the electoral college vote. Nor is it a function of party control of the House of Representatives. It would, of course, be what it is, a function—in major part at least—of the alignment of state delegations to the House. But since that alignment is basically irrelevant to any other decision that is made in the land, the once-in-a-lifetime choice of the president by the House would have precarious "democratic" ground on which to rest while laying claim to legitimacy.

If avoiding the contingent House procedure is taken as desirable, the only apparent way to do so in wholesale fashion is by constitutional amendment. But we have seen that constitutional amendment is always difficult, and would likely be especially so in the case of change in the electoral college.[40] Even if the House contingent procedure could be approached in isolation, the less populous states might be reluctant to give up the enormous power they command under that procedure. But there likely is no way to isolate that part of the process. Proponents of a nationwide popular vote, in particular, would likely greet any move toward constitutional change in a part of the process as an occasion to pursue their cause. For these reasons constitutional amendment seems likely to be a dead end in dealing with the House procedure.

Short of a constitutional amendment I know of no way to avoid all possibility of recourse to the House contingent procedure. But we have seen that there is a variety of causes of electoral college deadlock that may call the House procedure into play. There is more potential to limit the mischief of the procedure by attacking its causes than by trying to banish it altogether, though we shall see that some of the causes may be more susceptible to effective treatment than others. Chapters Six through Eight deal with the major possibilities, some of which present more pervasive problems than the risk of the House contingent procedure. We start in Chapter Six, however, with relatively manageable possibility that the House might be called to decide on account of an electoral college tie.

CHAPTER SIX

The Case of Two Candidates Ending Up
in an Electoral College Tie

At the present time there are 538 members of the electoral college, an even
number that could split down the middle, sending the presidential choice into
the House of Representatives.[1] To be sure, we have not had an electoral college
tie since 1800, and that was under a very different voting protocol, in which
each elector cast two votes, undifferentiated between president and vice president. The tied candidates in 1800, Thomas Jefferson and Aaron Burr, were candidates of the same political party, the understanding being that Jefferson was
the party's presidential choice. The 1800 tie could actually have been avoided if
the Jeffersonians had coordinated a little better, reaching an agreement beforehand with electors owing fealty to the party that a designated one of them (but
only one) would vote for Jefferson but not for Burr. That is apparently what the
Federalists did in that same election, with their electors casting sixty-five votes
for their presidential candidate, John Adams, but sixty-four votes for their vice-
presidential candidate, Charles Cotesworth Pinckney. There has in fact never
been a tie between presidential candidates of different political parties.[2] A moment's reflection suggests, however, that the possibility of an electoral college tie
in today's quite different political world should not lightly be dismissed.

Throughout our history American politics has mostly been characterized by
two dominant political parties. There has typically been an assortment of minor parties, but never three (or more) parties more or less evenly matched and
vying for dominance over any extended period of time.[3] H. Ross Perot ran as an
independent in 1992, and did capture almost twenty percent of the popular

vote. Perot ran again in 1996 under the banner of "his personally organized Reform Party,"[4] and won over eight percent of the voting population nationwide. In neither year, however, did Perot capture electoral votes, and while his efforts in those two years unsettle the picture a bit, the recent trend seems to be solidifying a pattern of two parties, more or less equally matched.[5] We will return in Chapter Eight to some of the likely causes of that trend. But with minor and quirky exceptions,[6] since 1968 only candidates of the Democratic and Republican parties have garnered votes in the electoral college. To be sure, most of the electoral college counts have been one-sided in those years. Still, when there are two formidable contenders for the same divisible prize, it should not be surprising if every once in a while each comes away with about half.

That is what happened in the 2000 election. After Florida's disputed twenty-five electoral college votes were secured for George Bush by the Supreme Court's decision, there were 267 electors pledged to Albert Gore and 271 to Bush. One of the Gore-pledged electors in the District of Columbia eventually abstained,[7] but almost surely she would have voted for Gore if her vote would have made a difference. On that assumption, there are any number of plausible scenarios which would have resulted in a 2000 electoral college tie.[8]

Pennsylvania's twenty-three electoral votes, for instance, went for Gore in 2000 by virtue of a popular vote margin for him in the state of a little more than 200,000 votes, about 4.3 percent. It is certainly not fanciful to imagine that Florida would have gone for Gore and Pennsylvania for Bush. Pennsylvania, after all, has two Republican senators and a House delegation of twelve Republicans and seven Democrats. This latter figure is apparently a result of a partisan gerrymander,[9] but in 2000 Pennsylvania was universally judged to be a "swing" or "battleground" state that could easily go either way in the presidential election.[10] Had Florida and Pennsylvania switched in this way in 2000—and the District elector voted for Gore—there would have been an electoral college tie, 269-269. The same would have been true if Tennessee, with its eleven votes, had gone for Gore and Maine and New Mexico, with a total of nine votes, had gone for Bush, or if Arizona and Nevada, with twelve votes, had gone for Gore, and Minnesota, with ten, had gone for Bush. Indeed, just by focusing on states where the popular vote totals were fairly close, it is possible to identify a dozen or more plausible possibilities for an electoral vote tie in the 2000 election.[11]

In 2004 the election was not as close as that of 2000, in either electoral college or nationwide popular vote terms. Thirty-five electoral votes eventually separated the two major candidates.[12] Nor was the popular vote margin in 2004 razor-thin in any state with a large clump of electoral votes, as it had been in Florida in 2000. But up until election day there were many predictions of a very close contest, both in the electoral college and in crucial swing states.[13] Indeed, there was a great deal of speculation about the possibility of an electoral college tie.[14] In the end, while close by historical standards in both popular and electoral votes, the 2004 election was not in the closeness league of the 2000 election. Nonetheless, the 2004 election provides additional examples of entirely plausible reversals in particular states that would have produced an electoral college tie.

The most realistic examples all depend on a switch of Florida's twenty-seven electoral votes, and the popular vote in Florida in 2004 ended up not terribly close. Almost 400,000 votes eventually separated the two candidates. Still, Florida had routinely been classified as a "swing" state in the days leading up to the election,[15] and a different 2004 outcome there hardly seems fanciful. Had Florida's twenty-seven votes gone for John Kerry, and either Minnesota or Wisconsin (each a swing state as well) given its ten electoral votes to George W. Bush, the result would have been a tie. Similarly there would have been an electoral college tie in 2004 if Florida, Ohio, and Nevada, with a total of fifty-two electoral votes, had gone for Kerry, and Pennsylvania, New Hampshire (one of the most closely contested states in both 2000 and 2004), and either Wisconsin or Minnesota, with a total of twenty-five, had gone for Bush.

In these terms, both the 2000 and 2004 electoral college tallies were close, but in neither year was there a cigar that exploded into the House contingent procedure. We did not have a tie in 2000 or 2004, and in any event the closeness of the 2000 contest may turn out to be the aberration. But long-term complacency about the tie possibility seems misplaced. In any given election a tie is surely unlikely, but for several reasons we would nonetheless do well to guard against the possibility.

First, there have been other elections with close electoral college contests. Rutherford B. Hayes beat Samuel Tilden in 1876 by just one electoral vote, when there was an odd number of electors. Woodrow Wilson beat Charles Evans Hughes in 1916 by twenty-three electoral votes. John F. Kennedy's electoral vote margin over Richard Nixon in 1960 was eighty-four, with fifteen votes cast for other candidates. In 1976 Jimmy Carter beat Gerald Ford by fifty-seven electoral votes. While the Kennedy and Carter margins may seem sizable, the 2004 hypothetical scenarios discussed above can be adapted to those situations as well. With most state delegations awarded on a winner-take-all basis, a shift in one or two competitive populous states, perhaps aided by a nudge or two from less populous competitive states, would have been sufficient to overcome the 1960 and 1976 margins and produce paper thin, or even tied, outcomes.[16]

Second, the country seems very closely divided politically at the present time, not only in overall totals of popular sentiment, but in divisions among the states as well. This is reflected in close divisions of the House and Senate, as well as in the last two presidential contests. It is also reflected in the pattern of presidential elections since Franklin Roosevelt, in which the two major political parties have more or less alternated in winning the presidency. American politics, and the society in which it is embedded, is sufficiently complex that we should hesitate to project the future on the basis of the past, but in a two-party environment frequent shifts from victory by one party to victory by the other might be expected as the long-run norm. After all, each party has an incentive to appeal to voters at the margin of the other party's constituencies. In any event, we should hardly be surprised to see a recurring pattern of presidential races closely contested between the two major parties.

Third, the technology of campaigning has advanced markedly in recent years. With the use of computers and detailed census data, competing candidates can more readily identify areas of strength and weakness.[17] They can then target their resources, and, other things being equal, that might be expected to lead to close elections. The closely fought 2000 and 2004 elections provide the best evidence of what the new campaigning environment might bring, and they provide no basis for complacency about the possibility of an electoral college tie.

Finally, even if an electoral college tie were thought to be quite a remote possibility, the costs of invoking the House contingent procedure that we discussed in Chapter Five would still make it advisable to take action now to forestall the possibility, at least if that action were itself relatively costless. That is, I think, precisely the situation we face. In the case of the tie possibility in the electoral college, there is a relatively straightforward measure—not requiring a constitutional amendment—that would greatly lessen the chances that we will have to bear the costs.

The size of a state's delegation to the electoral college is the combined size of its delegations in the Senate and in the House of Representatives.[18] In addition, the Twenty-Third Amendment provides for an electoral college delegation for the District of Columbia equal to that of the "least populous state." In toto, the size of the electoral college can thus be thought of as having three components: the size of the Senate; the size of the District's delegation; and the size of the House of Representatives.[19] The first is always an even number, since each state has two senators. The District's delegation will almost surely remain at its present size—the odd number three—for the foreseeable future.[20] But the third component can be changed without constitutional amendment, for the size of the House of Representatives is a matter for legislative determination.

The only constitutional limitations on the size of the House are that "[t]he number of representatives shall not exceed one for every thirty thousand [people in the census count]"—a limitation no longer of any practical significance—and that "each state shall have at least one representative."[21] The size of the House is now set at 435,[22] an odd number which combines with the other two components to yield an even number of electors. If the Congress were to increase the House size by one, the electoral college would similarly be increased by one member. The resulting odd number would greatly reduce the possibility of an electoral college deadlock and the consequent recourse to the House to select the president.

When I floated this idea in an earlier article,[23] I occasionally encountered the objection that an odd number of electors would come at the cost of an even number of members of the House, courting the possibility there of deadlock through tie votes. For several reasons, that possibility does not seem at all troublesome. First, vacancies in the House at the present time are common. By one account written in 2003, "[i]n the past 15 years 26 members of the House . . . died in office, and on average it was 116 days . . . until a successor was sworn into office."[24] And vacancies occur with some frequency through forced or voluntary resignation. In 2004, for instance, South Dakota's Congressman William Janklow resigned after he was convicted of manslaughter resulting from an automobile accident. Unless they occur late in the congressional term, those vacancies are filled by special elections[25]—as was Janklow's—but the result is that there is no telling whether the House at any given time will have an even or odd number of voting members.[26]

Second, there are probably no great costs associated with the prospect of tie votes in the House in any event. Legislation presents an essentially infinite set of possibilities for compromises that can change votes, so that ties can be avoided through trading and accommodation. If a tie is inevitable, moreover, that probably means that there is no imperative need for either side to prevail and that the country will survive just fine without the legislation under consideration. The only time a tie might cause real mischief would be when the House is organized at the beginning of a new Congress with the choice of a speaker and the designation of committees and their chairs. Deadlock on those matters might be troublesome, but there seems no reason why compromise should not be possible for them as well. Committees could be divided evenly between two parties, and chairs could either be rotated or shared. Even the speaker of the House could be changed by agreement in mid-term. Indeed, with a House that is evenly divided—or divided by one or two votes, for that matter—those compromises might be thought preferable to one party's domination of those levers of decision. In short, an even number of House members would probably go unnoticed, and when noticed might well do more good than bad. In any event, even discounting for its improbability, there seems to be no mischief in the tie possibility in the House that compares with what might befall us with the prospect of an electoral college tie.

An intriguing possibility for implementing a one-vote increase in the size of the electoral college is presented by the recent introduction of legislation that would temporarily increase the size of the House by *two members*. Congressman Thomas M. Davis III of Virginia, chairman of the House Committee on Government Reform, has proposed that the District of Columbia be given representation in the House, urging that this can be done through Congress's power to "exercise exclusive Legislation" over the District of Columbia.[27] At the present time a District representative would surely be a Democrat. To make the move more politically palatable, Davis's proposal would add a second new representative, which would likely go to Utah, and likely be a Republican. If this were done, the electoral college would only increase by one member, however, since the District would presumably not be entitled to an additional elector on account of its new representative. Davis's proposal would have the size of the House revert to 435 after the 2010 census, but that would include one representative from the District and hence would also leave the electoral college with an odd number of members thereafter.

This is not to say that a move to increase the size of the House of Representatives—whether through Davis's initiative or otherwise—would be uncontroversial, or without cost. The House undergoes a reapportionment—adjustment of the size of state delegations—after each decennial census.[28] If the size of the House is held constant, then the size of some delegations is likely to decrease. Understandably states resist any diminution in the size of their delegations and indeed covet additional seats that might be in prospect. To be sure, many, perhaps most, delegations are likely to maintain their size, and before the 1960s, the prospect of a delegation of the same size would have been relatively comfortable for states, allowing them to avoid redistricting and the dislocation costs that redistricting could bring to congressional incumbents. But in the 1960s, the U.S. Supreme Court required that states draw their congressional districts to make them equally populous.[29] Given that decision, births, deaths, and the mobility of the population virtually ensure that states must redistrict internally after each decennial census, regardless of whether the size of their delegations has changed. As a result, the attractiveness of stable size for state House delegations is greatly diminished, unless, perhaps, the alternative for a state is a smaller delegation.

These pressures would seem to create an institutional incentive for an ever larger House of Representatives. In the face of this incentive, it is quite stunning that the House has remained at it present size of 435 for going on a century now.[30] If the size of the House were the subject of serious legislative consideration, there might be understandable concern that the floodgates would open and a variety of states would push for an ever larger House of Representatives.

A larger House would allow a more favorable ratio of representatives to constituents, and for that reason there are contemporary proponents of an appreciably larger House.[31] But larger bodies raise the danger that the leadership increasingly makes all the important decisions. I won't undertake to resolve that tension here, but simply note that an increase through Congressman Davis's initiative, or of one member, or at most a small—odd—number, would effectively maintain the status quo in the size dimension.[32] This being said, simply opening up the question of the size of the House might set in motion a process of enlargement that would prove hard to contain. Congressman Davis's proposal suggests that he views such a risk as manageable. In any event, given the serious costs associated with the present flirtation with the possibility of an electoral college tie, the risk seems to be one worth running.

The same can be said of recurring controversy about the way in which the seats are allocated among the states, once the size of the House has been established. The approach to allocation has been a subject of controversy from the earliest days of the nation, generating a clash between Thomas Jefferson and Alexander Hamilton.[33] Two constitutional requirements create the allocation problem. First, each state is entitled to at least one representative, no matter how minuscule its population in comparison to that of other states.[34] And second, House districts must be wholly contained within states, so that each state has a whole number of representatives. But allocation of a limited number of House seats among the fifty states will almost inevitably lead to an "ideal" allocation for each state that contains a fractional element. That raises the question of whether and how to round the fractions up or down, and also whether to start with a set number of representatives to be allocated or instead allow the size of the House to vary depending upon how the fractions are falling out. If one starts with a given size for the House—as we essentially have for going on a hundred years now[35]—simply rounding up or down will seldom yield the right number, so other possibilities must be entertained.[36] The theoretical question is by no means settled,[37] but it does appear that the practical one is. The Congress opted for a method called "equal proportions" in 1941, and subsequent Congresses have seen fit not to reopen the question.[38] A move to increase the size of the House by one member would pose some danger of unsettling that status quo, but again the risk seems worth taking.

After the 2000 census Utah objected to a counting methodology of the Census Bureau that resulted in North Carolina, rather than Utah, being assigned the last available slot.[39] It thus appears that if the size of the House were increased by one at the time this is written, Utah would be most likely to receive the new position, almost surely making it a reliably Republican seat. As we have seen that is a premise of Congressman Davis's proposal. Outside the Davis proposal, this would make the addition of a single representative a matter of partisan contentiousness. For that reason, the Davis proposal apart, it would proba-

bly enhance the chances of achieving an increase in the size of the House to delay the effectiveness of the increase to a date after the next census, making it
considerably more unpredictable which state (or states) would benefit. This
would, of course, delay the effectiveness of the insurance against a tie in the
electoral college. But delayed insurance is surely better than none at all.

   The tie possibility to which an increase in the size of the House is a response
assumes that all members of the electoral college cast effective votes for one of
two major party candidates. Since passage of the Twelfth Amendment, the constitutional trigger for the House choice of the president is not the tie possibility
as such, but rather the failure of any candidate to obtain a majority of the electoral college. It would be possible to have an electoral college tie with the tied
candidates receiving votes of fewer than half the electors. This could come
about, for instance, if third-party candidates garnered some electoral college
votes, or some electors abstained, or were disqualified from voting. And any of
these could result in there being no candidate with a majority of the electoral
college votes, even though there was no tie. There are, in short, perils in the
electoral college process besides an even split of the full 538 electors that could
invite the House contingent procedure. Chapter Eight is devoted to the third-
party possibility. In Chapter Seven, I turn to the possibility of faithless electors
whose votes threaten to throw the choice of president into the House, or
worse.[40]

CHAPTER SEVEN

The Problem of Faithless Electors

To win in the electoral college, a candidate must command "a majority of the whole number of Electors appointed,"[1] and achieving that goal can be frustrated in a variety of ways besides an equal division between two candidates after a straightforward designation of electors in state-by-state popular elections. One of those ways is that one or more electors might abstain or vote for a candidate other than the one to whom they were committed beforehand. In the literature about the electoral college these are often called "faithless electors." The potential for mischief on account of elector faithlessness, moreover, reaches well beyond the possibility that the electoral college will tie or otherwise fail to achieve the required majority. For elector faithlessness could produce an entirely decisive outcome in the electoral college itself, just a different one from what the contemporary understanding of the presidential election process would have led the voters to assume was coming.

The members of the electoral college meet in separate state (and District of Columbia) meetings about forty days after each quadrennial presidential "election day." As we have seen, the meeting day is established by congressional legislation and is required by the Constitution to be the "the same throughout the United States."[2] When all goes smoothly at those meetings—and historically that has been most of the time—the electors simply go through prescribed motions, casting their votes for the new president and vice president. They vote for the candidates for whom they were pledged to vote, usually the national nominees of the political party that advanced them for the office of elector. This "pledge" may have taken the form of a formal oath, perhaps administered by the political party under authorization of state law.[3] Or it may have been more informal, at the extreme simply understood as what an elector on a party slate does in fulfillment of his or her responsibility as an elector. State laws may provide for candidates for electors who are "unpledged," and such unpledged electors have won on occasion over the years.[4] But states discourage unpledged electors, and in recent years electors who have won have been pledged—formally or informally—to one candidate or another and have almost always voted as they had committed themselves to vote.

There have, however, been occasional deviations from this pattern of commitment keeping. In the 2004 election, an unidentified Minnesota elector cast his presidential vote for John Edwards, his party's vice-presidential nominee. Whether he did this intentionally or inadvertently is not known.[5] In the 2000 election, Barbara Lett-Simmons, a District of Columbia elector, abstained rather than voting as pledged for the Democratic presidential candidate, Albert Gore. In the 1988 election, one Democratic elector cast her presidential vote for the party's vice-presidential candidate, and vice versa—apparently quite intentionally. Over the years there have been perhaps a dozen or more electors who have voted in the presidential contest contrary to a formal pledge or rather clear expectations they have aroused, going back by some accounts all the way to 1796, when Samuel Miles cast a vote for Thomas Jefferson even though he had been advanced for the office of elector by the Federalists, rivals to Jefferson's own party.[6]

While electors who deviate from their commitments have come to be called "faithless electors," as mentioned in Chapter Three there is something wonderfully ironic about the term. We have seen that the office of elector was originally conceived as one calling for independent judgment. It was assumed that those meetings of electors would be devoted to serious discussion about who would make the best president, and that the electors would cast their votes pursuant to judgments formed in those discussions. Contemporary electors who deviate from prior commitments might be thought rather "faithful" to at least a part of this original idea. At best they are typically faithful to the original idea of their role only in part, for contemporary "faithless" electors typically do not come to the elector meetings with deliberation in mind, and in casting their faithless votes they are more likely to be making a point about something other than who would make the best president. An abstaining elector, for instance, can hardly be making an affirmative case about who should be president. Thus Lett-Simmons abstained in the 2000 election as a symbolic protest about the fact that the District of Columbia has no full voting representation in either the House or the Senate.[7]

Sometimes no doubt the point a faithless elector wants to make is that the person to whom an elector was pledged would *not* make a good president. That may have been the point the 1988 Democratic elector had in mind. And in the days before the 2004 election, Richie Robb, a nominee for elector on the Republican slate in West Virginia, indicated that if elected he did not think he could vote for George Bush, the Republican nominee for president. Robb was vague about the person for whom he would cast his presidential vote, leaving the clear impression that his consideration of faithlessness was borne solely of doubts about whether Bush was suited for the job.[8] (As it turned out, Robb must have voted for Bush, because Bush carried the state, and all the West Virginia electors voted for him.[9])

The specter of the faithless elector who changes the outcome of the choice of president has captured the imagination of some commentators,[10] and a substantial number of states have passed laws that explicitly purport to "bind" electors to vote in accord with their prior commitments. These laws sometimes simply instruct electors to vote as committed,[11] but sometimes they provide penalties of one sort or another. North Carolina, for instance, imposes a fine of $500 for faithlessness, while New Mexico makes it a "fourth degree felony."[12] Some laws require political parties to extract pledges, while others have state officers composing and administering oaths of faithfulness.[13] Some states provide that a faithless vote constitutes resignation from the office of elector.[14] And there are occasional proposals for a constitutional amendment that would do away with electors altogether, leaving the present system for allocating electoral votes among the states intact, and requiring the winner-take-all approach to determining the distribution of each state's allocation.[15] Still the subject of faithless electors is treated by both the Congress and many states with surprising casualness. The laws of almost half the states do not address the issue with any explicitness,[16] and in the joint meeting counting session the Congress over the years has routinely counted "faithless" electoral votes as they were cast, declining to treat the prior commitments as rendering those votes illegitimate. In Chapter Three we discussed the example of Lloyd Bailey, a North Carolina elector in the 1968 election whose faithless votes for president and vice president were challenged but then counted as he cast them.[17]

No doubt part of the reason for inattention to the subject is that faithlessly cast electoral votes have been fairly rare over the years and have never threatened to change the outcome of a presidential choice.[18] It may even be that some electors are made more likely to cast one of those rare faithless votes because of the assumption that their votes will make no difference in determining who will be president.[19] No elector could be sure, of course, as long as other electors can be faithless as well. If given effect, faithlessness on a large scale most assuredly could change outcomes. At the extreme faithless voting could conceivably result in selection of a president who did not receive a single popular vote in the entire country. But electors surely read the newspaper accounts of presidential election "returns," and hence know the electoral college count that will obtain if all electors vote faithfully. They also know that faithfulness has been the overwhelming norm over the years, and hence they can calculate with a high degree of assuredness whether or not a faithless vote here or there will make a difference in the presidential outcome.

There are also complications in attempts to bind electors that may cause some state legislators to hold back. Thus it is frequently asserted that electors cannot constitutionally be bound, that they must be left free to vote faithlessly if they wish.[20] Members of a state legislature might agree with that assessment, but even if they did not, they might worry that theirs would not be the last word. They might think that a state or federal court would hold a state law binding electors to be unconstitutional. Or they might imagine that the joint meeting of the two houses of Congress at which votes are to be counted would take the position that the state had no power to bind electors.[21] If the state law had prevented the casting of a vote deemed to have constitutional endorsement, the court or the joint meeting might then disregard that vote altogether. Or if a vote had been cast and then overridden by the state law, the court or joint meeting might insist on counting it as initially cast rather than acceding to the state law.

Despite the questions and difficulties, the problem of faithless electors is deserving of the most careful attention, for the possibilities for mischief growing out of elector faithlessness are quite real. There actually was a dramatic example of faithlessness with (temporary) bite, albeit in a vice-presidential selection and in an earlier era when the judgment of faithlessness was not quite so easy to make. In the 1836 election, Martin Van Buren was the presidential candidate of the Jacksonian Democratic Party, the lineal descendant of the Jeffersonians. The party's vice-presidential choice was the colorful and controversial Richard M. Johnson. By that time in American history, most states chose their electors through a statewide popular vote, but the forms of the ballots varied. I have been unable to locate Virginia ballots from the 1836 election, so I cannot be sure that Johnson's name actually appeared on the ballots that voters used. In all likelihood the names of the electors did appear.[22] In any event, once chosen the Virginia electors voted for Van Buren in accordance with their prior commitments, but refused to vote for Johnson, apparently because of allegations that he lived with a black woman. In all other states that went for Van Buren, the two men captured the same number of electoral votes. The result was that Van Buren won the presidency outright, while Johnson fell short of the required majority of appointed electors. The vice-presidential selection was then relegated to the Senate, where Johnson did win handily, 33-16.[23] That is the only time in our history that the Senate fallback procedure for selection of a vice president has been required.

The vice presidency is, of course, a much less significant office than the presidency, and for that reason elector votes for vice president might be cast with more abandon than those for president would be. Vice-presidential elections may thus not be terribly probative of what is likely to happen in presidential elections. In addition, the 1836 election was a long time ago, and since that time there has been no more momentous faithlessness of electors in their vice-presidential balloting than in their choices for president. Still, the 1836 election does demonstrate the potential of elector defection, and there seems every reason to fear that the possibility might be wielded with effect in a close presidential election.[24]

The electoral college margin for George Bush in the 2000 election was five votes, or four if Lett-Simmons's vote is included in the Gore count. In Chapter Six we examined the possibility suggested by that close vote of entirely faithful electors producing an even split in a two-person electoral college race. But the close 2000 election with Lett-Simmons's abstention should provide equally as clear a warning of the power of elector faithlessness. In a close contest, elector faithlessness could break a tie, or create one, or otherwise deprive the major candidates of the electoral college majority necessary to keep the presidential choice out of the House of Representatives. And quite apart from flirtation with the House contingent procedure, there is enormous potential mischief in the possibility of elector faithlessness. Faithless electors can make an electoral college winner out of the putative loser. Indeed as mentioned, in theory elector faithlessness could at the extreme give us a president for whom not a single popular vote had been cast.[25] That is, of course, decidedly unlikely, but even the theoretical possibility suggests the haphazardness—and danger for the American body politic—that the problem of faithless electors can introduce into the presidential selection process.

In the 2000 election, even after the Florida contest was decided in George Bush's favor, if three Republican electors had (successfully) voted for Gore, the outcome of the election would have been changed. And if two Republican electors had (successfully) abstained or voted for someone other than Bush or Gore, the presidential selection would have been relegated to the House of Representatives for want of an electoral college majority. Gore—or others associated with him—was rumored to have investigated the possibility of Republican elector defections, and that is hardly surprising.[26] Gore had, after all, decisively captured more popular votes nationwide than had Bush. Even his loss of the pivotal Florida electors was razor-thin at best, and subject to much dispute at worst. It is possible to imagine some committed Republicans who concluded that the intervention of the U.S. Supreme Court in the 2000 election was a bad mistake justifying faithlessness. For one or more of these reasons, Gore might well have thought that a few "conscientious" Republican electors could be convinced to give him the nod.[27]

If such efforts were made on behalf of Gore, moreover, it may simply have been turned about fair play. In the period immediately before election day, many polls suggested just the reverse of what happened. There were predictions that Bush would win the popular vote but lose to Gore in the electoral college.[28] In the face of this possibility, it was reported that the Bush campaign was investigating the possibility of securing the defection of some Democratic electors. In his recent book George Edwards provides an account of the preparations:

> [the] campaign had prepared talking points about the essential unfairness of the electoral college and intended to run advertisements, encourage a massive talk radio operation, and mobilize local business leaders and the clergy against acceptance of a

Gore victory. . . . The goal was to convince electors that they should cast their votes for the popular vote winner and not the winner in the electoral college.[29]

Edwards, of course, tellingly misstates the situation, for there would have been no "winner in the electoral college," until after the electoral votes had been cast. And if Bush had won the popular vote, and the Bush campaign's reported effort had succeeded, the popular vote winner would have become the "winner in the electoral college." Be that as it may, whatever the truth to the rumors in 2000,[30] one earlier candid candidate made little secret of the campaign's intention to seek out electoral college defections in the case of a contest in that forum that promised to be a close one.[31] As election day in 2004 was approaching, again there were many projections of a Bush popular vote "victory," with Kerry nonetheless prevailing in the electoral college. I know of no reports of a Bush campaign plan to search out faithless electors in 2004, but it would hardly be surprising had there been one.

Nor would it be all that surprising if such an effort were one day to succeed. The same lore that suggests that state law would be unconstitutional if it bound electors to their pledges might suggest to some electors that they should not be modest in their conception of their role.[32] After all, it is almost unthinkable that the office of elector would have been created in the first place if no discretion was to be exercised in carrying out its duties. Given that background, at least some electors might easily convince themselves that breaking faith would be true to a better way of selecting the president than the one embodied in the rote voting of the modern electoral college. I will turn shortly to why the constitutional arguments for elector discretion are misconceived, and it is clear that elector defection does break faith with the modern conception about how we choose a president, a conception with much more claim on elector fidelity than one entertained more than two centuries ago and never really taken seriously in practice. But it is entirely plausible to imagine that the heady possibility of elector discretion might cause some who hold the office not to see it that way.[33]

More than that, a presidential candidate within shooting distance of an electoral college—or House of Representatives—victory has so much at stake that a great deal might be promised to induce defection by electors. To be sure, outright bribery would be illegal, and hence probably unlikely, but favoritism for an elector's pet governmental cause or project could easily enter into the discussion of defection. Promise of a coveted office could be put in play, probably without transgressing legal norms. We saw, for instance, that John Calhoun supported John Quincy Adams in the 1824 House election and then became Adams's secretary of state.[34] We also saw that rumors of promised office played a role in the 1800 House election drama.[35] The same was true in the prolonged decision-making process of 1876.[36] Calhoun was not an elector, nor were those who allegedly received promises in 1800 and 1876. But an elector in a close contest has just what those others brought to the table: a large measure of influence over the selection of the president. Regardless of the truth of the claim that deals were offered or made in those cases, it is entirely plausible to imagine that they might have been. Electors are typically party loyalists and hence unlikely defectors,[37] even in close contests, but just as in those other cases there is nothing bizarre about the suggestion that a few might on occasion be tempted.

A presidential election decided by faithless electors could be disastrous. Some warn that divergence of the electoral college result from the popular vote holds great peril. The 2000 election shows that the perceived danger there may have been exaggerated.[38] We touched on that and related questions in Chapter Four. But unless and until the rules of the game are changed, it is entirely fair that the presidency goes to the candidate who wins the popular vote in sufficient states (or districts where applicable) to command the required majority of the electoral votes. The same can hardly be said of an election decided by faithless electors. There are no well-established and well-understood rules of a presidential election contest that allow elector defection from their prior commitments to candidates. We have seen that there is a strong current of opinion that elector discretion—and hence defection—is constitutionally protected. But even if that conclusion were more unassailable than it is, it is accompanied by near-universal assumption—reinforced by explicit statutory provision in a large number of states—that elector defection is breaking "faith" with an obligation.

As early as 1796, Samuel Miles's vote for Thomas Jefferson, despite his prior commitment to the Federalist candidate John Adams, elicited the following response from an aggrieved Federalist: "What, do I chuse Samuel Miles to determine for me whether John Adams or Thomas Jefferson shall be President? No! I chuse him to *act*, not *think*."[39] Elected as a Republican elector in the contentious 1876 election, James Russell Lowell made the same point from the other side of the relationship of voter to elector. Urged to vote for the Democrat Samuel Tilden, he declined, saying:

> I have no choice, and am bound in honor to vote for [the Republican] Hayes, as the
> people who chose me expected me to do. They did not choose me because they had
> confidence in my judgment, but because they thought they knew what that judgment
> would be. . . . It is a plain question of trust.[40]

That vision of the role of electors would be virtually universal today among
voters who gave any thought at all to the question.[41]

The elector's obligation, moreover, is not simply a private one. A defecting
elector has been a party to a very large-scale public event—indeed probably the
signature event of American democracy—in which millions of actors took it
for granted that electors would vote as pledged. They were encouraged in that
thought by the fact that these days many, perhaps most, presidential "election"
ballots do not even contain the names of the electors. And as we saw in Chapter Three even when the names of electors do appear on the ballot, they are typically presented in such a way that the electorate is given every reason to believe
that it is voting not for electors but for the persons to whom the electors are
pledged. We will elaborate on that point shortly. In contrast, no breaking of any
obligation—public or private—is involved in electors' voting as pledged for the
loser of the nationwide popular vote in accordance with the understood oper-
ations of the electoral college. A fair number of voters no doubt assume that it
is the nationwide popular vote that determines the winner of a presidential
election. But there is no secret kept that in almost all states it is simply the
statewide tally that counts.

Elector faithlessness that changes an election outcome could thus pose a serious threat to the perception, and indeed to the reality, of an election's legitimacy. Widespread social turmoil, even widespread violence, could well result.
The validity of the defection would, no doubt, be challenged, and the legitimacy
of that challenge would be challenged as well. The outcome of the struggle
could remain uncertain for a long time, with unforeseeable results. One commentator has said that "the ensuing dispute over the legitimacy of the election
of a new President might well inflict grave injuries upon the nation."[42] But that
is to put it mildly. It is entirely plausible to imagine, for instance, that foreign
enemies might confront the United States in the atmosphere of uncertainty
that could prevail. And even if some settlement of the election outcome were
reached with reasonable expedition, there would likely be bitterness and dis-

sension in many quarters. It seems to me unarguable that the possible societal costs of an election decided by faithless electors are enormous, and in any event sufficiently high that we would be well advised to forestall them by action now if that is feasible.

While a few loose ends might be unavoidable, the problem of the faithless elector is one that can be brought under control. Perhaps the least of the problems is the suggested constitutional obstacle to binding electors to their prior commitments. Initially the constitutional claim seems appealing, but it loses that appeal upon serious examination. As we have seen, a large number of states have already taken action through legislation that directly challenges any assertion that elector discretion enjoys constitutional protection. And in a 1952 decision that is most directly in point, the Supreme Court clearly tilted in favor of those state laws, holding in *Ray v. Blair* that states may allow political parties to extract pledges of faithfulness from candidates for elector who seek to run in party primaries.[43] Nonetheless it is instructive to examine the constitutional question more closely.

The starting point for any constitutional question must be the enacted language. The constitutional text that might be thought to bear on elector discretion appears now in the Twelfth Amendment:

> The electors shall meet in their respective states and vote by ballot for President and Vice-President, one of whom, at least, shall not be an inhabitant of the same state with themselves; they shall name in their ballots the person voted for as President, and in distinct ballots the person voted for as Vice-President, and they shall make distinct lists of all persons voted for as President, and of all persons voted for as Vice-President, and of the number of votes for each, which lists they shall sign and certify, and transmit sealed to the seat of the government of the United States directed to the President of the Senate.

One could hardly claim that this language requires elector discretion with crystal clarity. It does not, for instance, say anything like "the electors shall cast their ballots for any eligible candidate they choose, in their sole discretion." Still, the picture that the language most naturally conjures up is of groups of electors making genuine choices and then recording those choices on their "ballots." Indeed use of the word "ballot" is often cited as strong textual support for elector discretion.[44] Many dictionary definitions of "ballot" include "secrecy" as a feature of ballots,[45] and there surely would be little point to voting in secret if the voter were simply to vote in a way that was already a matter of public knowledge.

But if the promulgated language is the starting point in application of a provision to a problem that arises, it is by no means the end of the process. Indeed language alone is just scrawl on a page, or grunts in the air. Despite the bravado of some constitutional or statutory "textualists" or "literalists,"[46] language can only be sensibly applied once it is appreciated as embedded in a linguistic, cultural, and social context where it is deployed to give expression to human ideas and human ends. That context shapes the meaning given to words is nicely illustrated by the word "ballot." If the word once connoted secrecy, it no longer does so, at least with any regularity. Rather "ballot" is now often used simply to indicate a device for recording a vote, no matter how open or foreordained that vote might be.[47] And even when the meaning of words is stable, instructions gleaned from them will draw on the human ends they are assumed to serve. Even textualists effectively concede this last point when they leave an escape hatch from some seeming literal application of enacted language if it would lead to "absurd results."[48] "Absurd results" cannot be tolerated, precisely because it is assumed that no plausible human agency would have enacted language in order to bring them about.

Particularly in constitutional interpretation, a common approach to bridging the gap between enacted language and problems to which it is to be applied has come to be called "originalism."[49] Originalism comes in several varieties, but in each the Constitution is said to be appropriately interpreted to do the work that it was originally envisaged as doing. One variant of originalism turns to the author's intentions in promulgating a constitutional provision that is said to be applicable. A second variant, ascendant in the more recent originalist writing, draws on the audience's understanding, rather than the author's. Proponents of this latter approach usually insist (without much explanation) that the relevant "audience" is the public at the time of enactment of the provision—or, more typically, some representative "reasonable" member of that public—rather than one that changes with the generations that live under the provision.[50] As we saw in Chapter Two, the electoral college constitutional provisions suggest elector discretion, and so it is hardly surprising that originalism is an approach to constitutional interpretation that might initially also seem to counsel protection for elector discretion.

Unlike constitutional language, originalism in each of its variations must initially come to grips with what I call a "summing problem," ascribing a "purpose" or "intention" to the product of a large number of individual actors. We touched briefly on this problem in Chapter Two, when we discussed the historical dispute about elector discretion. Unless the words used are painfully precise, it will often be problematic to assume that the various actors shared some "purpose" or "intention" when they assented to use of those words. And without broad accord, questions abound of whose states of mind matter, and of just how much coincidence in those states of mind is required. The problem exists even for a simple law passed by a unicameral legislature, but in American jurisprudence it is particularly acute for constitutional provisions, where formulation and promulgation of the document was dependent upon a layered complex of multimember bodies—the constitutional convention, the Continental Congress, and then the various state ratifying conventions. The single most plausible way through this dilemma is to reason backward from the words used, imagining what some idealized single "reasonable" lawmaker at the time might have wanted to accomplish by those words.[51] A search for original "understanding" would appropriately proceed in essentially the same way. For the construct of a "reasonable" member of the public—the audience—at the time the Constitution was adopted can only be deployed through use of a fiction that similarly condenses understandings about a multitude of individuals. This approach differs from textualism in principle because of its candid acknowledgment that the ultimate inquiry is about purpose or intention. And it differs from textualism in practice mostly in its insistence that the historical and social contexts in which words are used matter a great deal.

This approach may on occasion be initially suggestive of answers that seem "absurd" and hence could not plausibly be ascribed to the idealized lawmaker. Or it may come up empty for other reasons, leaving ambiguities and uncertainties to be resolved by other means. But when the enacted words give firm guidance, that guidance should be heeded in preference to comments of an individual here or there, for it is only the language that has garnered the votes required to become the law. This is in essence what we did in addressing the historical dispute in Chapter Two, and it easily led to the conclusion that electors were originally "intended" to exercise independent judgment and discretion.[52]

Many proponents of originalism as the key to constitutional interpretation

would stop right there, comfortably concluding that elector discretion is constitutionally protected. But sensibly understood, constitutional originalism jus-
tifies no such conclusion. For constitutional language fortified by our best reading of original intention or understanding about elector discretion can only
begin the process of addressing the sole question about the role of electors that
could possibly arise today, one that resides in *today's* social, political, and cultural contexts.

For these purposes, it does not matter which variant of originalism we employ. For purposes of discussion, I will talk of "original intention," but nothing
in the discussion would be different if we imagined an "original understander"
instead. In either case, it is entirely unreasonable to ascribe to the electoral college provisions some "purpose" or "intention" that could answer—or even provide much help in answering—the *contemporary* question of elector discretion.
For the original intender's assumption of discretion—and crafting of constitutional language—was itself embedded in a larger context that made it intelligi-
ble and workable. That context has been turned upside down over the years, so
that if our supposed original intender were asked the contemporary question of
elector discretion, he would hardly know where to begin in providing an answer.[53]

Consider, for instance, the fact that political parties now hover over every aspect of political life, nominating slates of electors with the assumption that they
will vote in accordance with decisions made by the parties themselves, often
through an electoral mechanism by the state's voters who affirm their affiliation
with the party. The original intender would not recognize this as the context in
which he had formulated his expectation of elector discretion.[54] It would not be
faithful to any serious projection of the original intender's state of mind to the
contemporary problem to decontextualize the notion of elector discretion and
simply plunk it down in today's party-dominated context.

Worse than that, if one took seriously the notion that original intention was
to govern contemporary constitutional questions about the presidential selection process, many existing features of the contemporary process would come
into serious question in addition to any attempt to restrict elector discretion.
The precommitment of most electors would surely be unconstitutional.[55] In
many states electors now commonly vote not by secret "ballot," but entirely out
in the open. This would have to be deemed unconstitutional if we seriously

sought to re-create the process that our original intender had in mind.[56] And political parties, deeply suspect at the time of the promulgation of the electoral college provisions, could hardly be made the agencies of the states in many parts of the process as they are now.

The "short ballot" that most states employ in the election of electors would present a constitutional nightmare. Nowhere on the short ballot do the electors' names appear. In some versions, the ballot says in fine print something like "electors pledged to" followed by the presidential and vice-presidential candidates' names. In other versions, the reference to electors is omitted entirely. By one count published in 2004, in "only eight states" were "the names of both the presidential candidates and the electors [to] appear on the ballots."[57] The Illinois absentee ballot that I filled out for the 2004 election, for instance, says the following (omitting the Spanish):

> For President and Vice President of the United States
>
> Vote For One
>
> John F. Kerry and John Edwards   Democratic
>
> George W. Bush and Dick Cheney   Republican
>
> Michael Badnarik and Richard V. Campagna   Libertarian[58]

In an environment defined by the short ballot, the election is formally one to choose electors only by virtue of a provision in the state election law that stipulates that a vote for presidential and vice-presidential candidates is "really" for the slate of electors pledged to them.[59] With or without the phrase "electors pledged to" or the like, the short ballot resembles nothing so much as a shell game if the electorate is really supposed to be voting for electors who will themselves exercise discretion.[60]

To see how bizarre such an election would be if taken seriously as one for electors, imagine a state law that provided that a vote for a presidential candidate constituted a vote as well for any senatorial or congressional candidate of the same party who was vying for election at the same time, even though the latter name[s] nowhere appeared on the ballot. The Constitution says that House members are to be "chosen . . . by the people of the several states."[61] Surely it would be held—should there be a way to bring the question up for judicial resolution—that a state law that made a vote cast for one person into a vote for another was not a meaningful "choice" as contemplated by the Constitution. In similar fashion, allowing state law to make a vote cast for a presidential candidate into a vote for electors does not make for any meaningful choice of electors.

Of course the constitutional language is not parallel in the two settings, though at one point the Constitution does use the word "choosing" to refer to the selection process for electors.[62] But however articulated, electors can no more be designated with meaningful attention to their qualities as individuals who will exercise discretion by casting a ballot for someone else than can choosing House members. The simple fact of the matter is that our contemporary way of selecting the president *has* made the electors irrelevant—almost all the time. That irrelevance is entirely inconsistent with the original conception of their role, but if we insist on their exercise of judgment and discretion as individuals in the name of original intention, we will surely be obliged to rescue them from their contemporary fate a good deal more fully.

Imagine the remedies that would be appropriate if we took seriously the claim of constitutional protection for elector discretion. The electors' names would have to be on the ballot, of course, but in addition there could be no party designation for them, for that would suggest precommitment rather than a resolve to debate and then decide. Nor could the names of candidates for president and vice president appear—let alone as a linked pair—for that too would suggest the forbidden precommitment. Voters would then come to the polls and cast ballots essentially in the dark—as they have come to understand light and dark in the present day. The error rate in voting would likely reach epic proportions.[63] In all likelihood the electorate would in large numbers simply stop coming. A presidential selection process reconfigured in that way would, in other words, so upset settled expectations of what we now mean by American democracy that it would simply be unthinkable for a court to order it. And if that is so, it would be thoroughly mischievous to insist on one element of an integrated system, the entire rest of which had been put beyond the pale.[64]

For this reason, if we could reify the author of the Twelfth Amendment language, educate him about what has happened in the meantime, and then bring him here for a talk about what he wrote, he would in all likelihood do whatever he could to interpret his language to allow states to forbid elector discretion. He might point to the contemporary use of the word "ballot," but failing all else he would be likely to say that his language should not be used to produce any re-

sult that would put contemporary American democracy at peril. And if he resisted any such bow to the modern world, we would have to send him back to
his bygone era. For better or worse, we are required to live in the present. Enacted language, in other words, simply cannot be allowed to reshape a reality
that has decisively broken loose from its constraints. The clearest direction of
the text has no capacity to free us from the reality that has taken a firm grip on
the presidential selection process.[65] In the case of the governing language on
"selection" by the electoral college, we should simply be grateful that the text
leaves us sufficient "wiggle" room to complete what we have mostly done already.[66]

In the case of the electoral college—luckily, but in truth fortuitously—we
are provided a measure of comfort with the constitutional interpretation I am
urging by the Twenty-Third Amendment and congressional action in response
to it. The amendment provides electoral college representation for the District
of Columbia, and it does so by likening the District to a state for electoral college purposes. For this reason, the amendment could be considered something
of a gloss on the earlier electoral college provisions. By the time of the Twenty-
Third Amendment, a number of states had undertaken to hem in elector discretion, and, as mentioned above, the Supreme Court had indicated sympathy
with such state regulation. In doing so, the Court relied on the "practical interpretation" of the Constitution over the years.[67] The amendment does nothing
to repudiate such state power, and then in its wake the Congress—here presumably acting as if it were a state legislature for this purpose—passed legislation authorizing political parties to extract pledges of faithfulness from their
slates of electors.[68] Such contemporaneous congressional interpretation of the
Constitution is often accorded a measure of respect.[69] Through this route the
Twenty-Third Amendment could help us conclude that the original constitutional electoral college provisions should at least now be understood to allow a
good measure of state regulation of elector discretion.[70]

To be sure, this aid from the Twenty-Third Amendment is really a
makeweight. Those involved in its passage may well have taken state power to
regulate elector discretion for granted, but not because they thought deeply
about the question of elector discretion as a matter of constitutional interpretation. They were living in a world defined by the contemporary understanding
of presidential selection, so that state authority to regulate could come natu-

rally, and for many no doubt, thoughtlessly. As I suggested earlier, we are effectively constrained to reach the conclusion that states can regulate if we are to have a system for choosing the president that is both coherent and relatively free of peril. And that would be so whether or not the Twenty-Third Amendment had come to pass.

The committed textualist will, I suppose, try to deny the force of this reasoning. The Constitution provides for amendment, and that route to change, it is often insisted, is exclusive.[71] But that badly misunderstands the process of interpretation of documents that are to govern over time. Words are merely a means to give expression to projects and purposes, and it is the purposes that must be served. The world changes about the words of governing documents, and there is no holding back that change. If they are to serve the purposes that justify them, governing words must be adapted to problems, many of which would be unrecognizable to the authors of the words. No doubt there is usually great virtue in following the words where they most naturally seem to lead. If we do not insist on that when we can, then the interpreter will rule, and the body with the authority to make our governing laws—the authority in the first place to devise the projects and harbor the purposes that are to be served—will be in danger of fading into insignificance. That is the justification for the textualist's dogma, but that dogma must have a safety valve lest it do more harm than good—by the lights of those who promulgated the words. To put this point another way, limits on the textualist dogma are as integral as the dogma itself to serving *its* purposes. That is what the so-called exception for "absurd results" provides. In the constitutional context, a version of this point is often captured by insisting that the "constitution is not a suicide pact."[72]

Obviously there is a tension, and a danger of abuse, in insisting simultaneously on the authoritativeness of enacted language and on the primacy of the language's purposes. What is clear, however, is that the tension and danger are occasionally met head on if enough seems to be at stake. An instructive example in the U.S. Supreme Court is provided by what are called collectively the "white primary cases" of the first half of the Twentieth Century, and in particular by *Terry v. Adams*.[73] Texas had sought to exclude blacks from voting in the dominant Democratic primary elections, and the Supreme Court struck down the state's initial overt efforts as violative of the Fourteenth Amendment's Equal Protection Clause. That provision operates, however, as a restraint not on individuals or private entities, but on states, and in response Texas sought to insu-late its efforts from constitutional challenge by delegating the authority to set voting qualifications to political parties, assumed to be nonstate actors.[74] In re-sponse, the court found the necessary state action in the delegation itself.[75]

Texas next withdrew the overt delegation and simply left the dirty work to the initiative of the Democratic Party, which was nominally a private entity and in truth needed no state guidance of its proclivity toward racial discrimination. The court's answer was that the necessary state action could be found in the holding of a primary election under state auspices.[76] With that move, a state could not allow a party that itself discriminated to take part in a primary elec-tion. The Democratic Party's seeming access to state offices seemed in jeopardy unless it stopped discriminating on the basis of race.

But that was not the end of the drama. An organization calling itself the Jay-bird Party undertook to hold a "primary election" that was preliminary to the Democratic primary and was held without any state aid or other seeming state complicity. The Jaybird Party made no bones about excluding blacks from its "primary," and the Jaybird winners then entered themselves in a "nondiscrimi-natory" Democratic primary, where they regularly prevailed. That led to the Court's decision in *Terry*, where it found the state action requirement satisfied by the state's permitting this overwhelmingly successful private political action to proceed within its borders.[77]

Over the years, there have been scholars who have urged that the "state ac-tion" requirement is meaningless and should be discarded, since the state re-quires, prohibits, or permits everything that goes on within its jurisdiction.[78] But the Supreme Court has never embraced that position, insisting instead that more active state complicity is required, except on occasion—as in the white primary context—where it seems that something at once monumental and sys-temic is at stake.[79] In this way, "mere" language has not been allowed to get in the way of the adjustment of constitutional norms to pressing political realities of the day.[80]

Who is to say if the white primary cases might be justified in the name of some modern projection of a mental state that we might ascribe to the explicit mention of states as subject to limitation in the Fourteenth and Fifteenth Amendments? There likely is no way confidently to trace our constructed "in-tention" or "understanding" through historical developments and the ingenious steps that the state of Texas devised to perpetuate racial discrimination in the electoral system. But what is clear is that faced with the deviousness of Texas, the Supreme Court did not hesitate long in subordinating its own best reading of the constitutional language in order to come to grips with the novel problems that the passage of time had conspired to produce.

The problem of elector discretion is actually much easier to solve in these terms than that of the white primary. This is not because the seeming instruction of the language for elector discretion is less clear than for state action, though that is probably so. Rather it is because even more—indeed, a lot more—is at stake in the question of elector discretion. Elimination of the white primary, even at the Jaybird Party end of the spectrum, did not bring racial discrimination to a halt in Texas generally, or in Texas politics. Genuine progress in that regard would have to await later developments. This was, moreover, reasonably foreseeable at the time. In that sense, the Court might have bowed to constitutional language in the white primary cases without overwhelming consequences. It would not have been a particularly proud moment for the nation's legal and political systems, or for the moral force of constitutional law. But the course of history and of political and racial progress would likely have been affected only modestly had the Court held back. In sharp contrast, it may well be that the continued stable functioning of American democracy would be put at risk by disabling states from reining in elector discretion—to say nothing of reordering election practices more generally in the name of some original conception. We could not be sure about such dire consequences until elector discretion had bitten. Indeed even then we might not be able to parse the causation, or be sure about the degree of stability. But a prediction of large-scale trouble is certainly a plausible one. No approach to constitutional interpretation can be taken seriously—or can be thought genuinely to serve the ends that inspire constitutional provisions—that remains oblivious to the possibility of such extreme consequences.

Faced with this imperative of constitutional interpretation, the interpreter must make his way on questions of elector discretion without much help from constitutional language or even what he can tease out of the historical record about animating purposes. His task is to work with existing practice to find guidance for novel questions that are posed. There is nothing new about judges, or other constitutional interpreters, taking instruction from practices that have developed. In the great early case of *McCulloch v. Maryland*, Chief Justice John Marshall faced the question of whether the federal government could establish a bank of the United States, even though the Constitution nowhere gives it the power to do so with any explicitness. In the absence of an explicit grant of the power, opponents claimed the ability of government to create banks remained exclusively with the states where it had seemingly resided before the Constitution was approved. Marshall affirmed the national power, relying in part on the fact that the very first Congress had established a bank, which had operated for a time before being allowed to lapse. The interpretational problem of adjusting the powers of states and national government, he insisted, "ought to receive a considerable impression from that practice."[81]

To say that existing practice is relevant, however, is only to identify a source of guidance. Existing practices can hardly be dispositive, where the interpreter will often face a challenge to one aspect of practice in the name of another. In *McCulloch*, for instance, the ultimate question that Marshall had to face was whether Maryland could impose a tax on the bank. The bank had resisted the tax, but Maryland had most assuredly levied it. Practice alone gave no decisive answer to the ultimate question in issue. And so it is with elector discretion. I have urged that existing election practice strongly counsels against elector discretion, but there is no doubt that the historical record is dotted with a few instances of it. And, as mentioned, the joint meeting of Congress has regularly counted the occasional faithless votes as they were cast. What the conscientious interpreter must do is try to bring coherence to an often unwieldy whole, seeking guidance in the task from sources outside of its own vision of the way the world should be ordered.

With this task in view, disapproving elector discretion is in many ways the easy part. We have already seen how out of touch that discretion is with the whole of presidential election practices in the United States, and how potentially disastrous it might turn out to be. But what does it mean to disapprove elector discretion? About half the states have no explicit prohibition of the discretion. Should the short ballot and related practices that prevail there be taken implicitly to forbid elector discretion, even when the state legislature has not done so explicitly? That would itself be contrary to some aspects of practice in those states, for faithless votes have typically been forwarded by state officials to the joint meeting, and then, as we have seen, been counted as cast. And what are the implications of refusal to count a faithless vote? The Constitution requires that a candidate receive a majority of the votes of "appointed" electors in order to avoid the House selection procedure, and a faithless elector whose vote was simply not counted would seem still to be an "appointed" elector. Failure to cast any vote on account of that faithless elector could then deprive a candidate of the necessary majority and throw the process into the House. Or should this bit of constitutional language be put to the side in the interests of a more coherent whole, or of avoiding the House contingent procedure? If we do that, then we may have to reckon with other questions of just what it means for an elector to have been appointed.[82]

Even if the answers to these questions were clearer, the courts are ill suited to address them, at least in the first instance. Courts only grapple with interpretational problems after controversy has gelled and a lawsuit has been filed. In the case of a faithless electoral vote that seems to change the outcome of a presidential election, that will be awfully late in the game. No doubt some will see the Supreme Court's intervention in the 2000 election process as suggesting that the Court can bring a measure of quiet to the most public of controversies, even after that controversy has achieved a good head of steam.[83] But whether that is so or not, a court's task will be more manageable, and considerably less societal turmoil will be in prospect, if the political process has paved the way. Particularly if those actions form some reasonably coherent whole, courts would be likely to bow to them, rather than bob about in uncharted seas. That is, in fact, just what we saw in *Ray v. Blair*, the Supreme Court's 1952 decision upholding state required pledges of faithfulness.[84] With this approach in mind, I offer a few suggestions for bringing the problem of faithless electors under control.

Initially, I put the possibility of constitutional amendment to the side. Actually it should be relatively manageable to convince the necessary supermajorities for amendment that forbidding elector discretion—or even at the extreme doing away with the office of elector—would be a desirable move. But once the possibility of amendment was on the table, many would no doubt push for more sweeping reform. We saw in Chapter Four that there is a great deal of sentiment in favor of a nationwide popular vote for president. It would be very difficult to subordinate this possibility to the effort to forbid elector discretion. The likely controversy might effectively scuttle the amendment route even to this benign, and relatively uncontroversial, reform.[85]

A more promising possibility would be a federal statute dealing directly with the subject of elector discretion. The Electoral Count Act that we discussed in Chapter Three is suggestive of how a federal statute might bring some order to an aspect of the electoral college process. But as we have seen, the governing constitutional language seems to repose primary responsibility for designating electors and for regulating their conduct in the state legislatures. Indeed, the Electoral Count Act itself operates in large part by inducing the states to order their processes more fully and effectively. The latitudinarian approach to constitutional interpretation that I suggested earlier might leave room for a federal statute to bring order to an unwieldy whole, but the effort seems quite risky at the present time. In recent years, the Supreme Court has been solicitous of state prerogatives in our federal system. This has been so even where the constitutional language provided little support for the protections for states that the court has found.[86] The contemporary court might well be wary of any wholesale preemption of state prerogatives where the constitutional language actually tilts decidedly in favor of those prerogatives. There may well be a role for federal legislation, but that role would more likely be salutary if it engaged the authority of the states.

If we turn to the state arena, there seem to be two major problems—not of power but of politics—in corralling elector discretion. One is the demonstrated indifference to the problem. As mentioned, only a little more than half the states have adopted laws that attempt to rein in elector discretion with some degree of explicitness. The indifference is puzzling, because the self-interest of state legislators themselves would seem to be advanced—or at least not harmed—by laws controlling elector discretion. Indeed, it is hard to see any significant public or private interest in American society that is served by elector discretion. The best explanation for the "inaction" is probably that the problems have not attained political visibility in a large number of states, or if visible have simply not been viewed as serious. This explanation is reinforced by the fact that most states that have witnessed elector faithlessness in recent times have soon thereafter enacted laws that restrain electors.[87]

The second problem at the state level is the danger of unfortunate variability among the fifty-one separate decision makers. Some states could move forward as others held back. And even if all states took action, their actions might occasionally work at cross purposes. It could be, for instance, that faithless votes were to be counted as if cast faithfully in some states, but completely ignored in others. This might then raise questions of whether faithless votes in states that ignored them were those of "electors appointed" for purposes of determining the electoral college "majority" that was necessary to prevail. This sort of variability is, of course, just what we observe in the pattern of state laws that have thus far addressed the problem of elector discretion.

What is required to address these two problems is some mechanism for getting the attention of the states and for focusing that attention on desirable elements of a common solution. There are actually two mechanisms that might address both these concerns at once. One possibility would draw the Congress back into the process, but in a way that would pose less risk of disapproval by the courts. This would make use of the leverage of the federal government's spending authority. In fairly opaque language, the Constitution gives Congress the power "to lay and collect taxes . . . to pay the debts and provide for the . . . general welfare of the United States."[88] The Supreme Court has construed this power rather expansively,[89] so that Congress can make money available to the states, but attach conditions to the state receipt of the federal largesse. The conditioning possibilities are not unlimited, but might well extend to rather precise requirements of state laws reining in elector discretion, in return, say, for generous federal funding of election expenses that might fairly be attributable to federal offices.[90]

A second possibility—not necessarily inconsistent with federal financial inducements—is an independent effort to enact a "uniform" state law. State laws must be passed separately in each state, of course, but that does not foreclose the adoption of identically worded statutes in a number of states. In the United States we do have two organizations in particular that specialize in formulating and recommending uniform state laws. These are the National Conference of Commissioners on Uniform State Laws (NCCUSL) and the American Law Institute (ALI). The former consists of commissioners from states and territories who represent official organizations devoted to producing uniform laws where they seem appropriate. The latter is a private organization devoted to the clarification and simplification of the law and its adaptation to social needs. Neither organization has waded into the electoral college process, though NCCUSL has been urged to do so on occasion.[91] Nonetheless, these organizations in particular would be well equipped both to generate uniform laws on elector discretion and, in the very act of doing so, call the attention of the states to the importance of the problem.

It would not be easy to accomplish universal adoption of uniform laws. Nonetheless, the effort seems worth undertaking to get control of elector discretion. First, as we have seen, the stakes are high. Second, widespread adoption of a uniform law would represent progress even if universal adoption proved elusive. But in addition it seems likely that once momentum built behind a uniform law on the subject of elector discretion, initially reluctant states would fall into line. I have suggested above that there is no obvious organized interest that seems to be served by allowing a faithless electoral vote. And if the move toward adoption gained visibility, states that held back would come to appreciate that they risked looking foolish if in a closely contested election their faithlessly cast votes should wreak havoc on the system.[92]

If one or both of these mechanisms provide cause for hope about state action to corral elector discretion, let me offer some thoughts on the content of a uniform law. First, state authority to regulate elector behavior should be viewed as comprehensive. Obviously a uniform law should forbid elector discretion, but it should do so in no uncertain terms, relying on a flat prohibition, rather than a pledge that might impliedly invite its breach. If a faithless vote is attempted, the law should simply substitute a faithful vote for it. Among other things, this would circumvent any claim that a disallowed faithless vote affected the number of votes necessary for outright victory in the electoral college and avoidance of the House contingent procedure.[93]

The law would have to deal with a variety of contingencies in which an electoral college result that did not reflect the popular vote for electors would be salutary, indeed essential, to avoid the House procedure, or worse. The most obvious possibility is where a candidate dies between election day and the date on which electors vote.[94] We saw in Chapter Three that that is what happened in 1872 with the Democratic candidate Horace Greeley. Greeley had lost the election, but electors still had to decide whether to cast their votes for a dead man. Only three electors did so, while sixty-three either abstained or scattered their votes for other persons.[95] In the joint meeting for the counting of electoral votes, the three votes cast for Greeley were not counted. In addition, in 1912 the Republican vice-presidential candidate James S. Sherman died before the election. With Theodore Roosevelt on the ballot as the presidential candidate of the Progressive Party, the Republicans ran a distant third, garnering only eight electoral votes. The electors pledged to Sherman voted for the prominent Republican Nicholas Butler instead.[96]

Should death or disability occur for a candidate who appeared to have won under these circumstances, it might seem that elector discretion had found a useful role.[97] At the present time, Tennessee state law explicitly provides for elector discretion in this circumstance, while Wisconsin state law does so a bit less explicitly.[98] But I do not think that elector discretion in this case is the lesson to be learned. That particular part of our past has been so thoroughly discredited that we do best not to proceed under any assumption that it remains just a little bit relevant today. Contemporary electors are no more suited to exercise discretion in responding to unusual problems like the death of a candidate than they are to making a discretion-laden choice more generally. The system must cope with an emergency, but that is no reason for recurring to an otherwise discredited device that is ill suited to the task.

In the case of the death of a candidate after election day but before the electors meet, of course, the electors should neither be required nor allowed to vote for the deceased. Neither Greeley nor Sherman had commanded the electoral votes to win, so their untimely deaths did not affect the outcomes of the election. But there is, of course, no guarantee that a candidate "victorious" on election day will survive until the electors have been able to seal that victory with their imprimatur. The Twentieth Amendment provides that the vice-president elect becomes president if the president-elect dies before his term begins.[99] This does not cover the present problem, however, because a candidate presumably becomes "president elect" (or vice-president elect) only after the electoral college has acted.[100] But there is no good reason why state law could not deal with this contingency without relying on elector discretion.[101] If the office in question was the presidency, the vice-presidential candidate is the obvious fallback. To be sure, in contemporary politics a party's vice-presidential nominee might well not have been chosen for the presidential slot had the now deceased winner not been in the picture. But the vice-presidential nominee would succeed to the office after the electoral college vote, and, of course, also after the two had been inaugurated.[102] There seems to be no particular reason to look elsewhere should the vacancy come a bit earlier in the process. Unlike the period before election day, a popular electoral stamp of approval would have been accorded the vice-presidential candidate. This solution is not enjoined upon the electors under current law, however, and it should be as part of a uniform law.[103] At a minimum this would take the wind out of the sails of any movement to have the choice depend on some free discretionary choice of electors.

Should a vacancy appear during this period before formal action in the electoral college on the choice of the vice president—but not the president—again the temptation should be resisted to think that we have finally found an occasion for elector discretion.[104] If we do reject elector discretion, however, we would do best to do so with explicitness in state law, for if state law remains silent, elector discretion would appear to be the default possibility and might just seem attractive if no other solution is already in place. One solution would be to allow the relevant political party to fill the void. For this time period, however, this would be a bit awkward, because unlike the situation just discussed, there would then have been no public processes engaged to replace a candidate who had triumphed in the popular election. A second possibility would be to leave the slot vacant until after the president assumes office, and rely on the procedures already in place for filling a vice-presidential vacancy. This, of course, has the drawback of leaving the system vulnerable to the additional loss of a president elect with no obvious substitute. Still, that may be the best solution to a problem with no terribly good one.

In the final analysis, it may not be possible to foresee all the contingencies that might arise. The residual uncertainty might counsel a residuum of elector discretion, but in truth there are no human institutions that are entirely free of the prospect of unanticipated contingencies. If the most obvious possibilities are provided for, it may be that others can be left to *ad hoc* solutions fashioned by legislative action at the time—or executive action in an emergency. That approach would have the virtue of allowing the complete removal of elector discretion, thus freeing the system from any continuing hint that elector discretion is somehow integral to it.

The comprehensive authority of the states would go for naught if the joint meeting of the Congress felt free to ignore state laws forbidding elector discretion in the process. We have seen that in the past the joint meeting has counted faithless votes as cast. These votes have not been in situations where they might affect the outcome of the elections, and hence are of questionable significance as precedent. And the suggested uniform law should ensure that faithful votes are certified and counted under the Electoral Count Act.[105] Still the possibility that the joint meeting would not feel bound by state law on the matter could haunt the effort. A joint meeting that asserted a prerogative to decide for itself in the face of state law could produce fully as much mischief as faithless electors encouraged by state law. A clash of state and federal laws on this matter could inject yet another element of uncertainty—produced in part by claims and cross claims of illegitimacy—into a precarious picture. Indeed the very possibility that the joint meeting might count a faithless vote in the face of state law that forbids it might cause states to hold back with regulation in the first place.

For these various reasons it would be advisable for Congress to make its intention to abide by state law reining in elector discretion. This would be a natural component of a federal law that employed the leverage of the spending power. But even without a spending program, congressional commitment could be accomplished by joint resolution or other articulated assurance by the Congress. While this technically might not bind a subsequent joint meeting, the commitment should have substantial persuasive force. At some point, the sound functioning of democracy must count on a measure of goodwill of a variety of actors in the process, and the precommitment of Congress seems more than sufficient to ensure that goodwill for the future.

CHAPTER EIGHT

Electoral Votes for Third-Party
(or Independent) Candidates

Yet another route to an indecisive electoral college vote that can send the presidential selection to the House of Representatives is electoral votes cast for more than two candidates. Over the years, American politics has usually been characterized by two major parties, and it is typically only candidates of those two parties who are able to win votes in the electoral college. That was the pattern in 2000 and 2004. Indeed, with the exception of a smattering of faithless votes, that has been the pattern since the election of 1968.[1] But presidential candidates are regularly advanced by minor parties as well, or mount campaigns independent of any political party. And occasionally those minor candidates[2] have succeeded in securing votes in the electoral college. It seems that the earliest instance was in the 1832 election when William Wirt captured seven electoral votes as a candidate of the Anti-Mason Party.

In more recent times, George Wallace appeared on the ballot in all fifty states in the 1968 election, and he received forty-six electoral votes as the candidate of the American Independent Party. In 1948 Strom Thurmond, with less than 2.3 percent of the nationwide popular vote, won thirty-nine electoral votes in a few Southern states under the banner of a breakaway segment of the Democratic Party, popularly called the "States' Rights" (or "Dixiecrat") Party (though labeled "Democratic Party" on some state ballots).[3] In neither of those years— nor in any other presidential election—has minor party command of electoral votes forced the selection into the House of Representatives.[4] But obviously the chances that the candidates of neither of the two main parties will win the re-

quired "majority of the whole number of Electors appointed"[5] is increased
when electoral votes are spread among more than just those two.[6]

The potential for mischief from recourse to the House on account of third-
party capture of electoral votes is, if anything, greater than the general problems with the House procedure that we canvassed in Chapter Four. If only two
candidates command electoral votes, and it is a tie between them—or perhaps
an abstention or two—that sends the selection to the House, the Constitution
specifies that the House's choice must be made between just those two. Each of
the two would necessarily come to the House with a very sizable bloc of electoral votes—and in all likelihood of popular votes as well.[7] If more than two
candidates receive electoral votes, on the other hand, under the Twelfth Amendment the House must choose from among the top three. If the electoral votes
for a minor party candidate came from a single state with the typical winner-
take-all rule for elector selection, for instance, that candidate could have been
propelled to the House standoff with just three electoral votes, the minimum
number assigned to a state.[8] The House choice from among three candidates is
required, of course, no matter how few popular votes the third-place finisher
obtained. Thurmond's 1948 showing demonstrates just how "efficiently" popular votes can be turned into electoral votes by a candidate whose appeal is concentrated in one or a few states.

Choice from among three opens up the possibility that a candidate with a
decided minority of the electoral—and popular—votes would be chosen by the
House to be president of the United States. As long as American politics is characterized by two major parties, however, the possibility of a distinctly minori-
tarian president through this route resides basically in the realm of theory. I
have been unable to conjure up even a barely plausible scenario under which
House delegations composed almost exclusively of adherents of the major parties would give the nod to a minor party candidate with just a smattering of
electoral and popular votes.[9]

The more serious problem is that, given the vagaries of the House process,
the participation of a minor party candidate might give that candidate leverage
that would weigh heavily in an otherwise close contest between the major party
candidates. The electors committed to a minor party candidate would not have
any votes in the House, of course, but representatives from states where he obtained his electoral votes might feel pressure to accede to his bidding. In the

1948 election, discussed below, the minor party candidate Strom Thurmond apparently envisaged the possibility that he could exert influence in the House proceeding.[10] And those representatives might just determine the outcome, given that, as we saw in Chapter Five, the allocation of authority in the House selection can be largely a matter of happenstance. The result could then be a president heavily indebted to a candidate who might have commanded a small fraction of the electoral votes—and possibly even a tinier fraction of the nationwide popular vote.

In their very useful study of the electoral college, Lawrence Longley and Neal Peirce discuss just such a possibility in the 1948 context. Of the 531 electoral votes at the time, Harry Truman, the Democratic candidate, received 303, thirty-seven more than the majority necessary at the time to win the presidency. But, as mentioned above, Strom Thurmond won thirty-nine electoral votes as a third-party candidate. If fewer than 13,000 voters in California and Ohio, which Truman had won, had cast their votes instead for Thomas Dewey, the Republican candidate, Dewey would seemingly have captured the electoral votes of those states, and no candidate would have commanded the electoral college majority necessary to keep the selection out of the House.[11] Longley and Peirce imagine what might then have happened in the House:

> Control of 25 delegations (a majority of the 48 states) would have been required to elect a president. Loyalist [*i.e.*, non-Dixiecrat] Democrats would have controlled 21 delegations, Republicans 20, the Dixiecrats 4. Three delegations would have been divided equally between the major parties. In fact, an election by the House was precisely what Thurmond and his Dixiecrats had hoped for. They would undoubtedly have brought pressure on Truman to hold back on civil rights legislation or other steps designed to further racial integration, in return for which the Dixiecrat states would have thrown their support to Truman to make him president. Thus a splinter party that had won only 2.4 percent of the national popular vote might have forced its terms on a president. . . . These calculations assume, of course, that House members would invariably vote for their own party's presidential candidate or, in the case of . . . the four Dixiecrat states, would vote the way the people of their states had voted in the fall elections. There might have been breaks in this lineup or peculiar types of deals under the pressures of the moment.[12]

While this imagined turn of events does not seem at all far-fetched, I do not want to exaggerate the *incremental* threat posed by invocation of the House procedure on account of the fractionation of the electoral vote. As we saw in

Chapter Five the House procedure is already ungrounded in any plausible normative vision of the political process. Given that sorry state of affairs, the presence of yet an additional element of arbitrariness may not do much additional harm. At a minimum, however, it seems fair to say that recourse to the House on account of a third-party candidate does nothing to brighten the gloomy picture that we took away from Chapter Five.

If the initial electoral vote count threatens to be indecisive, moreover, bargaining might move forward to the electoral college proceedings, unless the possibility of elector faithlessness has been satisfactorily contained. That very possibility apparently loomed large as election day approached in 1968. The third-party candidacy of George Wallace had no realistic chance of capturing the presidency, but it did seem quite possible that Wallace's presence in the race would prevent either Hubert Humphrey or Richard Nixon, the candidates respectively of the Democratic and Republican Parties, from capturing the required majority of the electors. Wallace's reported strategy in that event was to use the electors committed to him to bargain for concessions from Humphrey in exchange for electoral votes that would secure victory in that forum. That possibility in turn prompted some committed Humphrey elector candidates—including the novelist James Michener who was a candidate from Pennsylvania—to consider defection to Nixon in order to blunt Wallace's bargaining power.[13] None of these things happened, of course, when Nixon won outright in the electoral college, but the real possibility illustrates the interconnection of the dangers explored in the last chapter and in this one.

In contemplating this picture, I find no great consolation in the fact that third-party candidacies have not yet thrown the presidential selection process into the House (or threatened to after the "election day" results were in). That is, of course, also true of the tie possibility (in the post–Twelfth Amendment era) explored in Chapter Six, and of the faithless elector problem we treated in Chapter Seven. And in 1824 the electoral vote was split among multiple candidates associated with "factions" of a single party. In any event, in the modern day we shall see that much about American politics discourages vigorous minor party efforts. It is thus possible that third parties have already been sufficiently marginalized that they pose even less of a threat now than they have in the past to a decisive vote in the electoral college. But there is no way to reach a conclusion about this with assuredness, and in any event the risks of House selection are sufficiently great that we should at least explore ways to deal with the mischief invited by that procedure, even if the chances of its coming about are relatively small.

I think that recourse to the House on account of third-party candidacies can be avoided, but any suggested reform raises delicate questions. We could attack the problem of faithless electors with abandon, essentially striving to forbid the practice. This was possible because in contemporary American politics there are no significant redeeming virtues to elector faithlessness that call out for inclusion in a balance that must be struck. Similarly the tie possibility could be corralled with little more pain likely than that caused by temporary—and rather minor—disruption of accustomed ways of doing things. With third parties, in contrast, the possibility of garnering electoral votes is closely related to participation in presidential elections more generally. And that participation is in turn part of a larger and complex role in American politics, in which there are undoubtedly important elements of positive contribution. Any move to avoid the House procedure must strive to remain sensitive to the ripple effects that might be felt in other parts of a complex whole.[14]

Most obvious among the effects, third-party candidates can affect presidential elections without capturing electoral votes. This can happen as part of a challenge that poses a real threat to the major party candidates.[15] Thus as we saw in Chapter Six, running as an independent in 1992, H. Ross Perot won close to twenty million votes, almost nineteen percent of the total. He also won more than eight million votes in 1996 running under the banner of the "Reform Party" that was organized for the effort. In each of those elections Perot's vote total exceeded the margin of victory between the major party candidates in a large number of states. And yet Perot did not capture a single electoral vote in either election.

That Perot came up empty in the electoral college in the 1992 election is particularly stunning. In 1912, then former President Theodore Roosevelt, running as the candidate of what proved to be the evanescent Progressive Party, came in second to Woodrow Wilson in both popular and electoral votes, beating William Howard Taft, the candidate of the Republicans, the other "major" party at the time. (In that same election, Eugene Debs, running as the Socialist Party candidate, captured six percent of the popular vote, though no electoral votes.) With the exception of this 1912 showing by Roosevelt, Perot's 1992 nineteen percent exceeds the popular vote percentage of any third-party candidate in the nation's history. Perot's failure to win electoral votes in 1992 was because he enjoyed popularity spread fairly evenly over the states. Had his support been as large overall but concentrated in fewer states, Perot, like Roosevelt, might well have captured a substantial number of electoral votes.[16]

The 2000 election in particular provides a stark example of a minor party candidacy for the presidency making its presence felt without posing any significant threat of taking electoral votes. Running under the banner of the Green Party that year, Ralph Nader received close to three million votes across the nation. This was less than three percent of the nationwide popular vote total, and at no time did Nader have any real chance of becoming president. Nor did he come close in any single state to the plurality necessary to win the state's electoral votes. Nader's vote total in eight states was, however, larger than the margin of victory in those states between the candidates of the two major parties. And it is generally assumed that a much greater number of those who voted for Nader would have both voted, and voted for Albert Gore as opposed to George Bush, had Nader not been on the ballot. On those assumptions, Nader's third-party candidacy likely changed the outcome of the election, because Gore would probably have won both Florida and New Hampshire in a two-person race between Bush and himself. And if nothing changed in the other states, electoral votes for Gore from either Florida or New Hampshire would have changed the outcome in the electoral college balloting.[17]

These forms of direct participation in presidential elections provide the most visible effect of third parties on American politics, but they are by no means the only ones of importance. Third parties generate ideas and substantive programs which then feed into—or otherwise influence—the programs of the major parties.[18] Third parties also have incentives that the major parties do not to challenge aspects of the system that arguably serve mostly to entrench American two-party politics.[19] On occasion they even command such widespread support that they manage to supplant one of the two major parties.[20] And then, perhaps most importantly, because of the possibility of displacing a major party, the very existence of third parties likely produces a more lively and healthy competition between the two major ones.

This is not to suggest that the effects of minor party activity are uniformly or uncontroversially positive. The fact that Nader's candidacy likely changed the outcome of the 2000 election, for instance, has aroused great resentment.[21] That may be a function of partisan alignments, but more generally it is often as- sumed that the stability of the American political system is a product in impor- tant part of there being two, and only two, major political parties.[22] For obvious reasons, adherents of the two contemporary major parties also have an incen- tive to champion the stability-enhancing virtues of the two-party system. But respect for the two-party system, on account of the order and stability it brings to American politics, is by no means confined to major party partisans.[23]

The result of these cross-cutting considerations and incentives is a regula- tory environment that in a large variety of ways favors a system dominated by two major parties. This is hardly surprising, given that adherents of the two parties occupy almost all the various governmental positions in the country where formal authority over decisions about the structure of the system resides. Perhaps most fundamental of all in providing succor for a two-party system is the prevalence of single-member legislative districts, with a plurality of the popular vote sufficient for victory. Some democracies conduct their legislative elections as a single integrated nationwide contest among parties. Legislative seats are then allocated among the parties in proportion to their shares of the popular vote. In such a system of "proportional representation" smaller parties will typically be able to obtain some legislative representation even if they can only command a small fraction of the total vote.[24] In a system of single mem- ber legislative districts, in contrast, a minor party candidate will seldom have any realistic chance of winning. For, as we saw in Chapter Four, to the extent that voters are drawn to voting "strategically," they will tend to avoid "wasting" votes on minor party candidates, and appreciation of that disinclination will tend to discourage such candidacies from the outset.[25]

There are also a variety of other measures that state and federal governments have taken that have the purpose, or at least the effect, of favoring the two ma- jor parties. These include petition requirements for access to the ballot,[26] re- striction of third-party candidacies to those without some prior specified sorts of attachments to a major party,[27] bipartisan gerrymandering of legislative dis- tricts,[28] and campaign finance support that differentiates between major and minor parties.[29] Because of these and other laws, moreover, the United States seems to have built a culture of two-party competition that then further discourages minor parties.[30] As just one example, highly publicized face-to-face debates have become an important part of the presidential campaign process, and participation in those debates is typically limited—by sponsors or even by insistence of the candidates themselves—to "major" contenders.[31] And the parties regularly employ primaries to nominate candidates for office, encouraging the expression of dissatisfaction within major party structures rather than outside of them.[32]

Acting variously in the name of freedom of association, freedom of speech, and of the citizen's right to vote, the courts step in occasionally to maintain some semblance of balance in this system. But perhaps understandably they have produced no clear vision for the tradeoff of ordered democratic decision making, on the one hand, and vigor of the system in stimulating responsiveness to the full array of interests and sentiments in the polity, on the other. Here is the U.S. Supreme Court, for instance, singing the virtues of stability in a 1997 decision upholding a Minnesota ban on "fusion" candidacies, in which one party is prohibited from having a candidate for an office on the ballot who is already the candidate of another party:

> States . . . have a strong interest in the stability of their political systems. This interest does not permit a State to completely insulate the two-party system from minor parties' or independent candidates' competition and influence. . . . That said, the States' interest permits them to enact reasonable election regulations that may, in practice, favor the traditional two-party system, and that temper the destabilizing effects of party-splintering and excessive factionalism. The Constitution permits the Minnesota Legislature to decide that political stability is best served through a healthy two-party system. And while an interest in securing the perceived benefits of a stable two-party system will not justify unreasonably exclusionary restrictions, States need not remove all the many hurdles third parties face in the American political arena today.[33]

In this passage the Court is not inattentive to the importance of minor parties, but the emphasis on the contribution they make to a healthy level of competitiveness in the system was much more pronounced in a 1968 decision striking down an Ohio ballot access limitation:

> There is of course no reason why two parties should retain a permanent monopoly on the right to have people vote for or against them. Competition in ideas and governmental policies is at the core of our electoral process and of First Amendment

freedoms. New parties struggling for their place must have the time and opportunity to organize in order to meet reasonable requirements for ballot position, just as old parties have had in the past.[34]

This then defines the dilemma for any attempt to cabin the role that third-party candidates can take on in the electoral college process. There is probably no way to minimize the chances that third-party candidacies will relegate the presidential choice to the House of Representatives in complete isolation from other effects on the political role of third parties and of independent politics. And yet it is well beyond my present ambitions to navigate the waters of these open seas, to provide any global accounting of the advantages and disadvantages of third parties in American politics. The best I can offer in this context of both debate and uncertainty is an attempt to remain sensitive to the larger effects of reform proposals, and wary lest reform courts more trouble than it corrals. I have made no secret of the fact that I think mischief lurks in the possibility that third-party candidacies may throw the presidential selection into the House of Representatives. Recognizing that this may tend to skew my conclusions, I will try to retain a healthy skepticism about recommendations that might dampen incentives for third-party efforts.

With these cautionary notes, let us turn to the tools that are available to prevent electoral votes for third-party or independent candidates from forcing the presidential selection into the House. They largely inhere in the constitutional authority of state legislatures to determine the "manner" in which electors are appointed.[35] In recent times, the states have been decidedly unimaginative in using this authority. As we have seen, all but two of the states assign all their electoral votes to the slate associated with the winner of the statewide popular vote. The two dissenters—Maine and Nebraska—use popular election in intrastate districts to allocate some of their electors, a method with ample precedent in early days of the electoral college.[36] And in the 2004 election Colorado did consider the possibility of allocating its electoral votes in proportion to the statewide popular vote.[37] Still, there is every reason to think that states have the authority to experiment much more boldly in this realm. And with a bit of boldness may come a satisfactory solution to the problem posed by the possibility of third-party command of electoral votes.

In the 1892 *McPherson* case,[38] the Supreme Court confronted a challenge to the decision of the Michigan legislature to employ districts for election of electors, instead of the statewide winner-take-all elections that even then had become the norm among the states. The Court rejected the challenge and in doing so characterized the power of state legislatures in very expansive terms. It concluded that "decisive" practical construction of the constitutional language over the years had reposed "plenary power . . . [in] the state legislatures in the matter of the appointment of electors." According to the Court, "the . . . mode of appointment of electors belong[s] exclusively to the states under the constitution of the United States."[39] And much more recently the Supreme Court's decision bringing the 2000 election recount in Florida to a halt reiterated the wide range of state legislative prerogatives in deciding how electors will be chosen.[40] The state discretion over the manner of selection of electors has attracted some colorful characterizations over the years, as in the case of the early Nineteenth-Century New York congressman who said that "there is nothing to prevent . . . [a state] from vesting that power 'in a Board of bank directors—a turnpike corporation—or a synagogue.' "[41]

Despite the Supreme Court's expansive language, state legislative discretion over the "manner" of choosing electors is certainly not unlimited. The *McPherson* opinion itself acknowledged the limitations imposed by the Fourteenth and Fifteenth Amendments, once a state has opted for popular election of its electors.[42] Since that time other constitutional amendments have constrained state choices in ways that are just as surely applicable to popular election of electors. We touched briefly on these in Chapter One. In addition to race and previous condition of servitude treated in the Fifteenth Amendment, the states cannot discriminate on the basis of sex, or against those over eighteen years of age.[43] Nor under the Twenty-Fourth Amendment may they impose poll taxes as a condition for voting in federal elections, explicitly including "for President or Vice President."[44] There may also be limitations on state discretion that are not made so explicit in the text of the Constitution. If states do select electors from geographic districts, for instance, they surely are bound by the requirement of equal population that the Supreme Court has imposed for state legislative districts in the name of the Equal Protection Clause.[45] And despite the colorful language, delegating the power of appointment to a synagogue would likely violate the constitutional prohibition on establishing a religion.[46] And then finally, there remains a large measure of uncertainty about whether the Court might at some later time qualify state discretion over the way in which electors are chosen if the states are severely curtailing the political role of third parties.[47]

Recognizing a measure of uncertainty, states would seem to have ample room to maneuver in addressing the danger that third-party candidates will force a presidential selection into the House. We have seen that popular election of electors has swept the field as the states' preferred "manner" of appointment, but in the first few presidential elections there was a good deal of state experimentation that the *McPherson* Court surveyed with no hint of disapproval. In the 1792 election, for instance, New Hampshire adopted a convoluted process that began with popular election and then employed contingencies if earlier proceedings proved indecisive. In the final contingency the New Hampshire Secretary of State drew "names of [those still in contention] . . . out of a box."[48] Massachusetts did not leave things quite so much to chance in the 1796 election, and its approach is particularly suggestive. All but two of the Massachusetts electors were to be chosen by popular election in districts, but with a limitation that a mere plurality of the popular vote would not suffice. If none of the candidates for elector in a particular district obtained a popular majority, the "deficiencies shall be supplied from the several districts, respectively, by joint ballot of the [state] Senate and House of Representatives."[49] In generally parallel fashion, four years later the New Hampshire legislature chose five electors outright from the ten people who had received the highest number of votes in a popular election.[50]

Remnants of this kind of contingent procedure, moreover, could still be found in Georgia as late as 1968. For a four-year period starting in 1964, the Georgia election code provided generally for a runoff election "where no candidate [for 'public office'] receives a majority of the votes cast."[51] While this provision did not explicitly refer to elections for electors, the state election code's definition of "public office" was seemingly comprehensive.[52] And then Georgia amended its code in 1968 specifically to disavow the requirement of a majority for selection of electors, providing instead that a prevailing slate of electors need only have received "the highest number of votes cast."[53]

Given this history, and the Supreme Court's repeated insistence on broad state discretion in the selection of electors, there would seem to be no obstacle to a state's seeking to avoid the House fallback selection procedure by introducing contingent selection into its own choice process for electors. In the first phase of a state's selection process, for instance, state officials with responsibility for determining election winners could be charged with collecting the first-cut electoral vote results from all states, counting the state's own electoral votes in whatever way the state would otherwise employ. For most states this would presumably remain the winner-take-all approach. This "first-cut" electoral vote calculation for the nation as a whole would await certainty for any state where the result was in doubt (and mattered for determination of a winner),[54] but otherwise would be like that regularly undertaken by the news media on presidential election night.[55] If that first-cut calculation produced an electoral vote winner, there would seemingly be no danger that the House would get into the act, and the state's electoral vote would be awarded without recourse to any contingency, just as it is now.

In the event that a comprehensive first-cut calculation showed that no candidate commanded a majority of the electoral college, however, the state officials would make additional calculations. If the state's winning candidate had placed third (or worse) in the first-cut nationwide electoral vote tally, the state's electoral votes would be awarded to the first- or second-place national electoral vote finisher, whichever had placed higher in the state's own popular vote.[56] This might be done even if the state's popular vote winner had commanded a majority of that vote, but a plurality showing was the trigger for the early Massachusetts and New Hampshire contingent processes mentioned above, and a more cautious measure would limit the contingent award to instances where the statewide winner had commanded only a plurality of the popular vote.

If this approach were adopted by all the states in the strong form where even a candidate with a majority in the state could lose the state's electoral votes, there would always be a decisive winner in the electoral college balloting, unless perhaps there was a tie, or some electors cast no vote, inadvertently or intentionally.[57] For electoral votes for third-party candidates that threatened to send the selection into the House would be turned instead into votes for one of the two candidates with the highest first-cut national electoral vote totals. For that reason, consideration might be given to incorporating this approach in the uniform state law on faithless electors that we discussed in Chapter Seven—or of fashioning a separate uniform law on the subject. But even if just those states most in jeopardy of vigorous third-party candidacies were to adopt this system, the chances of the presidential selection being sent to the House on account of electoral votes for such candidates—already rather small—would be all but eliminated. If some or all states adopted the weaker form of the contingency in which a candidate who commanded a majority in the state could not lose the state's electoral votes, there would remain a possibility of recourse to the House, but the chance would probably be quite minimal. And once a few states had moved the contingent selection of the president to the electoral college in this fashion, it is conceivable that other states would quickly fall in line, particularly if the process got under way well before an election loomed in which the contingent choice of electors seemed likely to be required. The state legislatures that would be required to adopt the contingent process are themselves dominated by the two major political parties that would be the most immediate beneficiaries of the suggested change.

A number of legal and policy concerns with the suggested procedure require attention. It may aid in considering them if we digress a bit to consider possible limits on state legislative power over the "manner" of choosing electors that were just offstage in the 2000 election drama in Florida. When the popular vote count in the state was proving so contentious, there was a move in the Florida legislature to have the legislature itself name Florida's electors, preempting the vote tabulation that was both under way and in litigation.[58] There is no serious doubt that the Florida legislature would have had the legal authority to name the state's electors directly, if it had never provided an electoral process for the choice in the first place. A number of state legislatures had done just that in early presidential elections, and the *McPherson* court discussed those precedents with no hint of disfavor.[59] The constitutional language reposing power in state legislatures over the "manner" of elector appointment, of course, leaves room for such direct legislative designation of the electors. But the Florida legislature was considering preemption of an election, the balloting for which had already been conducted. That prospect raised serious additional questions.

An 1874 Senate committee report said that the state legislature had the "right . . . to resume the power [directly to name electors] at any time, for . . . [that power] can neither be taken away nor abdicated."[60] This passage was then quoted with approval in *McPherson*.[61] In calling a halt to the Florida recount, the U.S. Supreme Court quoted the language again, with apparent—though perhaps somewhat measured—approval.[62] It is certainly possible to give this language an interpretation that would permit the preemptive action that the Florida legislature was considering. But the Senate Committee that had first used the language was referring to a decision to reintroduce legislative appointment after the state had employed popular election of electors at one or more presidential elections in the past. There would be nothing particularly awkward about confining the "at any time" language to new election cycles, rather than giving it a literal reading that would encourage last minute legislative manipulation of the presidential selection process.

When the selection method being renounced is popular election, moreover, "taking back" the choice treads on sensitivities associated with the right to vote. It is one thing to renounce popular election as a method of selection, but when that renunciation is done in the midst of a vote count, the suspicion is sure to arise—as it most certainly did in Florida—that the legislature's change is motivated by partisan disapproval of the likely (or at least feared) outcome of the election.[63] In the legislative apportionment context, the Supreme Court has said that the "right of suffrage is a fundamental matter . . . [so that] any alleged infringement of the right of citizens to vote must be carefully and meticulously scrutinized."[64]

There was an additional question raised by the preemptive action that the Florida legislature had under consideration. As we saw in Chapter Three, the Constitution explicitly gives Congress the power to "determine the time of choosing the electors,"[65] and it had long opted for the November date that we think of as election day. Any later date at which the Florida legislature might have designated electors would seem to violate a congressional determination that was itself clearly authorized by the Constitution. But Congress has also long provided that if a "[s]tate has held an election for the purpose of choosing electors, and has failed to make a choice on the day prescribed by law, the electors may be appointed on a subsequent day in such a manner as the legislature of such [s]tate may direct."[66] This statute is comfortably accommodated by the congressional power over the timing of the choice of electors. The legality of the contemplated Florida preemptive action then seemed to turn on whether the contentious election represented a failure "to make a choice on the day prescribed by law."[67]

Some who supported the preemptive action that the Florida legislature was contemplating sought to make the election into a "failure" by characterizing the popular vote as a "tie."[68] The election was close enough that talk of a "tie" was a permissible figure of speech. Indeed if the difference in the reported vote totals for the two leading candidates was greater than the likely "margin of error" that inevitably plagues any real world process of counting, it might be fair to call the election a statistical "tie."[69] But there was never a tie in Florida in the literal sense that would provide no winner. "Mere" statistical margins of error have never before stood in the way of determining a winner in close elections in the United States, and it would thus be stretching things to include such a statistical "tie" as a statutory "failure to make a choice." Others more plausibly argued instead that the turmoil surrounding the counting justified a conclusion of "failure."[70]

The preponderance of the expert commentary at the time, however, seemed to conclude that there was no "failure" that might justify the legislature's stepping in.[71] The final results were still not known, to be sure, but it is decidedly awkward to interpret Congress's use of the word "failure" to include a close election where time was required for the normal process to play out through which a winner would eventually be declared. After all, as we saw in Chapter Three, the Electoral Count Act encourages states to establish judicial or quasi-judicial procedures by which electoral college voting disputes can be resolved with some promptness. Prompt resolution of election disputes can hardly be expected, however, on the same day as the election.

The question of a statutory "failure" takes on a somewhat different cast, however, if viewed through the lens of the concurring opinion filed in the Supreme Court's 2000 election decision by Chief Justice William Rehnquist and joined in by Justices Antonin Scalia and Clarence Thomas.[72] They put special emphasis on the assignment to the legislature—as opposed to the state as an entity—of the power over the manner of designation of electors. The concurring opinion found serious fault with the Florida Supreme Court's interpretation of state law, insisting that in a number of respects it had stretched the language of the Florida statute beyond any plausible boundaries. The concurring opinion said that under the circumstances "the text of the [Florida] election law itself, and not just its interpretation by the [Florida] courts . . . takes on independent significance."[73] Now statutory interpretation is anything but an exact science, and the fault that the concurring opinion finds with the Florida Supreme Court failed to enlist a majority of the Court and has itself been subject to serious scholarly criticism.[74] From the perspective of the concurring opinion, however, a conclusion of "failure" to make a choice on election day becomes plausible. An out-of-control state court would have made it so.

None of the objections leveled at Florida legislative preemption of the election have much force, however, as applied to the suggested contingent award of electoral votes designed to keep the presidential selection from going to the House of Representatives. The Florida legislature was considering displacing an election result that might well have changed the outcome of an election that had already been held, under legislation it had itself passed. The contingent procedure, in contrast, would have been adopted before any election for which it would be effective. In addition, the contingent procedure would take electoral votes from a candidate with a real chance to become president only in the most remote of circumstances—where a minor party candidate would have won in the House of Representatives. The contingent procedure might, of course, change the eventual outcome of the process, producing a victory for one major party candidate when the other might otherwise have triumphed in the House. But the possibility of affecting outcomes is presented by virtually any change in procedure that goes beyond the purely cosmetic. The motivation for the contingent approach would be "neutral" between the major contenders in a way that the Florida legislature's contemplated action would not have been.

The contingent procedure would, in a sense, displace the decision of the state's voters. It might thus be claimed that the state had compromised the citizenry's right to vote for electors by awarding its electoral votes to the second-place finisher in the popular vote tally. To be sure, the suggested procedure would be more "democratic" than the 1796 Massachusetts approach, since it would at least require selection of the second-place finisher. But in addition, the contingent second phase would come into play only upon a finding that the "winning" candidate was decidedly unlikely eventually to prevail in the presidential contest. The procedure is thus akin to a "runoff" election, which is pretty standard fare both in democratic theory and at least occasional American practice.[75] In addition, any objection on voting rights grounds seems to miss the mark when leveled at a selection mechanism designed to forestall the much more democratically problematic recourse to the House of Representatives.

A variant on the claim that the suggested procedure is undemocratic because it interferes with the right to vote is that it ties an enacting state's choice to the election outcomes in other states, to a choice that had been made by "irrelevant" voters. While the 1796 Massachusetts approach did not have this feature, any such objection seems terribly formalistic. It is simply not true that each state's selection procedure operates at the present time in isolation from what happens in other states. Admittedly, there is no contingency provision in present practice that draws on the election results in other states, but political parties already operate in today's political world as very powerful mechanisms for coordinating the selection processes of the various states.[76] We saw in Chapter Two that there was concern at the time the electoral college provision was being devised that local orientation of the electors would dominate the process. That concern has greatly receded over time, precisely because the choices open to a state's voters are so much a function of the interstate operation of political parties. In that environment, there would not seem to be anything untoward about drawing on the implications of what other states have done in a state's allocation of its electoral votes.

In addition, we should bear in mind that the focal point of an election procedure is the determination of a winner. There are surely other purposes that elections serve—important ones, like fostering a sense of involvement on the part of the electorate.[77] But these other purposes would quickly be drained of their meaning if elections did not routinely yield "election" results in the form of winners and losers. The suggested contingent procedure that draws on what voters outside the state have decided is brought into play only after it becomes reasonably clear that the in-state winner will not have finished first or second in the body with initial authority to determine that election winner, and indeed that the in-state winner would be decidedly unlikely eventually to prevail in the House contingent procedure that is being displaced. In those circumstances voters who voted for the candidate being displaced would not seem to have much election-based cause for complaint.

Nor should the timing problem that was raised in connection with the preemptive action the Florida legislature was considering cause any problems. The first-cut electoral vote tabulation might not be completed on election day because counting takes time, or because of disputes in some states that require a process of resolution that takes time. For that reason, a state that had adopted the contingent approach might not be able to make a final determination of its electors on election day. But it would be bizarre to find this to be a statutory failure "to make a choice on the day prescribed by law." As we saw in discussing the Florida legislative preemption possibility, delay in determining winners of elections is actually contemplated by the Electoral Count Act. In those circumstances, the statutory reference to making "a choice on" election day should be taken to refer to the casting and collecting of the votes, not to a decisive determination of the result that flows from those votes.[78]

One important objection to the suggested contingent procedure is that the state's voters might have preferred the third-place finisher to the second-place one, had that been the choice presented initially.[79] The problem is similar to one that inheres in any election where a single choice is to be made from three or more candidates. Several possibilities for addressing the problem in the electoral college context come to mind. First, it might be urged that a residuum of elector discretion could deal satisfactorily with secondary voter preferences. If a third-party candidate prevailed in a state, but had no realistic chance of taking the presidency either in the electoral college or in the House, the electors pledged to him might well capture the second choice of the candidate's supporters if simply allowed to abandon their pre-election commitments when they cast their electoral votes.

For a number of reasons, I do not think that this response is very attractive. First, it is hard to see how this possibility for elector discretion could be retained without also retaining the discretion to force the selection into the House. Second, even if the electors did express their supporters' secondary preferences in the electoral college, they, and the third-party candidate to whom they were pledged, would have the self-same temptation to bargain in the electoral college context that seems so unattractive when deployed in the House proceedings. And finally, retaining this residuum of elector discretion might suggest some redeeming virtue to the possibility of elector discretion that would poison the effort to purge it more generally from the system.

Another possibility is an adaptation of the runoff election. A second round of voting is sometimes employed where a first round has proved indecisive. The typical "indecisiveness" is that the first round did not produce a single candidate who commanded a majority of the total votes, or perhaps a stated percentage short of a majority. In Chapter Four, for instance, we saw that the nationwide popular vote proposal of a special commission of the American Bar

Association called for a runoff if no candidate obtained forty percent of the vote in an initial round. In the electoral college context, a runoff between the second- and third-place candidates in a state might be held if it was determined that a minor party candidate who finished first—either with a plurality, or even a majority of the popular vote—had no chance of winning the presidency.

A runoff is never a full answer to this democratic dilemma of voter preferences beyond a chosen favorite, because a voter's second choice may have been eliminated before the runoff occurs. The short time frame in which presidential elections are held, moreover, may make a runoff impracticable.[80] The time between election day and the meetings of electors could be changed through legislation,[81] though both tradition and the constitutionally prescribed January 20 date for the beginning of the president's term[82] do impinge on the possibilities for two rounds of voting. For this timing problem, however, there is a solution. Two separate rounds need not be held.

Instead of a genuine two-stage runoff, the electorate's "second choice" might be gauged through an "instant run-off" system like that employed in Australia, where each voter rank orders the various candidates in a single round of voting.[83] After the votes are tabulated initially, if no candidate commands a majority of the (first-place) votes, the candidate with the least votes is eliminated, and his votes are spread among the remaining candidates according to the second choices indicated on the ballots cast for the eliminated candidate. This process continues with the elimination of each successive remaining candidate with the least votes until a single candidate commands a majority of the total number of voters. While it was first devised in this country in the 1870s, the instant runoff system has not caught on widely here.[84] Nor does the instant runoff provide a perfect answer to the democratic dilemma in capturing the complex array of voter sentiments through an inevitably simplified process of balloting. For just as with the first round of a two-stage runoff, a voter casting an instant runoff ballot might be tempted to make some of his choices "strategically." He might, for instance, think that his "true" second choice would be eliminated in an early round, and hence substitute a third or lower choice which seemed to have a better chance of surviving to subsequent rounds. The strategic calculations in an instant runoff, moreover, are more complicated than in a standard American-style single round election. That may be part of the reason that instant runoffs have not found warm reception in the United States. Be that as it may, if politically feasible the instant runoff should be given serious consideration as an alternative to the contingent procedure I have suggested.

We should consider a few additional challenges that might be leveled at the suggested contingent selection procedure. Perhaps most obvious of all, it could be claimed that any attempt to subvert the House role in the selection process is unconstitutional for that reason alone. The Constitution does after all provide for a fallback procedure in the House, not the contingent manipulation of the electoral college I have suggested. A form of that objection could, of course, be made to the proposal of Chapter Six to avoid ties, and indeed to the Uniform State Law on elector discretion suggested in Chapter Seven. The whole point of the one, and a good part of the other, is to avoid selection of the president by the House of Representatives. I doubt that this objection should be taken very seriously, however, for reasons similar to those discussed in Chapter Seven for finding state authority to do away with elector discretion. The simple fact of the matter is that the contemporary electoral college bears scant resemblance to the mechanism the constitutional framers thought they were installing. It would simply be foolhardy to forbid states from working within the constitutional language to make the best of inevitable awkwardness that creeps into the process as it adapts to today's vastly different political world.

There remains the very real policy question—perhaps a legal one as well—of whether the suggested contingent approach unduly interferes with the operation of minor parties in American politics. Under the contingent approach, minor parties would, of course, be disabled from commanding electoral votes in close national contests. That is the whole point of employing the contingent procedure, and I will take its desirability as a given. The relevant question then is whether the measure seriously handicaps minor parties beyond this core interference. The rather clear answer, I think, is that there is no such intolerable burden.

It seems unlikely at the present time that third parties are energized in any substantial measure by the prospect of throwing the presidential selection into the House. The rewards from doing so—while likely not including a shot at the presidency—are surely not trivial. As we have seen, third parties might well be attracted by the possibility of obtaining leverage in the House procedure over major party candidates seeking their votes. It may be doubtful that that prospect should weigh on the positive side of the balance, but we should hesitate to be too particular in evaluating possible rewards that may energize third parties. Major party incentives, after all, are themselves not always so wholesome. If in fact third parties were energized in some substantial measure by the prospect of throwing an election into the House, that might give us pause, since we seek to minimize interference with the role that third parties play in American politics. But we have seen that third parties have not yet thrown a presidential election into the House. Their chances of doing so surely remain remote. Despite that fact, third parties have played vigorous roles in recent elections, and we can probably conclude that they would retain a large measure of incentive for political activity even if the prospect of action in the House were effectively taken off the table.

It would seem that a much more tempting target for a third party is the possibility of affecting the electoral vote outcome between the major party candidates in one or more states—as Ralph Nader apparently did in the 2000 election, for instance—or even of bargaining to withdraw from a state to remove that threat. The substitute fallback procedure that I have outlined should do very little to discourage a third-party candidacy aimed at those more realistic third-party goals. Nor should it dampen the incentive of third parties to affect the agenda of the major parties, or even the hope that they might replace one of the major parties. A third party that was denied a bloc of electoral votes on account of the contingent assignment would nonetheless have been able to demonstrate its ability to win a statewide race. That demonstration would be fully apparent both to the major party actors and to others around the country who might over time be drawn to the third party's message.

Indeed, one criticism that might be aimed at the suggested contingent electoral vote assignment is that it ignores the more important problem of a third-party candidacy changing the outcome of an election, à la Nader in 2000. My own view is that that problem *is* more important than the threat that third parties create of House selection of the president, simply because it is much more likely. But that problem is also entirely separable—and indeed separately solvable—through the instant runoff procedure discussed above. If it is true that Nader voters overwhelmingly favored Gore over Bush as their second choices, then an "instant run-off" system in Florida, for instance, would have resulted in a Gore victory in 2000. But it is also true, as mentioned above, that instant runoff voting has not gained political traction in the United States. Thus even after the experience of the 2000 election, I know of no movement to institute instant runoff voting in the choice of presidential electors in Florida. Whether or not instant runoff voting catches on in the United States, however, the threat that third parties will throw the presidential selection into the House will remain. Even acknowledging that this is the lesser problem of the two, there seems to be no reason to neglect smaller problems just because we may lack the will to solve some larger ones.

Finally, there might be practical problems in implementing the suggested contingent procedure. The first-cut determination of an electoral vote winner would depend on the voting returns from the other states, and some of those might be delayed. If the delay were greatly prolonged, it might impinge on the state's ability to name its electors. We will defer discussion of the problem of collecting the required information until Chapter Ten, where we take up another approach to elector selection that makes one state's choice dependent on what happens in other states. The problem presented in Chapter Ten is one where the other states may have an incentive to withhold cooperation. For the contingent procedure suggested in this chapter, however, there is no apparent reason why a state that had voted for the candidate of one of the two major parties should resist making the winner known. For that reason any practical problems of serious delay should be rare and ultimately manageable.

CHAPTER NINE

Miscellaneous Pitfalls in the
Electoral College Process

The reforms suggested in Chapters Six, Seven, and Eight are informed by what I have called the "contemporary understanding of the presidential election process." Pursuant to this understanding, political parties nominate one candidate each for president and vice president, and each state, and the District of Columbia, then holds a popular election to determine how its allotted electors will cast their ballots for one of the party slates for the two offices. While this contemporary understanding is solidly embedded in today's American political culture and practice, the presidential selection process is periodically troubled by questions or occurrences that seem quite disconnected from that understanding. While perhaps initially surprising, this disjuncture becomes easy to understand once it is appreciated that the constitutional provisions for the electoral college were inspired originally by a vision of the way the process would work that is worlds apart from the contemporary understanding.

The last three chapters dealt with the most awkward possibilities, ones that present special dissonance with the contemporary understanding. An electoral college tie when only two candidates gain electoral votes, faithlessly cast electoral votes, and electoral votes gained by minor party candidates can upset and indeed despoil the process in two different ways. They can force the choice of president into the contingent procedure in the House of Representatives (and the choice of the vice president to the Senate), while the second or third can produce an aberrant presidential or vice-presidential choice in the electoral college itself. The problems of those three chapters are not, however, the only ones with the potential to throw the system off course. In this chapter I continue to take the contemporary understanding of the presidential election process as an organizing ideal and turn to a grab bag of other peculiarities in the system, asking whether modest correctives here and there might be both feasible and useful in furthering that ideal.[1]

Some of the potential pitfalls in the process are not bottomed in constitutional peculiarities of the electoral college, but rather are variations on problems with which any large-scale electoral system must come to grips. One of these is the death of a candidate or a candidate's patent inability (or even simple unwillingness) to serve for some other reason. Another is vote tabulation controversies, sometimes grounded in voter eligibility questions, and sometimes a matter of simple counting difficulties. While not confined to the electoral college process, these problems do take somewhat different forms because of unusual features of the way we choose our president.

For the most part the contemporary understanding of the electoral college counsels that we strain to ensure that the electoral votes of any given state adhere to the popular vote in that state, even when a now anachronistic provision would seem to contemplate elector discretion. But if after the popular election and before the electoral college has met a candidate dies or becomes disabled, or even simply decides that he cannot assume office, nothing is to be gained by ensuring that electoral votes are cast for him anyway. Our only experience with untimely death of a presidential candidate was in the 1872 election when the Democratic candidate Horace Greeley died in this period.[2] Despite this, several electors cast their votes for him. They could do so without facing momentous consequences, since Greeley had not been victorious in the election. The congressional joint meeting decided not to count the votes cast for Greeley, rejecting what the insistent electors had done. Had Greeley won the election, however, something would obviously have had to give, either before or after the electors had voted.

I urged in Chapter Seven that if the untimely loss of a candidate comes in this period between the popular election and the meetings of electors, we resist the temptation to think that we have finally found a useful role for elector discretion in the contemporary context. But loss of a candidate might also come either before the popular election or after the electors have cast their votes. On three different occasions we have actually had to face the problem of the death

or withdrawal of a vice-presidential nominee in the period after initial nomination but before designation of electors on "election day." In each of the three
instances, the void was filled by action of the relevant political party's national
committee.[3] Since a state's electors are those of a political party and pledged to
that party's candidates, any future vacancy in this time period for president or
vice president would presumably—and should—be handled in the same manner.[4] Should the vacancy occur in the presidential slot, the most likely substitute
would be the vice-presidential candidate, but there seems to be no great harm
in leaving that choice to party processes.

This leaves the period after the electoral college has met, but before the date
for the president and vice president to assume office. If up until then all had
gone smoothly in the electoral college process, the Twentieth Amendment an-
ticipates the problem, providing that the "Vice President elect shall become
President." This should govern the situation even if the problem arises before
the votes are counted in the joint meeting.[5] But as we saw in Chapter Five,
things may not have gone smoothly. The electoral college may not have provided a decisive winner, and the contingent procedure in the House may face
the question of what to do when one of the candidates from which it was to
choose is no longer with us.

If we were entirely unencumbered by the niceties of the electoral college
provisions, the ideal solution under those difficult circumstances would probably track the solution suggested in Chapter Seven when the disability comes
before the meetings of electors. The vice-presidential candidate of the same
party would seem to be the most appropriate substitute for the unavailable
presidential candidate. But there are two quite serious obstacles to reaching this
outcome. First, in all likelihood the electoral college selection of the vice president would have been indecisive as well, and that choice, relegated to the Senate, might still await an outcome. And second, whether or not the Senate had
made its choice, the Twelfth Amendment instructs that the House choice is to
be from among the three candidates who received the highest number of electoral votes for president. In all likelihood the vice-presidential candidate of the
party of the unavailable presidential candidate would not have received any
electoral votes for president, and hence would not be available for selection by
the House.[6]

There seem to be two possibilities for dealing with this dilemma. The most straightforward is for the House to choose another candidate from those made available under the Twelfth Amendment. In most cases—where only two presidential candidates had received electoral votes—there would actually be just one other candidate, and his name would thus be the only one formally available to the House. The other possibility, however, would be for the House to hold back from any decision, a result which could presumably be produced in a one candidate context by abstention by twenty-five or more states. In that case, if the vice president had been chosen by the Senate, under the Twentieth Amendment he would, as we have seen, assume the powers of the presidency on inauguration day. This would actually not accord fully with the ideal solution mentioned above, because under the Twentieth Amendment, the president not having yet "been chosen," the vice president would not "become President," but rather be an "acting" president. An acting president would serve in an important way at the sufferance of the House, which could at any time break its deadlock and name as president one of the original candidates (or the only one still available) who had received electoral votes.

Neither of these outcomes is fully satisfactory, and any other would seem to require a constitutional amendment. Short of an amendment, probably the better of the two solutions, should this (unlikely) choice fall to the House, would be to choose the remaining presidential candidate with the most electoral votes. He would, after all, almost surely have come to the House process with virtually the same support as his now unavailable rival. He might well end up with a vice president of a different party, but we have seen that that bit of awkwardness seems tolerable. It should be noted, however, that precommitment of the House to this outcome will almost surely never be forthcoming (and would not likely be binding if it were), so that there is no way to ensure that the House will not opt for the alternative that will keep an "acting" president obliged to it for his continuation in office. Given the other problems in the process, we can probably count either of the outcomes as at least tolerable, in these exceedingly unlikely circumstances.[7]

The other standard concern is that of voter eligibility determinations and related counting problems in tabulating the vote. This is, of course, the set of problems that transfixed the nation as it watched the 2000 election play out in the state of Florida. One electoral college peculiarity that hovers over counting disputes is the winner-take-all approach to selecting electors that is now all but universal among the states. Since this approach makes a state's entire slate of electors depend on the resolution of any counting controversy in a given state, it greatly magnifies the significance of what might otherwise be relatively trivial disputes. This becomes important in those states with electoral college delegations large enough—singly or in combination—to change an election's outcome. In razor-thin elections like that of 2000, this could be so for even the smallest state delegations.

Historically the disputes have sometimes gelled into rival slates of electors. Instead of engaging in some judicial or other contest at the state level, rival slates may meet separately and, ostensibly as instructed by the Constitution,[8] send their separate results on to the president of the Senate. In Chapter Three we saw that the 1876 election produced rival slates of electors in four different states, and that both before and after 1876 there has been a scattering of other instances of rival slates. The engagement of the federal courts in the Florida tabulation controversy forestalled the development of rival slates on that occasion, but the possibility was not far offstage.[9]

Actually the rival slate problem is now reasonably under control. In Chapter Three we looked at the provisions of the Electoral Count Act (ECA) that undertake to regularize the counting of electoral votes in the constitutionally prescribed joint meeting of the House and Senate. In the case of competing slates of electors from a state, the ECA provisions give a decided edge to a slate that the state's governor has certified. While little is certain in this largely uncharted territory, that "edge" would probably have been sufficient to resolve the Florida dispute had the Supreme Court not gotten involved.[10]

There is a lingering question of the constitutionality of the ECA. The statute recognizes that very substantial authority resides in the individual states to resolve controversies about electoral votes, but it also asserts congressional authority in a variety of situations. It is sometimes argued that Congress has no authority to divide up responsibility in this fashion between the states and the joint meeting, that state authority to select electors and tabulate their votes is exclusive.[11] This argument would have raised no question about any governor-certified slate in the Florida 2000 context, but it could cast a shadow over any joint meeting decision that rejects a slate that comes with a gubernatorial imprimatur.

Constitutional language on the division of authority is sparse. The state legislatures are given authority to determine the "manner" in which the state's electors are to be "appoint[ed]," but the joint meeting is where the votes "shall . . . be counted."[12] The language seems suggestive of a routine counting process, and that is the basis for challenging congressional authority to exclude state-approved electoral votes. This interpretation is perhaps reinforced by the fact that Congress is assigned other limited duties in the process—basically to determine matters of timing—and that this is done with rather explicit language.[13] There are, however, two basic problems with insisting on exclusive state authority over controversial questions about electors and their votes. One is that the Constitution does place explicit limits on electors, such as their own qualifications, and the qualifications of those for whom they can vote.[14] The second is that the state is not a monolith—and even if it were it still might be necessary to interpret what that monolith had done. Many of the controversies about electors that have arisen over the years have involved questions of just who speaks for the state.

There is no complete solution to this problem in saying that the state "legislature" is the organ of the state to which the Constitution assigns authority. There could actually be more than one body laying claim to being the legislature.[15] Sometimes there will be controversy about how a legislature does its speaking.[16] But most importantly the legislature typically speaks in a very formal and stylized way—enacting language—and then turns to other things, or even adjourns. Some additional body will typically have to interpret just what it is that the legislature has done, and then whether others acting pursuant to its instructions have done so properly. That, of course, is one way to think about what happened in the controversy over Florida's electoral votes in the 2000 election, where it was the Florida Supreme Court and then the U.S. Supreme Court that did the interpreting. But when the courts do not step in, it should hardly be surprising if the task of determining the fact and legitimacy of what the state has done would occasionally be assumed by the joint meeting.

The approach to constitutional interpretation that I sketched in Chapter Seven is apropos here. Even if the constitutional framers assumed that the counting process would be routine, experience has taught us to the contrary. In such a context, the "original intention" behind the sparse constitutional language tells us little about how to resolve the controversies that do arise. Some authority must make final determinations, and it makes a good deal of sense for that authority to reside in a single body that can bring a measure of regularity and consistency to the process. The courts are one possibility, but the joint meeting has an entirely plausible claim on the authority, if for no reason other than that it is already called upon to do the counting. Through the ECA's division of authority between the states and the joint meeting, the Congress has risen to that challenge, and thus far done so with apparent success.[17] In this context we would do well to accept that solution and move on to remaining problems that are much less under control.

Another electoral college peculiarity that helps shape tabulation disputes is the time pressure. Any electoral system will require time to resolve the eligibility and other counting disputes that will inevitably arise on occasion in any competitive large-scale electoral environment.[18] But there is a special urgency for presidential tabulation disputes, because unlike a multimember legislative body, the executive branch can hardly function without a definitive determination of who is entitled to exercise the power of the president. In the American system, this determination is squeezed among dates that initially seem to have relatively little give in them.

The Twentieth Amendment establishes January 20 as the beginning of the president's term. Election day is set by statute under Congress's constitutional authority to "determine the time of choosing the electors."[19] For a long time Congress held back from prescribing a uniform date, in part at least in deference to state legislatures which still chose electors directly in some cases.[20] As we saw in Chapter Three, however, in 1845 it opted for the first Tuesday after the first Monday in November, and that date has held as "election day" ever since.[21] The meetings of electors obviously must come between these two dates, as must the congressional joint meeting where the electoral votes are to be counted.

The times of both those meetings are set by statute. As a part of the original electoral college provisions, Congress is given authority to set the elector meeting date, which is then required to "the same throughout the United States."[22] In 1887 the date was set at the second Monday in January, but under pressure from the Twentieth Amendment's new January 20 date for the new president to take office,[23] it was moved in 1934 to the first Monday after the second Wednesday in December.[24] This had the effect of shortening the time between election day and the electors' meetings, and hence of shortening the time for comfortably resolving tabulation disputes. I say "comfortably" because the meetings of electors might be thought irrelevant under the modern conception of presidential elections, in which popular votes are supposed to translate formulaically into electoral votes. It is only because of the residual hold of the notion of elector discretion—as well as some statutory provisions to which we will turn shortly—that the meetings of electors seem to be of real importance. In any event, the December meeting date for electors has also held for almost three-quarters of a century.

Were it not for the artificial significance attached to the meetings of electors, the real outside date for resolving tabulation disputes would be the joint meeting counting session. In addition to establishing January 20 as the inauguration date for the new president, the Twentieth Amendment separated the dates for the beginning of the terms of the executive and of the legislature, setting January 3 for the latter.[25] This in turn allowed the new Congress, rather than a "lame duck" one, to carry out any presidential selection duties enjoined upon the Congress. Most vitally these duties entail any proceedings under the contingent selection provisions, but they also encompass the counting of the electoral votes in the congressional joint meeting. After passage of the Twentieth Amendment Congress responded by setting the congressional joint meeting date as January 6, two weeks before the scheduled inauguration and soon after the new Congress would have taken office.[26]

The net result of these various dates is to leave a little more than forty days between election day and the meetings of electors, and an additional two to three weeks before the congressional joint meeting (a period, however, that includes the year-end holiday season). The shorter period did not prove sufficient in Florida in the 2000 election, nor in Hawaii in 1960.[27] And use of the longer period is complicated by the Electoral Count Act, at least as it was used by the U.S. Supreme Court in the decision that called a halt to the Florida recount in the 2000 election.[28]

In its decision the Supreme Court quoted the Florida Supreme Court as saying that the Florida legislature wanted the state's electors to " 'participat[e] fully in the federal electoral process."[29] It was this that led the Supreme Court to assume that Florida would want to meet the "deadline" of the safe harbor provision—"six days before the time fixed for the meeting of electors." This seems quite questionable, on two grounds. First, in its several pronouncements on the election dispute, the Florida court had put considerably more emphasis on the

importance of ensuring that all votes were counted correctly, noting in particular the Florida constitutional provision that "all political power is inherent in
the people."[30] Second, and more importantly for our purposes, the safe harbor
provision does not preclude Florida's "full" participation in the election even if
controversies have not finally been settled six days before the meeting of electors. The provision deprives the state of the guarantee of a "safe harbor," but
that does not mean that disqualified votes are to be discarded. Whether or not
they have lingered for a time in the safety of a harbor, the state's votes can come
to rest in the port of the electoral college meetings any time before those meetings are held.

It is this question of timing that could use some attention in rationalizing
the electoral college process. In Chapter Three we discussed some of the continuing ambiguities and difficulties of the ECA. Still, the act does provide a reasonably satisfactory process for the joint meeting to follow in resolving tabulation questions that may arise, very importantly including choices between rival
slates of electors. The integrity of this process is, however, dependent on the
earlier state processes. Those have come a long way since the ECA was passed,
in part under the prodding of the act's safe harbor provision.[31] But the Florida
2000 litigation painfully revealed that time can prove short in addressing disputes at the state level.

As of this writing, some nerves may still remain raw from the contentious
2000 election. For that reason, it may be premature to pursue the statutory reform I have in mind. When the time seems propitious, however, a few simple
measures could provide a greater margin of comfort in the timing at the state
level for resolving tabulation controversies. First of all, the Electoral Count Act's
six-day provision for a safe harbor serves no discernible purpose. It is not clear
that there was ever much reason for the requirement,[32] but with today's modern communication, it is hard to see why state resolution of a tabulation controversy at any time before the electors are to meet should not suffice. Second,
for the reasons we adverted to earlier, no obvious purpose is served by resolving controversies before the meetings of electors rather than after. In an era
where the electors were to deliberate and exercise real judgment, it made sense
to sort out just who they were well before the time for them to meet. But contemporary electors have nothing to deliberate about. At least when this is made
quite clear by the Uniform State Law, as suggested in Chapter Seven, or other-

wise, resolution of any controversies at the state level prior to the official counting at the joint meeting should suffice.[33]

Applying these lessons to the 2000 Florida controversies, had the court assumed that the Florida legislation contemplated continuing a recount even at
the risk of losing the ECA's harbor safety, there would have been six additional
days to pursue the recount. Had the Court gone even further and assumed that
a recount could proceed all the way up to the electoral vote count at the congressional joint meeting, it would have gained an additional two and a half
weeks or so. Even the first, and certainly the second, should have been sufficient
to complete a wholesome recount.[34] Statutory changes that make these desirable steps clear should be undertaken at the earliest time that the politics of the
matter provides a decent chance for the effort to succeed.

A series of other points of electoral college contention is traceable exclusively to the peculiarities of the constitutional provisions. We have encountered
several of them in our earlier discussions. Recall, for instance, the objection that
was raised to one of the Oregon electors in the 1876 election. He was a postmaster at the time of his election, and it was urged that that disqualified him,
because the Constitution provides that "no . . . person holding an office of trust
or profit under the United States shall be appointed an elector."[35] After the postmaster resigned both as postmaster and elector, his fellow Republican electors
chose him to fill the elector vacancy created by his own resignation, thus posing the further question of whether an elector disqualified when elected could
nonetheless serve once he had eliminated the cause for his disqualification.
That Oregon controversy was resolved in a way that allowed the suspect elector
to cast a vote that was in sync with the popular vote in the state,[36] but it is certainly possible to imagine that there might have been a less happy outcome.

The Oregon governor at the time, a Democrat, had attempted to substitute
the elector candidate with the next highest number of votes—not so coinci-
dentally a Democrat as well—which would have resulted in a partisan split in
the Oregon electors.[37] Had that approach prevailed, Oregon's electoral votes
would not have all gone to the statewide winner among presidential candidates,
but they also would not have been particularly out of touch with the popular
vote in the state. As we saw in Chapter Four, over the years states have considered—and employed—a variety of ways of translating the popular vote into an
allocation of electors. There are great debates about which of the ways is the

most democratic, but in truth as we also saw in Chapter Four, there is no magic route on this question to some democratic truth. Had the Oregon governor succeeded in his gambit, the process would have yielded a definitive electoral college result, one that could hardly be charged with being disconnected either from party politics or from the Oregon popular vote.[38] The governor had brought in new rules late in the game, and his designation of a Democratic elector might well have been rejected on that ground. But there was nothing inherently "undemocratic" about the split in the state's electoral vote that his designation produced.

Another plausible solution to the Oregon dilemma would have been to disqualify the vote of the miscreant elector altogether. In that case, Oregon would have cast fewer votes than its share under the prevailing electoral college allocation among states. While this solution does not have much appeal to modern sensibilities, it would not seem to be particularly foreign to the original conception of the way the college was to operate. The electors were to choose the president by exercising judgment and discretion. Their independence was important—hence the limitation on holding an official federal position—but not particularly their numbers. In this way of thinking about the operation of the electoral college, if one member of a state's delegation was unavailable, the others could simply decide without him or her. To be sure, the original conception was more complicated than this—after all the states were assigned delegations with specific and varying numbers of electoral votes—but for those who came up with the system there would probably have been nothing jarring in simply doing without the vote of an elector who turned out to be ineligible. If the simple disqualification route had been pursued, all other things being equal, there would have been an electoral college tie vote in 1876. This would presumably have thrown the choice of president into the House, where Tilden would likely have won on account of Democratic control of the requisite majority of House delegations. In addition, this would presumably have sent the selection of the vice president to the Senate, where the Republicans had a majority. The result could then easily have been a split administration.[39]

Even more serious would be disqualification of a state's entire delegation. This was a possibility presented by the votes of the Wisconsin electors in 1856 and the Arkansas electors in 1872. As mentioned in Chapter Three, in 1856 a blizzard prevented the Wisconsin electors from meeting and casting their votes on the day designated by Congress. As we have seen, once that date is set, the Constitution says that it is to be used throughout the country. The electors had accordingly met on that day in all the other states. Despite the seemingly forbidden delay, however, the Wisconsin votes were counted in the congressional joint meeting—though only after the most heated controversy.[40] The 1872 Arkansas electors were not treated so kindly. The joint meeting refused to count their votes, ostensibly—at least in part—because the certificate of returns that they submitted did not bear the "great seal" required by federal statute.[41] In neither election were the votes in question capable of changing the electoral college outcome, but disqualification of votes on grounds that arise after the selection of electors does court the danger of an indecisive electoral college outcome and hence recourse to the House and Senate to choose our executive officers.

The precise effects of disqualified vote, moreover, may depend upon the twists and turns of another electoral college peculiarity. The "majority" required to keep the presidential and vice-presidential selections out of the House and Senate is of "the whole number of electors appointed,"[42] a formulation apparently chosen originally to provide a ready decision even if "some states should neglect to appoint Electors or . . . some Electors should neglect to attend the College."[43] And there have been such instances of failure of appointment. In the very first election, for instance, the New York legislature, among others, resolved to appoint electors directly. In New York alone, however, the choice proved so contentious that none was ever made, and New York cast no electoral votes.[44] That is surely the purest sort of case of electors who were not "appointed." But we could have arguable cases of failure of appointment even today, with potentially troublesome implications.

In bringing closure to the 2000 Florida election controversy, for instance, the Supreme Court concluded not that George Bush did or would have won in a full and fair count of the Florida popular vote, but that there was insufficient time remaining to conduct such a (re)count. The Court's resolution was to leave the count where it had been before the final phase of the recounting process had been set in motion, with Bush holding a small lead. That may well have been the best resolution under the circumstances, but an alternative certainly suggests itself. Like New York in 1789, Florida could have abstained in the electoral college. By this way of thinking about the situation, no decision had been reached on the choice of electors, because a full, fair, and timely count had proved impossible.[45]

Had the Court opted for a Florida abstention in the 2000 context, for instance, Florida would presumably not have "appointed" any electors, and Albert Gore would have commanded a majority of the "electors appointed," though not of the full complement of slots in the electoral college. And the same would presumably be true if, even without the intervention of the nation's highest court, counting difficulties caused a standoff in a state's selection of electors that could not be resolved satisfactorily in a timely fashion. There would surely be resentments from the failure of a state to submit electoral votes. But with plausible claim to the votes available to each side, the resentments might lose traction without gelling into something worse.[46] And normally no great offense would be done to the contemporary understanding of presidential elections if no electoral votes are recorded for a state on account of such a close race that a winner could not be named.

Still, the 2000 election also taught us that the "normal" is not always what we get. We should prepare for the abnormal, and the question of whether an elector was "appointed" could be the breeding ground for more enduring damage. The determination of "appointment" itself might not be so clear, and whichever way the determination comes out, it could throw the electoral vote count into troubled territory. Suppose, for instance, that there are questions about two or more electoral votes on the ground that electors were ineligible to serve, as in the case of the disputed Oregon Republican elector in 1876.[47] But suppose further that the facts on which the claim of ineligibility is grounded become known to other electors only after the state's electoral votes have been cast and sent to the president of the Senate. Or suppose that, even if known, the constitutional significance of the electors' positions was uncertain, or was only appreciated after the meetings of electors. If the joint meeting rejected those votes on the ground of constitutional ineligibility, the electors' status as "appointed" could be debatable. The Constitution says that an unqualified person shall not be "appointed,"[48] but in this case it could be urged that there had been a *de facto* "appointment" nonetheless. An argument about "appointment" could then be put to strategic use in a partisan struggle, with either outcome courting trouble. A determination of disqualification but "appointment" would not change the size of the majority required to win in the electoral college, but could lead to neither candidate's achieving that majority. A determination of disqualification and hence nonappointment, on the other hand, would decrease the size of the required majority, raising the possibility of a decisive electoral college outcome, just one different from what a full count of electors would have produced. The result could be choice of the president in the House or an electoral college decision widely viewed as illegitimate.

In Chapter One I mentioned another electoral college provision that could similarly cast a dark shadow over the prospects for a decisive electoral vote. The Constitution provides that the electors cannot vote for an "inhabitant of the same state with themselves" for both president and vice president.[49] To date this has never caused an electoral vote tabulation problem,[50] but the 2000 election gave us a peek at its capacity to do so. Both George Bush and Dick Cheney had called Texas home in the period leading up to their selection as the Republican nominees for the two offices, and that at least raised the possibility that the Texas electors would be disabled from voting for both of them.[51] This co-inhabitancy cloud did not coalesce in 2000 into more than a cumulus, as the counting controversy in Florida took and held center stage in the election drama. But the possibility does serve to highlight the potential mischievousness of the provision.

If electors from Texas—or any other state—should be disabled from voting for their party's candidates for both president and vice president, it seems clear that the electors would be "electors appointed" for purposes of determining the necessary majority. After all, they could hardly vote for even one office if they had not been "appointed." In the 2000 election, if the Texas electoral votes for Cheney had been disqualified at the congressional joint meeting, then Cheney would not have had the requisite majority to be selected vice president, but neither would Joseph Lieberman, the Democratic vice-presidential candidate. The Senate would have been called upon to decide. That would have been bad enough, but in addition the Constitution treats the two executive offices as fully equivalent for the inhabitancy limitation. Had a challenge been successfully leveled at votes for Bush rather than Cheney, it would have been the greatly more troublesome House procedure that was called into play. The result could then have been a Bush-Lieberman administration, or a Gore-Cheney one. While not in accord with the prevailing party-based understanding of the way the system is to operate, I suggested in Chapter Four that these possibilities might not in themselves be the worst fates to befall the land. But the process of getting there would surely be rancorous in the extreme.

While courting problems, none of the bases mentioned for disqualifying electoral votes serves any contemporary purpose.[52] In a system where the electors are basically to cast votes determined at an earlier popular election, the day on which they meet, federal offices they might hold, the form of the certificates they submit, or indeed any procedural defect in their performance is irrelevant to fulfillment of their rather simple charge. Indeed, the very existence of electors as live functioning human beings[53] is irrelevant to fulfillment of their contemporary function as vessels for predetermined votes.

The situation is somewhat more complicated with the co-inhabitancy limitation, but not, I think, all that much. The original idea behind the limitation seems to have been to prevent the electors from voting parochially, at least with both their votes.[54] If the electors were to exercise judgment and discretion, then it might make sense to remove a temptation to favor local boys that might cloud their judgment. In truth, however, as I have been at pains to emphasize, the modern operation of the college leaves no legitimate room for elector discretion.

In contemporary terms, it is not elector but popular parochialism that might be thought at issue.[55] Popular parochialism is surely real, but it seems a relatively insignificant problem in the modern context of national political parties and of ease of travel and communication. We may know more about local figures, but information about our fellow citizens throughout the land is readily available. Moreover, there is already in place a better antidote for popular parochialism than the co-inhabitancy limitation. Political parties already seek a geographically balanced ticket in order to enhance their electoral chances.[56] Thus even the selection of Dick Cheney—the only modern example that even flirts with a co-inhabitancy transgression—was hardly the parochial choice of a local boy.[57] Cheney had been a congressman from a state other than Texas, and had held high national appointed office as well. In any event, the co-inhabitancy limitation serves no present-day purpose that seems at all comparable to the disservice it might do to having the electoral college processes conform to the contemporary understanding of the operation of the American presidential election.

We might choose to leave resolution of potentially mischievous electoral college problems like these to a future day when they might arise. The 1876 post-master problem, for instance, was handled correctly at both the state and the national level. The delayed Wisconsin votes were similarly handled properly in the joint meeting, if only after some soul searching. And in the 2000 election the Bush campaign seems to have appreciated the co-inhabitancy problem. It thus took preemptive steps by having Cheney distance himself from Texas.[58] The issue was never even joined at the joint meeting, and it seems most likely that any attempt to disqualify Texas electoral votes for either Bush or Cheney would have failed. It is true that the 1872 Arkansas electoral votes were mishandled, but that may well have been in part because of the leftover trauma of the Civil War.[59] Given this history, we might on balance simply trust to the good judgment of the various actors in the process, and in particular to the judgment of the joint meeting where the final decision in any future iteration of these questions would presumably be made.[60] Still, partisan juices can flow at that joint meeting. If one ground of objection is leveled, another could come in retaliation. And there do seem to be some steps that might be taken now to help ensure that the electoral college does not misfire on account of a collection of electoral college constitutional anachronisms.

Perhaps the simplest approach would be a formal precommitment through congressional resolution—or even legislation—that the joint meeting will count electoral votes reflective of a state's popular vote just as cast. This might be dressed up with some nominal sanction for a transgression, such as a formal admonition to the state to adhere in the future to required formalities. With or without the sanctions, this may strike some as disrespectful of the Constitution, but it should not. The Constitution, after all, is silent on the appropriate sanctions in each of the cases we have been discussing, and the joint meeting has typically counted the votes as cast. Indeed, as early as 1796, Thomas Jefferson took the position that the substance of electoral votes should be heeded regardless of procedural irregularities.[61] The simple fact of the matter is that these particular constitutional "infirmities" have—in the terms that should count—been rendered trivial by the march of time. Our constitutional law has never treated all provisions of the document as equally important, and it would be the height of folly to do so.[62] There should be nothing particularly jarring about nominal sanctions for violations of norms that have only nominal contemporary significance.

To be sure, it might still be possible for the joint meeting to ignore its prior commitment, indeed even to ignore legislation that instructed counting the votes in question. The meeting could plausibly insist that the requirements that were violated appear in the Constitution, so that the meeting has a constitutional duty to take them seriously, regardless of any legislation to the contrary. Partisan pressure could stimulate such an argument, and there is no way to forestall it, short of a constitutional amendment. Still, in the face of precommitment, precedent, and the democratic credentials of the votes that would be overridden, the call of the contemporary understanding of the presidential election process should be reasonably secure.

In closing this excursion into miscellaneous pitfalls in the electoral college process, I do not mean to suggest that we have exhausted the possibilities of problems, let alone provided airtight and comprehensive solutions to those we have discussed.[63] Even the simplest and most carefully constructed of election procedures can generate problems over time, for two related reasons. Social organization is simply too complicated to allow the wisest of decision makers to foresee all the problems that the march of time may throw in its way, even in relatively constrained contexts like elections. And inventive partisans can find give in any verbal formulation that attempts to corral the future. In the case of the electoral college, however, these ordinary infirmities are compounded many times, again for two related reasons. The system that we were given was not a simple one; and its practical operation has changed dramatically from what was originally envisaged. Short of starting all over—presumably through a constitutional amendment—we face the prospect of recurrent struggles. But we will do better in those struggles if we insist that it is the contemporary conception of the electoral college that must be served, rather than some awkward amalgam fed by elements that ceased long ago to serve any useful purpose.

CHAPTER TEN

Popular Election of the President
Without a Constitutional Amendment

The nonconstitutional reforms suggested in Chapters Six through Nine would go a long way toward taming the electoral college, reining in its potential for producing an accidental, a perverse, or a particularly costly choice for president of the United States. But there are those who insist that nothing short of a nationwide popular vote for president will do. I argued in Chapter Four that the case for such a nationwide vote is overstated, but also that the arguments offered in opposition are often strained as well. If those arguments pro and con are thought to be more or less in equipoise, the argument might be resolved against a nationwide popular vote because of the common assumption that it would require a constitutional amendment.[1] Constitutional amendment is difficult under the best of circumstances, but poses special problems for any direct move to substitute a nationwide popular vote for the electoral college provisions now in place. In this chapter, however, I want to suggest that constitutional amendment might not be necessary, at least at the outset, for institution of a nationwide popular vote for president.

As we saw in Chapters One and Four, amendment of the U.S. Constitution basically requires proposal by two-thirds of each house of Congress and then ratification by three-fourths of the states.[2] In some sense each and every person whose vote would be required for the change represents a particular state, either in the national legislature or in that of a state. This poses an initial formidable obstacle, because a large number of states either would be disadvantaged by a move to a nationwide vote, or officials within those states could well perceive that they would be disadvantaged.

To start with, opposition would almost certainly be widespread in less populous states. A state's electoral college delegation is equal to its total representation in the House and Senate, with the District of Columbia effectively given the state minimum of three electoral college votes by the Constitution's Twenty-Third Amendment.[3] The two-elector "bonus" that each state receives on account of its Senators gives less populous states a more favorable ratio of electors to population than is accorded to the more populous states. I will turn momentarily to why a perception of smaller-state favoritism may not reflect the political reality, but whatever the reality the favorable ratio gives great staying power to the perception that the electoral college favors the less populous states.[4]

The reality may actually be just the opposite, and appreciation—or at least a sense—of that reality would probably generate opposition among populous states. As we saw in Chapter Three, all states but two have long employed a winner-take-all system for selecting their electors. In winner-take-all states (including the District of Columbia), no matter how close the statewide popular vote, the entire electoral college delegation goes to the slate advanced by the party of the victor. Assuming faithfulness of electors, a voter in a populous state thus helps determine more electoral college votes than does a voter in a less populous state. The net result of the two elector "bonus" for less populous states and the winner-take-all rule is that voters in the states with very large delegations actually cast mathematically weightier votes than do voters in other states.[5] If we knew nothing about the distribution of political sentiment across the various states, in other words, we would have a greater chance of changing the outcome of the presidential selection process by changing the votes of a given number of voters in one of the most populous states with a winner-take-all rule than we would by changing the votes of the same number of voters in a less populous state (with or without a winner-take-all rule). The mathematical demonstration of a large state advantage is not nearly as straightforward as the small state favorable ratio, but it seems likely that officials in large states have an intuitive understanding of it nonetheless.

Of course, while we are not omniscient about the distribution of political sentiment across the various states, we do know a good deal more about it than "nothing." And it is obvious that a voter in a state that is closely divided among presidential candidates effectively casts a weightier vote than does one in a similarly populous but politically lopsided state. At least in recent years, there has been no mystery about this "swing state" importance, as candidates for president lavish time—and promises—on politically competitive states to the virtual exclusion of those where the outcome is foreordained.[6] This is not to say that candidates have free rein with regard to politically lopsided states. Those states presumably become politically one-sided in response to positions with which parties and candidates have been associated in the past. Radical change in those positions could jeopardize one current candidate's status, opening the way for gains by another. But there surely is a good deal of staying power to candidate and party positions, and to state inclinations. In combination, for any given election these provide a good deal of confidence in the inclusion and exclusion of states as capable of "swinging" one way or the other.

And finally, any attempt to define "winners" and "losers" from a move to a nationwide popular vote would take voter turnout into account. At the present time the states vary greatly in the turnout of eligible voters at the polls.[7] This is irrelevant to the size of a state's electoral college delegation, but would obviously take on great importance in a nationwide popular election. Greater turnout would give a state more say in selection of the president. To be sure, voter turnout would probably be affected by institution of a popular election. Indeed, one argument for the change is that it would encourage political parties in all states to "get out the vote." But if it can be assumed that a degree of turnout differential would continue, and that the present pattern gives some substantial indication of the likely pattern after the change, turnout identifies yet another perspective from which some states might gain and others lose from the move to a nationwide popular vote.[8]

The complications in identifying winners and losers from a nationwide vote might actually be thought to smooth the way to change. For if the change seems otherwise attractive, uncertainty about one set of consequences might cause the possibility to recede in perceived importance. But in fact the advantages of change are often difficult to grasp. Problematic elections like that of 2000 generate reform movements, but the victors in those elections will usually be unenthusiastic about change from what brought them success. And problematic elections are unusual. If several were to come in a row, a momentum for reform might grow, particularly if each of the major parties took some knocks along the way. But until that happens, the uncertainty about winners and losers from reform is most easily deployed to slow any reform movement down until the next election's normalcy brings it to a halt.

For these various reasons, direct election by constitutional amendment faces a tough uphill battle. There have been repeated attempts to fight that battle over the years, and they have ended in defeat after defeat. But there is a simple way to skirt the necessity of amendment. Some lessons about how this might be done are provided by the history of elections for the U.S. Senate.

The Constitution originally provided for selection of senators by state legislatures—the same bodies still charged with determining the "manner" in which presidential electors are to be chosen.[9] The Seventeenth Amendment now provides for direct popular election of senators, but that amendment was not the simple result of convincing a reluctant Congress and then lining up the requisite number of states. Instead a number of states introduced direct election into their own processes in more and less informal ways, thus forcing the issue at a national level well before the Seventeenth Amendment was finally ratified in 1913.

Some of the pressure built spontaneously. In the 1858 Illinois senatorial battle, for instance, the two major political parties had made their senatorial favorites known before the state legislative elections. The fabled series of debates around the state between the Republican Abraham Lincoln and the Democrat Stephen Douglas took on their formal electoral significance as arguments for state legislative candidates who, once seated, would cast their votes for the one senatorial "candidate" or the other. When the debates concluded, the state legislators could hardly have felt completely free to turn to others than the debaters for their choice.[10]

As populism and the progressive movement gained steam toward the end of the century, a number of states then experimented with measures that would draw the electorate into the process in more structured ways. With Oregon often taking the lead, states experimented with nonbinding senatorial primary, or even general, elections and various forms of pressure on state legislators to accede to the popular choice.[11] By one estimate, the result was that by 1910—three years before adoption of the Seventeenth Amendment—fourteen of the thirty newly chosen senators had been the product of *de facto* statewide popular election.[12]

Now what does this teach about the electoral college? We saw in Chapter Eight that state legislatures are said to have "plenary" power in establishing the "manner" of appointment of electors.[13] As we also saw in that chapter the emphasis on the expansiveness of state power led to quite serious discussion during the Florida counting drama following the 2000 presidential balloting about the possibility that the state legislature would repudiate the electoral mechanism for choosing electors and itself name a slate of electors—after the election had been conducted. While a postelection preemptive move like that would have raised serious constitutional questions,[14] it seems clear that in the period leading up to the balloting a state legislature's "plenary" power would extend to doing away with popular election of electors and naming the state's electors itself.

Several state legislatures opted to name the electors in the first several presidential elections. That was, of course, before popular election became the norm for selection, and today renunciation of popular election of electors may not be politically feasible for any state legislature—save perhaps in the sort of politically charged atmosphere that prevailed in Florida as the recount was proceeding. But there is every reason to think that the legal power remains. In Chapter Eight, we fashioned an approach to dealing with the disruption that third-party candidates might cause by indulging in an assumption that a strictly binding statewide popular election for electors was not required. Contingencies could be introduced, as they had been in early presidential elections. Proceeding on a similar assumption here that states retain a degree of flexibility can open the way to a mechanism through which a small number of state legislatures might break a path to a nationwide popular election.

There would seem to be no obstacle to a state legislature's providing *beforehand* that its electoral college delegation would be that pledged to the winner of the *nationwide* popular vote. At the extreme, if states with just 270 electoral votes—the required majority in the electoral college given its present size of 538—adopted such an approach, the popular vote winner would perforce win the presidency. Under the electoral college allocations that were produced by the 2000 census, a mere eleven states—those with the largest populations, of course—controlled 271 electoral votes.[15] Eleven states is, of course, many fewer than the three-fourths required for a constitutional amendment (to say nothing of the requirement of congressional approval by a two-thirds vote of each house).

To be sure, those populous states might be reluctant. We have seen that arguably some of them have the most to lose. But *de facto* popular election could be accomplished by fewer than eleven states. If just California and Texas—the two states that, starting with the 2004 election, had the largest electoral college delegations,[16] and which seem to have opposed party inclinations at the present time—would adopt such a rule, the chances of a disparity between the electoral college and popular votes would be pretty close to the vanishing point.

To begin with, California and Texas had eighty-nine electoral votes between them after the congressional reapportionment worked by the 2000 census.[17] If the popular vote loser started out eighty-nine or more votes behind, he would be hard pressed to overcome that obstacle.[18] In addition, the move would affect campaigning. At the present time, candidates employ "electoral college" strategies, targeting states with sufficient electoral college votes to win. They can do this basically without independent concern about the nationwide popular vote. With the suggested move by California and Texas, however, presidential candidates would be forced to alter that approach radically, devoting energy and resources to getting out the vote in all states. Deprived of the ability to pursue an electoral college strategy single mindedly, they would be even less likely than they have been historically to secure an electoral college win without winning the popular vote. There would still be a mathematical chance of their doing so, of course, but much less of a real world chance.[19]

Of course, California and Texas are among the states that arguably have the most to lose. We will return to that complication shortly, but it seems quite likely that even less populous states could start a ball rolling. Adoption by the swing (and occasionally adventuresome) state of Wisconsin—with ten electoral votes in the last election—would tilt the system toward popular election. Combinations of states with a larger total of electoral votes—Colorado and Oregon with a total of sixteen votes, for instance, or Missouri and Minnesota with a total of twenty-one—would increase the odds further.

The incentive to pursue the nationwide popular vote would operate to some degree even if adopting states were all of the same political complexion, but in a closely competitive political context, that incentive would presumably be felt more strongly by the party that had had parts of its reliable base put at risk. For that reason, the move would probably be politically feasible only if undertaken by a combination of states across the political divide. I chose the states mentioned above because at the present time they appear to meet that condition.

When I first suggested this possibility at a conference held at Northwestern University after the 2000 election, it was greeted with some skepticism by several knowledgeable electoral college commentators.[20] The skepticism was not about the legality of my suggestion, but about its political practicality. While the doubters did not elaborate, the skeptical argument presumably goes something like this: in a state that leans solidly in presidential elections toward one of the two major political parties, adherents of that dominant party would be risking the loss to its candidate of the state's electoral votes, with nothing to show in return. And even in a state fairly evenly divided between the major political parties, those holding political power from each of the major parties would be wary of having the state's electoral votes possibly go to the loser in the statewide popular vote. Any party that was temporarily ascendant in such a presidential "swing" state, moreover, might hope to translate that ascendancy into presidential votes under the present system, and indeed into presidential "coattails" for state and local candidates. These possibilities would be lost by adoption of the nationwide popular vote.

This analysis seems largely sensible, but the political calculus might be more complex, leaving room for advocates of "reform" to employ arguments of political self-interest. Consider, for instance, populous lopsided states like California and New York in both the 2000 and 2004 elections. As we saw in Chapter Four, at present these states are largely neglected by presidential candidates, because it makes no sense under an electoral college strategy to expend resources there—for either the presumptive winner or loser. This would change if the nationwide vote mattered, and party operatives in the state—of both major parties—might occasionally find the change beneficial. They might, for instance, relish the coattail effect for state and local candidates. Both parties could simultaneously harbor this sentiment, either because they assessed the net effects differently on races for the same state or local offices, or because they focused on different offices. The same might be said to a lesser extent of smaller lopsided states, for if the president were chosen through a nationwide vote, those states would surely receive more campaign attention than they now do.

Next, putting aside a state's political leanings, the two-senator "bonus" and winner-take-all advantages for small and large states respectively do leave a group of states that are clearly disfavored by electoral college math. For the 2004 election, for instance, and still assuming that we know nothing of the political complexion in the states, Montana had voters with the least chance per voter to change the presidential outcome. This is because it was the most populous state with just three electoral votes. Counting Montana, a total of thirty-one states, ranging in population up through Maryland (ten electoral votes), had presidential voting power in the 2000 election less than 1.2 times that of Montana voters.[21] In comparison, California voters had 2.663 times the chance of a Montana voter of changing the electoral outcome, while Texas voters had 1.891 times. If they came to appreciate this mathematical weighting in favor of the most populous states, a selection of states in this broad middle of the population spectrum might view a move to nationwide popular election quite favorably.[22] Those thirty-one states commanded 181 electoral votes in the 2000 election.

And finally, receptivity to change might be affected by continuing political fallout of the 2000 and 2004 elections. With a favorite son who won the presidency twice in the new century—once with the popular vote on his side and once without—lopsided Texas (thirty-four electoral votes in 2004) would seem unlikely to view the change with sympathy. For Floridians (twenty-seven electoral votes) and Ohioans (twenty electoral votes), in contrast, a nationwide popular vote might hold some appeal. Those two states received special attention in turn in the last two elections, because they were closely contested populous states on which the election outcomes seemed likely to turn. Given that background each might find that a nationwide popular vote would cast it back into a welcome state of relative electoral anonymity.

I am not necessarily suggesting that the time is ripe for a move to a nationwide popular vote. Given the relatively decisive victory of their candidate in the 2004 election, Republicans are likely to be wary of change. But the complications do counsel that the state and local incentives may not be so monolithically adverse as is sometimes assumed. A coalition of twelve to fifteen states in the middle of the population spectrum, for instance, could put together a package of electoral votes that would be hard for candidates to resist. Or, if just a few states traditionally associated with reform were to team up with anonymity-seeking Florida and Ohio, an irresistible package of one hundred electoral votes to be awarded to the winner of the nationwide popular vote would be easy to achieve.

Whatever the possibilities for one state going it alone, or some combination taking the action independently, it seems clear that one state would be more likely to make the move if it could be assured that others would join in. The less populous states could only hope to have a dramatic impact if a significant group of them banded together. And resistance would surely be fierce to any populous lopsided state going it alone. Success might thus depend crucially on whether there are mechanisms available by which states could act in concert. There would seem to be three possibilities for facilitating such coordination. These are: (1) political proselytizing by private groups and individuals; (2) overt agreement among several states; and (3) contingent legislation passed independently in several states. I take up these possibilities in turn.

One of the most visible and dramatic political reform movements in recent years has been that behind legislative term limits. Spurred on in many cases by wealthy individuals, no fewer than twenty-two states adopted term limits between 1990 and 1994.[23] The term limit movement is thus suggestive of the influence private individuals might bring to bear in any struggle for a popular vote for president. One very important similarity between the term limit movement and any push for popular election of the president is that in each context a state acting alone would arguably pay a substantial price for doing so. In the case of popular election of the president, a state might see its popular vote winner lose the election because of its move. In the case of term limits—for federal legislators—the most obvious cost was loss of the opportunity for a state's legislators to accumulate seniority and the greater influence in Congress that typically accompanies seniority. Because of this price, most congressional term limit measures made the action contingent upon similar action in a stated number of other states.[24] I will turn shortly to the possibility of contingent legislation in a move for nationwide popular election of the president. But the term limit example does show that even a large political price need not be fatal to a reform measure.

At the same time, term limit proponents may have had a very important advantage over those who might advocate popular election of the president. In the initial rush of requirements, the popular initiative process was used in all term limiting states but one, and even in the one legislative action was prompted by the threat of a popular initiative.[25] It seems fairly clear that a determined group pushing for a measure that might disserve a state's political interests would have more chance with the initiative process than with hard-headed—and self-interested—state legislators. But the Constitution provides that a state's electors are to be appointed "in such manner as the legislature thereof may direct."[26] It is an open question whether the popular initiative qualifies as action by the "legislature" under this provision. As we saw in Chapter Four, Colorado had a popular initiative on the ballot in the 2004 election that would have awarded its electors in proportion to the popular vote. The initiative had been challenged in court on several grounds, including that an initiative is not action by the state legislature.[27] But the initiative went down to defeat, and we have no definitive decision on this question. If popular initiative is not a viable option for changing the "manner" of state designation of electors, the lessons from the battles over term limits are much less compelling.

Still, a group of states might agree among themselves that each would pass nationwide popular vote legislation. Agreement might, for instance, be reached initially by the chief executives of the states or by officials responsible for administering election laws. These officials could not bind the state legislatures. Indeed a state legislature could not foreclose its ability to change the method of selection for future presidential contests. But an agreement among officials from a variety of states might be a mechanism for getting the process under way.

The Compact Clause of the U.S. Constitution has to be reckoned with, however. That clause requires congressional approval when one state enters into "any agreement or compact with another state."[28] Congressional approval seems quite unlikely for a nationwide popular vote initiative, but I doubt that approval would be required for this state cooperation. First, since the eventual decision is for the state legislature, and it would not be bound by any understanding reached by executive officials, it is not clear that any "agreement or compact" would be involved for any executive-based understanding, even giving those words a literal reading.[29] In addition, the Supreme Court has construed the clause narrowly, even as applied to binding agreements with legislative action.

There is some language in Supreme Court decisions that might suggest that the clause applies. The standard most generally employed for Compact Clause applicability is that the clause is "directed to the formation of any combination tending to the increase of political power in the States, which may encroach upon or interfere with the just supremacy of the United States."[30] Standing alone this might not be troubling, for presidential selection is organized around the states. No "supremacy of the United States" would thus be challenged by a move to a nationwide popular vote. But in the most recent case using this formulation, the Supreme Court also said that it did not "see how the statutes in question either enhance the political power of the . . . [agreeing] States *at the expense of other States* or have an 'impact on our federal structure.'"[31] The case involved coordinated activity by Massachusetts and Connecticut to move toward regional banking, a matter far afield from presidential selection. And more generally, the litigated Compact Clause cases have largely concerned boundary settlements or commercial and regulatory initiatives by groups of states. Given this context, "enhancement" of political power might be taken to refer solely to attempts to encroach on regulatory power at the federal level, where nonagreeing states would otherwise have a say through their elected representatives. This would also seem to accord with the animating purpose of the clause, which, as suggested above, was to ensure that the then quite powerful states did not encroach on the just powers of the nascent federal government.[32] Whatever the background of the use of the phraseology, however, the language of "enhancement" of political power "at the expense of other States" could invite Compact Clause challenge to state legislation incorporating the nationwide popular vote in the state's designation of its electors.

Even if understood to apply to such legislation, it is far from clear that "compacting" states could be seen as violating the clause because they were "enhancing" their political power.[33] Florida or Ohio might seek cover from any post-election limelight, but as large competitive states the *real world* voting power of its voters would, as we have seen, be severely *diminished* by the suggested change. The large, politically lopsided states, in contrast, might seek more candidate attention. While that could be understood as seeking more political power, we have also seen that a nationwide popular vote would arguably diminish the *theoretical* voting power of their voters.

Among the states that might be tempted to make the suggested change, it is the mid-level population group that could most plausibly be charged with seeking enhanced political power. Even as to these states, however, any judgment of "enhancement" requires a baseline for comparison. Against a baseline of the present exercise of presidential voting power, those middling population states would be seeking enhancement. But the present allocation that disfavors them is largely produced by the move to winner-take-all, which is anything but inherent in the electoral college scheme. If the baseline were derived solely from the textual provisions for electoral college apportionment, electoral college voting power per voter would presumably diminish as state population grew. That is the effect of the two-senator "bonus," the only explicit constitutional provision that bears on relative state influence in the choice of president. By this measure, the midpopulation states would not be "enhancing" their political power, but recapturing power lost mostly to the larger states with the move to winner-take-all.

More generally, there is a decided awkwardness in assessing the suggested change in terms of the allocation of state political power. After a move to a nationwide popular vote, every voter would have a fully equivalent say in the election of the president. The states would not retain their individual significance *qua* states in the selection process. In this sense there would be no state power after the change with which to judge the enhancement question. If one reached out for a measure of state power after the change, moreover, the most plausible candidate would be the state's proportion of the nationwide vote (or perhaps of eligible or registered voters). That proportion would be related only roughly to some present measure of state power. In fact, incentives would change radically under a nationwide popular vote. Voter turnout might increase generally, as candidates scrambled for votes wherever they could find them. The degree of turnout in any particular state would depend on political calculations by candidates and on incentives of state party organizations. A state's influence after the suggested change, in other words, is highly contingent and unpredictable, providing only the most fragile basis for making any "enhancement" judgment.

Reasonably close analogues to a move to a nationwide vote facilitated by state coordination are found in the several attempts over the last twenty years or so to institute regional presidential primaries. These have been facilitated by understandings produced by regional Governors' Associations, Legislative Conferences, and Councils of State Governments. Model legislation to rotate regional primaries was produced by the National Association of Secretaries of State.[34] These efforts have likely been motivated by concern that states that hold primaries alone and late lose effective say in the choice of presidential candidates. Thus against a baseline of the *status quo ante*, these were efforts to "enhance" political power in the presidential selection process. And as with the suggested coordination of moves to a nationwide popular vote for president, the individual states remained free to adopt or reject the regional primary possibility after the interstate coordination. None of these efforts seem to have met any Compact Clause challenge. Perhaps this suggests a judgment by those states that would have lost political power from regional primaries that no such challenge was likely to succeed.

For these reasons, a degree of state coordination in the move to a nationwide popular vote seems likely to survive any Compact Clause challenge. But while existing precedents are far removed from the presidential selection context, language in them is sufficiently suggestive that the possibility of a successful challenge cannot be entirely discounted. For that reason, the mechanism of state coordination that seems most promising is contingent legislation, to which I now turn. Here I build on the use of contingencies that we introduced in the discussion of third-party candidacies in Chapter Eight.[35]

A state that was attracted by the nationwide vote possibility, but concerned about going it alone, could pass legislation that made the selection of its electors by reference to the nationwide vote contingent on similar moves by other states. The initial states might, for instance, move cautiously at first, by tying their electoral votes to the nationwide popular vote only if a stated number of other states (or of states with a given number of electoral votes) followed suit. Or if they were politically lopsided states concerned with ensuring political balance in the move, they could express the contingency in terms of political balance, perhaps by reference to how state electoral votes were cast in the prior election. Too much inventiveness might, however, be the enemy of success. Adoption of a variety of devices by different states might weaken the chances of any one of them catching on. Still, if a few states took the plunge in one form or another, others might well follow, just as the movement for popular senatorial elections gained momentum over time. Opposition to a constitutional amendment could then quickly dissolve, just as it did back then.

In finding that a regional banking initiative pursued through statutes passed by Massachusetts and Connecticut did not violate the Compact Clause, the Supreme Court mentioned "several . . . classic indicia of a compact." One of those was that neither state's "statute is conditioned on action by the other State." In isolation, this might cast a Compact Clause shadow over contingent legislation. But the shadow does not seem to be a particularly dark one. We have seen that not even overt cooperation between states would likely run afoul of the Compact Clause. And in its list of "indicia" of compact, the Court also mentioned that a state be bound not to "modify or repeal its law unilaterally." Contingent popular vote legislation would not bind a legislature. And finally, the Court listed "reciprocation" of banking privileges as "most important" among its "indicia" of a compact.[36] In the case of contingent nationwide popular vote legislation, there is no occasion for reciprocation.

Contingent legislation *simpliciter*, in short, does not involve the sort of exchange relationship that would seem to be the *sine qua non* of a compact among states. There is also ample precedent for state legislation where effectiveness is contingent on action by other states. Reciprocal privileges of various sorts became "common in state legislation" long ago.[37] We saw that congressional term limit initiatives made use of requirements that a stated number of other states adopt comparable measures. For these reasons, contingent legislation seems to present no serious legal problems as a vehicle for a nationwide vote provision.

Implementing legislation should also deal with problems that might develop in the determination of just who is the winner of the nationwide popular vote. As we saw in Chapter Three, each state conducts an official canvass of the statewide popular vote, and under federal law submits the totals to the archivist of the United States as part of the state's "certificate of ascertainment." These are reported as totals for "electors pledged to" a particular candidate, or the like, but there is no obstacle to translating that designation into popular votes for the candidates. That is what the mass media regularly do. Until recently a small number of states allowed individual votes for electors rather than requiring the selection of an entire slate associated with a particular candidate. Even in those states, however, the names of the presidential candidates now appear, and voters regularly denominate one of them, with the state then translating that into a designation of the entire slate of electors pledged to that candidate.

To be sure, states have in the (distant) past dispensed with the popular vote as a mechanism for choosing electors, and they could presumably do so in the future. The possibility that some state might end the popular vote for president seems sufficiently remote that legislation could safely ignore it. But in an excess of caution an enacting state might want to deal with the possibility that less than the present fifty-one jurisdictions would calculate the popular vote. This could be dealt with by providing that the nationwide popular vote would be used if a stated minimum of states provided statewide counts, by dispensing with the popular vote mechanism if any jurisdictions did away with popular election, or simply by using the popular vote in those states that did employ it.

A potentially more serious problem in determining the nationwide popular vote winner is timing. State law typically requires an "expeditious" canvass of the state vote, but under federal law the certificate of ascertainment containing the state count need only be filed "as soon as practicable after the conclusion of the appointment of the [state's] electors,"[38] that is, election day. We have seen that electors meet and vote about forty days later.[39] A lopsided state that wanted to be uncooperative might conceivably be able to designate a popular vote winner—and hence its electors—without a definitive popular vote count. As far as *federal law* is concerned, the state might then in the name of "impracticability" delay its definitive calculation until near the end of that forty-day period, creating difficulty for states that made the nationwide vote determinative.

Allegations of fraud or other irregularities, such as those the nation witnessed in Florida in the 2000 election, could also create counting problems. We have seen the argument that making the nationwide vote determinative would encourage additional challenges on these grounds throughout the country.[40] And an uncooperative state might refuse to take allegations seriously if its own popular vote left no doubt about the identity of its electors. Long overdue improvement of voting machinery and procedures in many parts of the country would facilitate the counting process, but even without such reform, these counting problems seem largely theoretical. If it were understood beforehand that the nationwide popular vote is relevant, greater diligence by those concerned with the vote totals could be expected, in close and lopsided states alike. Pressure from news media and interested constituencies would make it very difficult for wary election officials to keep secret the information they did possess. It would then be surprising if a state's popular vote total were not available at least a few days before the electors meet. And a state statute could make the nationwide vote decisive even if a precise count were not available at the time electors had to be named. For even if one state's votes were being recounted or challenged up to the last minute—or one or more state officials was being uncooperative—the vote in the rest of the nation would have to be unusually close to put the winner of the nationwide popular vote in doubt. The problem would become truly serious only in extraordinarily close elections—even closer than the 2000 election, where the popular vote margin of over 500,000 was quite close by historic standards. While these practical considerations make it unlikely that useable nationwide vote totals would not be available in time for a state requiring them to designate its electors, the possibility could also be dealt with through contingencies in the legislation. The choice of electors could, for instance, be referred initially to the statewide vote and then to the nationwide vote only where it could be ascertained with some stated degree of confidence.

This route to change also finesses—initially at least—some tricky subissues. It avoids the question of whether a popular vote winner need obtain a majority of the vote, or only a stated plurality instead—as well as the associated question of whether a runoff should be required if no candidate receives the stated plurality. We discussed these problems in Chapter Four. Each state could define its own popular vote trigger and provide for contingencies (within its control) if that trigger proved indecisive.

In addition, any full move to a nationwide popular vote would have to take seriously the definition of eligibility to vote for president. As we saw in Chapter Four, under the original constitutional scheme, qualifications to vote were set at the state level and in fact varied quite a bit. We also saw that state discretion is now greatly hemmed in by constitutional and statutory restrictions. States cannot discriminate with regard to the vote on the basis of race or sex or against those over seventeen. They cannot impose poll taxes or English literacy tests or onerous residence requirements. But states retain the formalities of control over voter qualifications, and a number have exercised that discretion, most notoriously to withhold the vote from classes of felons and ex-felons. A very few states allow even incarcerated felons to vote, while others go to the opposite extreme and extend the disability to ex-felons. Observers of the 2000 election will recall that large numbers of Floridians were disenfranchised on this ground, and that confusion about the eligibility of some persons entered into the Florida counting controversy.[41] In addition, states impose varying registration requirements for voters (including varying deadlines), and these can be powerful determinants of voter turnout in a state.[42] In any event, there is a decided dissonance in instituting a nationwide popular vote for president but continuing state-by-state variations in eligibility requirements. We touched on that point in Chapter Four. The suggested change in a state's approach to designating electors accepts that dissonance, leaving resolution to any later full adoption of a nationwide vote.

State adoption of the nationwide vote as the determinant of its award of electoral votes would also avoid the question of the voting status of U.S. citizens who live in overseas territories of the United States or in foreign countries. The sure if halting movement in the United States over the years toward "universal" adult suffrage[43] has largely ignored the voting status of these American citizens, but if they are seen as genuine "members" of the American polity, it is not immediately apparent why they have no say in the electoral process. Puerto Ricans constitute the largest group of these citizens, and at the present time they have no vote in the choice of president unless and until they take up sufficiently stable residence in a state to establish voting rights there. There is a federal statute—of doubtful constitutionality[44]—that allows Americans living abroad to vote in federal elections through a state with which they had some substantial prior relationship, but no vote is accorded to those without such a prior state relationship. If we ever got to the point of serious consideration of a constitutional amendment instituting a nationwide popular vote, proponents of a nationwide vote might opt for the status quo in order to avoid controversy about the issue. But the question of extension of the franchise to one or both of these categories of U.S. citizens might prove sufficiently contentious that it alone would doom the effort.

The nonconstitutional mechanism suggested here for instituting a nationwide popular vote for president would initially skirt this set of issues, since it would simply leave the calculation of the nationwide vote to whatever state laws contribute to the totals in each state. This would mean, however, that state variations not only in qualifications to vote, but in other matters that affect election turnout, gave some states disproportionate say in the nationwide count. In addition to felon enfranchisement patterns, and other variable voting qualifications, for instance, states differ in the stringency of the procedures they require for voter registration. Over time pressure to regularize requirements across states would likely build, and recognition of that issue might well bring the overseas territory and foreign residence issues into focus as well. Such regularization would presumably require constitutional amendment. The result might be to force a constitutional amendment onto the nation's agenda, just as happened with state experimentation with the process of selecting U.S. senators.

Despite the problems, this indirect approach to a nationwide popular vote for president is actually more enticing in some ways than was the insinuation of popular voting into senatorial selection. The action of one state in moving toward popular election of senators brought no leverage on other states, save as the example might embarrass other states, or persuade on the merits. In the presidential context, on the other hand, a very few states have the capacity dramatically to tilt the entire system toward direct election. While I certainly would not predict it, the appeal to reformist zeal just might prove tempting.

CHAPTER ELEVEN

Conclusion

The electoral college is much too complex for its own good. The complexity is a product of several reinforcing influences. One is the division of function between the federal government and the fifty-one separate jurisdictions entitled to electors. The states and the District of Columbia determine the "manner" of selecting electors, but the Congress determines some matters of timing for those electors, and in addition the electoral votes are counted before a joint meeting of the two houses of the Congress. A second source of complexity is the original idea of the electoral college as a far-flung set of independent deliberative bodies, chosen in various ways as each state should decide. The march of events has left this vision behind, in favor of a very different modern electoral college in which political parties nominate candidates for president and vice president, and each state holds a popular election to determine how its allotted votes will be cast for the two offices. A simple cumulation of those allotted votes determines the winners. Because of the original conception, however, the constitutional provisions for the college contain a number of requirements that are unnecessary for—and fit quite uneasily into—its modern operation. Those requirements are "constitutional," however, and for that reason alone are difficult to put aside.

Yet a third generator of difficulty is ongoing uncertainty about many elements of the first two. Ironically, this can be traced to the usual success of the electoral college in designating a presidential winner. By the lights of the modern conception of the way the college is to operate, the choice of the nation's president and vice president typically proceeds rather smoothly. Human beings are notoriously given to discounting too much the likelihood of some unlikely events. This inclination seems often to be compounded in the political process. This then contributes to a nagging uncertainty about many elements of the electoral college scheme, as possible but unlikely difficulties from the division of function among state and federal bodies and from anachronistic constitutional provisions are ignored. The result in the case of the electoral college is that the meaning and implications of many of its elements are not probed, and there is seldom any move to anticipate problems and deal with them before they arise.

But every once in a while, one or another of the elements that was readily ignored causes trouble. The system responds awkwardly, but seldom more comprehensively than is necessary to get through the difficulties of the moment. In part this is because public decision making in the United States is heavily reliant on the same political parties that have become central actors in the contemporary understanding of the presidential election process. They often approach in partisan fashion the resolution of electoral college problems that do arise. Once the immediate problem is resolved, the most comfortable next step is typically to put the recent troubles out of mind, lest accustomed prerogatives come under attack. The next election is likely to proceed smoothly enough, and when that happens the country embraces again the assumption that all is well in the modern operation of the electoral college.

That seems a fair description of what happened in the first two elections of the Twenty-First Century. In the 2000 election, the popular vote in Florida in particular was very close. The state's statutory provisions for challenges and recounts had not previously been applied in presidential elections, and many of its requirements were confusing or uncertain in that context. Federal statutory time limits clearly impinged on the state processes, but less clear was how severely they impinged, just how much time the state had to come up with a final determination of the winning slate of electors. Also unclear were the implications of inability to resolve those uncertainties in whatever time was available. Perhaps the Florida legislature could step in to preempt the counting difficulties. Or perhaps the state would simply abstain in the final tabulation. The outcome of the presidential election could turn on resolution of such questions. And partisan decision making seemed to lurk in every corner, both on a state and a federal level.

In 2000, the way out of the difficulties was unexpectedly forged by the U.S.

Supreme Court. The judicial solution was awkward at best, with the Florida electoral votes determined without a full recount of the popular vote. The Supreme Court interpreted the Florida statutes to constrict the time frame for a recount, and on that basis concluded that there was no time to obtain a better count. Public commentary on the court's intervention was sharply divided, but the country seemed to accept the judicial solution. The most thoughtful of those who approved of the court's action did so on the ground that with partisan actors seemingly around every turn the court was the only body that could bring a degree of calm to a threatening storm.[1] Initially, many calls for electoral reform were heard, and a federal statute was passed that provided funds for improved balloting practices at the state level.[2] Interest in the mechanism of counting, and in the electoral college more generally, was then heightened as the 2004 election promised another cliffhanger. Instead, the second election of the century produced a reasonably smooth result by the lights of the contemporary understanding of the presidential selection process. The calls for reform then seemed to subside.

I know of no easy way comprehensively to sweep away the layers of electoral college complexity that threaten trouble every now and then. Had the 2004 election brought judicial intervention a second time, and particularly if that intervention had produced a different partisan outcome than that of 2000, perhaps the political forces in the country would have mustered the will for comprehensive reform. But comprehensive reform might provide no cure all, for there are widely divergent views on just what about the electoral college needs fixing. While a few items appear on most reform agendas, there is the most heated controversy about whether the modern operation of the electoral college—without the hidden complexities—is basically satisfactory. If the reform was pursued through a federal statute that compromised among different visions of a better way, it might just give us a different set of complexities and questions.

In addition it is commonly assumed that the most simple and sweeping of reform efforts would require constitutional amendment. Probably the single most popular of the reform proposals is a nationwide popular vote for president. Even that suggestion shrouds many important questions, including qualifications to vote in that election, and administrative responsibility for the count—and for any recount. Some workable resolution of those questions could probably be forged among those in favor of a nationwide vote, but amending the Constitution requires the assent of many actors who would perceive that a nationwide popular vote—or for that matter, any conceivable reform that would radically streamline the process—would disserve their constituencies. For this reason alone any reform through constitutional amendment would be very hard to achieve.

In an effort to find a way out of this tangle, I have offered a set of nonconstitutional solutions to the most serious problems that pose a threat to the wholesome contemporary operation of the electoral college. The two most glaring dangers are the possibility that "faithless" electors will determine the outcome of an electoral college choice, and that the electoral college will not be able to decide, necessitating recourse to the House of Representatives for selection of the president. This latter possibility could be produced by faithless electors, but it could result from a variety of other causes, including an electoral college tie between just two candidates and electoral votes for more than two candidates.

Some of the nonconstitutional solutions I offer are relatively straightforward and simple. Thus the possibility of an electoral college tie between the nominees of the two major parties could be significantly reduced if the size of the House of Representatives was increased by one member. That could be done by federal legislation and would result in a concomitant increase in the size of the electoral college, producing a college with an odd number of members instead of the present even number. A tie would still be possible, if there were one or a few abstentions or disqualifications of electors. But an odd number of electors would remove the most likely generator of an electoral college tie.

Solutions for other problems that I have identified are not so simple. To deal with the faithless elector problem I have suggested a uniform state law, to be adopted by each of the fifty-one jurisdictions that are entitled to electoral votes. A uniform law would, no doubt, have complexities, though nowhere near the present hodge-podge of varying state laws that often completely ignore the problem of faithless electors, but also often deal with that problem in one way or another. There are venerable American organizations that specialize in devising and advancing uniform laws. Some of the content of a uniform law on the faithless elector problem might prove contentious, but faithless electors serve no apparent purpose, so that widespread agreement on the need for such a law, and on much of its content, should be forthcoming.

The most serious problem in dealing with the faithless elector problem is getting the attention of legislatures in those states where faithless votes have never been cast and the problem thus might seem to be purely theoretical. A move to adopt a uniform state law would have the added advantage of providing a degree of visibility for the reform effort that might just cause normally distracted states to pay attention. Adoption of such a law by all fifty-one jurisdictions that choose electors would, to be sure, require a great deal of time and effort. But if successful—even to the point of widespread if not universal adoption—the effort would be amply rewarded by dampening the risk of what is probably the single most disturbing possibility for electoral college trouble.

A uniform law at the state level might also be the vehicle for addressing the possibility of sending the selection process to the House on account of electoral votes for three or more candidates. The approach I suggest for dealing with that possibility is the introduction of contingencies into the states' elector selection mechanisms, so that in any case where third-party command of a state's electoral votes would cause an indecisive electoral college outcome the state votes would be diverted to a candidate with a real chance of prevailing in the electoral college. Recourse to the House would then not be necessary. But much more than with the faithless elector problem, use of a contingent approach to elector selection might, at least initially, prove divisive, and for that reason might appropriately be pursued outside the ambit of a uniform state law.

Justice Louis Brandeis once famously sang the praises of the states as the engines of experimentation to meet "changing social and economic needs." A "single courageous state," he urged "may . . . serve as a laboratory."[3] In the case of the electoral college, the invitation to experiment is especially clear, as the Constitution—fortified by Supreme Court decisions—vests the states with wide-ranging control over the "manner" of selection of its electors. In recent years, however, the states have basically given up experimenting as all but two have opted for a straight winner-take-all popular election of its slate of electors. I am no advocate of experimentation for its own sake, but the possibility of a stalemated electoral college on account of electoral votes for minor party candidates is real, and potentially quite destructive. If state contingencies in the award of their electors were to catch on in one or a few "courageous" states, others might then be tempted to explore the possibility.

There are also reforms beyond increase in the size of the House of Representatives that might usefully be pursued at the federal level. The joint meeting of the two houses of Congress where electoral votes are counted has assumed the authority to reject votes where infirmities appear. The process is to a great extent governed by the federal Electoral Count Act which was passed after the tumultuous 1876 election. That act is complex and ambiguous in ways that could cause problems. I have explored some of those difficulties and suggested responsive reforms, but others have probed the act in even greater detail.[4] Revision of the Electoral Count Act would no doubt be difficult to achieve as a political matter, but clarification of several points would be salutary.

Even more useful would be some indication from Congress in the form of a resolution that the joint meeting would abide by state results that were dictated by the uniform act on elector discretion that I have suggested. A resolution could also make clear that electoral votes would be counted even if they failed to comply with some of the requirements for the electoral college that remain in the Constitution, but that serve no contemporary purpose. These include requirements of the timing of meetings of electors and the procedures to be followed. But they also include qualifications of electors and an anachronistic limitation on the persons for whom a particular state's electors might vote. In the modern embodiment of the electoral college, none of these requirements serves any significant purpose. The chances of their nonetheless being put to partisan use could be considerably lessened by the suggested congressional resolution.

Even if the entire reform agenda I have suggested were adopted, the electoral college process would remain a complex one. Indeed, the suggestion of state experimentation with contingencies in their elector selection mechanisms might, at least initially, add to the complexity. Still, the agenda as a whole would simplify the process considerably and, more importantly, would introduce important insurance against unlikely, but potentially disastrous, events. This is not to say that the suggested reforms would address all conceivable problems. I am not sure that it is even possible to foresee all the problems that might plague the electoral college process. Inventive minds have certainly come up with many unlikely though possible electoral college scenarios that would spell trouble.[5] In this book I have only touched lightly on the range of possibilities, because I did not want to divert our focus unduly from what I judge to be the most pressing concerns.

I have not advocated an integrated nationwide popular vote for president, even though that would displace the electoral college complexity with a simplified process, the pitfalls in which would be much easier overall to anticipate and address. My hesitation is produced by a confluence of several admittedly uncertain assessments. I do believe that a nationwide vote would represent a degree of improvement if it could be achieved costlessly and quickly. At the same time I am doubtful that that degree of improvement would be more than modest if the most troublesome problems with the electoral college were corralled by the reform agenda I have presented. And institution of a nationwide vote would come neither costlessly nor quickly.

This would clearly be the case if a constitutional amendment were required. Short of two highly troublesome presidential elections in a row, adoption of a constitutional amendment providing for a nationwide vote is simply not in the cards. I have suggested, however, that a constitutional amendment might not be necessary for effectively bringing about a popular vote for president. Here too a few "courageous" states might forge the way through experimentation with the way they designate electors. For those whose cost/benefit calculations tilt decidedly in favor of a nationwide vote, this route provides an opening toward salutary reform. But there should be no illusion about the ease of accomplishing a nationwide vote through the nonconstitutional approach I have outlined.

Discussion of the electoral college and possible reforms would benefit greatly from more tempered rhetoric. Advocates of a nationwide vote should appreciate that, with or without the change they favor, decision making in American democracy will remain much more complex than the simple ideal associated with their plea for "one person, one vote." And advocates of retaining the electoral college must test their own preconceptions as rigorously as they question those of advocates of a nationwide vote. Defenders of the electoral college, for instance, decry the incentives that might accompany a nationwide popular vote, but romanticize the incentives that the electoral college creates. These defenders rightly point out that the electoral college process typically produces an outcome the country readily accepts, but they avoid taking seriously both the pain produced by the occasional mishap, and the far worse pain that lurks in the shadowy complexities of the electoral college scheme.

One glaring example of the excess of rhetoric is the attempt simultaneously to depict the electoral college as a brilliant invention of our constitutional framers and as wonderfully adaptable over time.[6] Whether or not the adaptation has been wonderful, the modern version of the electoral college bears scant resemblance to what those who devised it had in mind. It is not made up of discretion-laden electors, as they intended. Political parties are central to its operation, rather than absent—or at best peripheral—as they hoped and expected. The separate state meetings are not the disconnected deliberations they envisaged, but rather staged and coordinated proceedings orchestrated by those same political parties. The only respect in which the modern electoral college resembles what the constitutional framers had in mind is the allocation of electoral voting strength by states. And even that has been importantly transformed by near-universal state adoption of winner-take-all rules for awarding a state's electoral votes, a development that electoral college supporters tend to laud rather than lament. For better or worse, the system we have will have to find its justification in the way it actually operates—or perhaps in the pain associated with alternatives—rather than in some imagined attachment to the framers' farsighted brilliance. I am a great fan of the American constitutional system, but it cheapens the framers' accomplishment to lump their flawed innovations with their particularly insightful ones.

A dampening of the rhetoric would be particularly useful in allowing us to see the important areas of agreement about problematic aspects of the electoral college mechanisms. While there surely would be pockets of dissent, there is actually a broad consensus among serious commentators that both faithless electors and the contingent procedure for selection of the president in the House of Representatives are potentially quite mischievous. If those concerned about the electoral college could concentrate for a time on these areas of agreement, real progress might be achieved. There is, of course, nothing wrong with strenuous debate about the merits and demerits of a nationwide vote for president. But both supporters and detractors of the electoral college should appreciate that that debate could be rejoined after more serious problems are under control. Indeed, if the problems of faithless electors and of the House backup procedure were remedied, the more basic question of how to choose our president could be discussed with less distraction, and hence more clarity.

The electoral college is not the only aspect of American elections that merits reform. We need to improve the mechanics of voting,[7] and we sorely need to insulate the processes of voting and counting votes from officials with partisan politics prominent in their responsibilities and mentalities.[8] While difficult to address, these problems are easy to see, in a way that so many electoral college problems are not. Because it is both complex and usually successful, the electoral college is easily relegated to the background of the nation's reform concerns. That, however, is unfortunate. Selection of the president is the single most important and gripping event in American democracy. It engages the nation, as it does the world. There is no more serious concern we should have about American democracy than that the process of selection may work very badly.

In closing, let me mention an unavoidable concern I have felt throughout this effort. Much of my analysis is dependent on assessment of risks and of the quantum of damage to the body politic if one or another risk is realized. For instance, I believe that an electoral college tie between two candidates is more likely than an electoral college outcome dictated by faithless electors. At the same time, I believe that an electoral college vote that is determined by elector faithlessness would be much more troublesome even than selection of the president in the House of Representatives. I do not find the possibility of a president and vice president of different parties a seriously damaging prospect. And I have largely dismissed the possibility that the House, if called upon to choose among three candidates, would opt for the one who obtained the smallest number of votes in the electoral college. Similarly, I have found fit to put to the side the possibility in today's political world that if we moved to a nationwide popular vote a presidential candidate would win overwhelmingly in the largest states and lose overwhelmingly in all the rest. These and many like assessments have informed my discussions throughout this book. I would have preferred scientific measurement, but judgment after study and reflection was all I could provide. Others can, of course, second guess my assessments, but I do plead that perfection in that regard is not available, and that as far as the electoral college is concerned inaction in the face of uncertainty is the problem rather than the solution.

REFERENCE MATTER

Notes

Chapter One

1. This book courts enough trouble without delving into calendar controversies. I simply follow convention in placing the year 2000 in the Twenty-First Century rather than at the end of the Twentieth Century.

2. At least as a formal matter. It may be that the members are invited as individuals to inauguration events, and the like.

3. In the past commentators have regularly assumed that the public was largely ignorant of the role of the electoral college. *See, e.g.,* Lucius Wilmerding, Jr., The Electoral College vii–viii (Beacon Press 1958); Michael J. Glennon, When No Majority Rules 19, 67 (Congressional Quarterly, Inc. 1992); Robert M. Hardaway, The Electoral College and the Constitution: The Case for Preserving Federalism 101–2 (Praeger 1994); Lawrence D. Longley & Alan G. Braun, The Politics of Electoral College Reform 2, 68, 84 (Yale University Press 1972).

4. The modern use of the term "election day" is accurate enough, because the electors are chosen in elections, and in addition state and local elections are held in conjunction with the selection of presidential electors. In 1800, however, the term was used to refer to "the day designated by Congress for the presidential electors of each state to assemble in their respective capitals and vote." John Ferling, Adams vs. Jefferson 2 (Oxford University Press 2004).

5. *See* Glennon, *supra* note 3, at 23. Because of the other elections held at the same time, *see supra* note 4, the ballots can actually be quite long. The term is used to distinguish those ballots on which the electors' names do not appear (a "short ballot") from those on which they do.

6. *See* Chapter Seven.

7. *See* U.S. Const., Am. XII.

8. Neil R. Peirce, The People's President 93 (Simon & Schuster 1968). Those words

were written well before the 2000 election. They remain true unless, of course, the 2000 election is counted as part of the Twentieth Century. *See supra* note 1. In addition, it is possible that the 1960 election should be counted as one where the popular vote loser won in the electoral college. As discussed in more detail in Chapter Three, it is impossible to know who won the nationwide popular vote in 1960, since the Alabama ballot at the time listed only the electors. *See* Lawrence D. Longley & Neal R. Peirce, The Electoral College Primer 2000 46–59 (Yale University Press 1999).

9. *See* Chapter Four. The term derives from David W. Abbott & James P. Levine, Wrong Winner: The Coming Debacle in the Electoral College (Praeger 1991).

10. William H. Rehnquist, Centennial Crisis: The Disputed Election of 1876 3 (Alfred A. Knopf 2004).

11. *See* Chapter Three.

12. *See* Jones v. Bush, 122 F. Supp. 2d 713 (N.D. Tex. 2002), *aff'd without opinion*, 244 F.3d 134 (5th Cir. 2000), *cert. denied*, 531 U.S. 1062 (2001).

13. *See, e.g.,* State ex rel. Chappell v. Martinez, 536 So. 2d 1007 (Fla. 1988).

14. *See* Roe v. State of Alabama, 43 F.3d 574 (11th Cir. 1995); Roe v. State of Alabama, 52 F.3d 300 (11th Cir. 1995); Roe v. State of Alabama, 68 F.3d 404 (11th Cir. 1995).

15. Bush v. Gore, 531 U.S. 98 (2000) (*per curiam*).

16. The Court's remedy—calling a halt to the recount—has come in for especially harsh criticism across the ideological spectrum. *See, e.g.,* David A. Strauss, What Were They Thinking?, in The Vote: Bush, Gore & The Supreme Court 184, 188–89 (Cass R. Sunstein & Richard A. Epstein eds., University of Chicago Press 2001); Michael W. McConnell, Two-and-a-Half Cheers for Bush v. Gore, in The Vote, *supra*, at 98, 117–20.

17. In the 1876 election, a special commission played a large role in resolving election controversies, and that commission's membership included Supreme Court justices. *See* Chapter Three.

18. For just a sampling, *see* The Vote, *supra* note 16; The Longest Night: Polemics and Perspectives on Election 2000 (Arthur J. Jacobson & Michel Rosenfeld eds., University of California Press 2002); The Unfinished Election of 2000 (Jack N. Rakove, ed., Basic Books 2001); Richard A. Posner, Breaking The Deadlock: The 2000 Election, The Constitution, and the Courts (Princeton University Press 2001); Abner Greene, Understanding the 2000 Election (New York University Press 2001).

19. *See* U.S. Const., Art. I, § 2, cl. 1 ("The House of Representatives shall be composed of members chosen every second year by the people of the several states, and the electors in each state shall have the qualifications requisite for electors of the most numerous branch of the state legislature.") Under the original constitutional scheme, members of the U.S. Senate were chosen by the state legislatures. U.S. Const., Art. I, § 3, cl. 1. The Seventeenth Amendment now provides for popular election of senators as well,

with qualifications similarly tied to state electoral qualifications. U.S. Const., Am. XVII, cl. 1.

20. *See* U.S. Const., Ams. XV ("race, color, or previous condition of servitude"); XIX (sex); XXIV ("failure to pay any poll tax or other tax" for federal elections); XXVI (age, for those eighteen years or older); Harper v. Virginia State Bd. of Elections, 383 U.S. 663 (1966) (failure to pay poll tax in state elections); Katzenbach v. Morgan, 384 U.S. 641 (1966); Gaston County v. United States, 395 U.S. 285 (1969); Oregon v. Mitchell, 400 U.S. 112 (1970) (statutory limitation of English language literacy tests upheld).

21. In 1913 Illinois extended the right to vote for presidential electors to women, even as it held back from fully enfranchising women. This partial step was then emulated by a number of other states prior to the passage of the Nineteenth Amendment in 1920. *See* Alexander Keyssar, The Right to Vote: The Contested History of Democracy in the United States 401, Table A19 (Basic Books 2000).

22. *See generally*, Keyssar, *supra* note 21, at 62–63, 162–63, 302–3, 308. The Supreme Court rebuffed a constitutional challenge to this practice in Richardson v. Ramirez, 418 U.S. 24 (1974); *but cf.* Hunter v. Underwood, 471 U.S. 222 (1985).

23. *See* The Law of Democracy 43 (rev. 2d ed., Samuel Issacharoff, Pamela S. Karlan, & Richard H. Pildes, eds., Foundation Press 2002).

24. *See* Abby Goodnough, Election Troubles Already Descending on Florida, N.Y. Times, July 15, 2004, at A20, 24; Eric Lichtblau, Confusing Rules Deny Vote to Ex-Felons, Study Says, N.Y. Times, Feb. 20, 2005, http://www.freerepublic.com/focus/f-news/1347956/posts (last visited 02/02/05). The issue remains alive in the courts as well. *See* Linda Greenhouse, Supreme Court Declines to Hear 2 Cases Weighing the Right of Felons to Vote, N.Y. Times, Nov. 9, 2004, at A19.

25. After the People Vote xiii (3d ed., John C. Fortier, ed., AEI Press 2004). In the wake of the 2000 election, a privately supported commission on election reform was organized, with luminous membership and ample funding. Former presidents Ford and Carter served as honorary co-chairs. The commission made a series of recommendations, ranging from ensuring that ex-felons are allowed to vote to a host of measures designed to ensure greater turnout and fair processing of the vote. No recommendations were made for changes in the electoral college process. *See* National Commission on Federal Election Reform, To Assure Pride and Confidence in the Electoral Process (2001).

26. *See* Henry E. Brady *et al.*, Law and Data: The Butterfly Ballot Episode, in The Longest Night, *supra* note 18, at 50–63.

27. States can obtain federal funds for "improving, acquiring, leasing, modifying, or replacing voting systems and technology and methods for casting and counting votes." Help America Vote Act of 2002, § 101(b)(1)(F), Pub. L. 107–252, 116 Stat. 1666, 1669.

28. Perhaps most importantly provisional voting, stimulated by Section 302 of the Help America Vote Act, *supra* note 27. *See also* Edward Walsh, Enthusiasm Wanes For Election Changes; Bush, Hill Slow on Funds, Commission, Wash. Post, Sept. 16, 2003, at A09; Matthew Rodrigues, Mass. Election Overhaul Faulted Group Says State Lags in Two Areas, Boston Globe, Jan. 23, 2004, at B2.

29. *See* Jack N. Rakove, The E-College in the E-Age, in Unfinished Election, *supra* note 18, at 201–2.

30. In Chapter Four we will discuss some other proposals for reform of the electoral college, but "[t]he most popular reform plan is direct election." Judith Best, Weighing the Alternatives: Reform or Deform?, in The Longest Night, *supra* note 18, at 349. Illinois' Senator Richard Durbin's proposal for a constitutional amendment to institute a nationwide popular vote for president received particular attention. *See* 146 Cong. Rec. S11618 (daily ed. Dec. 6, 2000). *See also* Robin Toner, The 2000 elections, The Electoral College, Election Quandary Prompts Pop Civic Test, N.Y. Times, Nov. 9, 2000, at B8.

31. U.S. Const., Art. V.

32. *See* Alexander Keyssar, The Electoral College Flunks, New York Rev. of Books, March 24, 2005, at 18.

33. Abbott & Levine, *supra* note 9, at 139.

34. *See* Keyssar, *supra* note 32, at 18; Sanford Levinson & Ernest A. Young, Who's Afraid of the Twelfth Amendment, 29 Fla. St. U.L. Rev. 925, 973 (2001).

Chapter Two

1. *See generally* Tadahisa Kuroda, The Origins of the Twelfth Amendment 9 (Greenwood Press 1994). Quite apart from the issues on which we concentrate here, it is interesting to speculate on the incentives that a nationwide popular vote for president would have had for subsequent American history. For instance, assuming that states retained the discretion over voting qualifications they had long enjoyed, *see* Chapter One, a nationwide popular vote might well have resulted in women obtaining the right to vote much earlier than they did. Depending upon the other qualifications that were imposed, that move might have been an easy way for an individual state to double its say in the selection of the executive.

2. For a contemporary expression of this concern, *see* Judith Best, Weighing the Alternatives: Reform or Deform?, in The Longest Night: Polemics and Perspectives on Election 2000 347, 353 (Arthur J. Jacobson & Michel Rosenfeld, eds., University of California Press 2002).

3. U.S. Const., Art. I, § 2, cl. 3.

4. *See* Matthew J. Festa, The Origins and Constitutionality of State Unit Voting in the Electoral College, 54 Vand. L. Rev. 2099, 2109–20 (2001).

5. U.S. Const., Art. II, § 1, cl. 2.

6. U.S. Const., Art. II, § 1, cl. 4.

7. An Act relative to the Election of a President and Vice President of the United States, ch. 8, §1, 1 Stat. 239 (1792). *See* Kuroda, *supra* note 1, at 53. In 1845 Congress made the date for selection of electors (what we call presidential "election day") uniform as well. *See* 3 U.S.C. § 1 (2000), originally enacted as Act of Jan. 23, 1845, ch. 1, 5 Stat. 721. By that time, popular election was the "manner" of selection chosen by all states. *See* McPherson v. Blacker, 146 U.S. 1, 29 (1892).

8. *See* Jules Witcover, Crapshoot: Rolling the Dice on the Vice Presidency 12–26 (Crown Publishers 1992) (chapter 2, titled "Founding Fathers' Afterthought").

9. U.S. Const., Art. I, § 3, cl. 4.

10. U.S. Const., Art. II, § 1, cl. 6, now superseded (though not essentially changed in these respects) by the Twenty-Fifth Amendment.

11. *See* U.S. Const., Art. II, § 1, cl. 3. As we shall see, this was changed by the Twelfth Amendment, but even before it was passed, at least the Rhode Island electors in the 1792 election made explicit their separate choices for the two offices. Kuroda, *supra* note 1, at 60.

12. Federalist 68; *see* Federalist 64 (Jay) ("As the select assemblies for choosing the President . . . will in general be composed of the most enlightened and respectable citizens, there is reason to presume that their attention and their votes will be directed to those men only who have become the most distinguished by their abilities and virtue, and in whom the people perceive just ground for confidence").

13. U.S. Const., Art. II, § 1, cl. 2.

14. U.S. Senate Rep. No. 395, 43rd Cong., 1st. Sess. 3 (1874). A sampling of other authority to the same effect is collected in note 23, *infra*. The Senate Report continues:

> That the candidates for electors should be pledged in advance to vote for particular persons was not only not contemplated by the framers of the Constitution, but was expressly excluded by their theory. They were to be independent, not influenced by previous committals or engagements, so that when they came together they could deliberate with perfect freedom for the best interests of the Republic. How completely this theory has been overturned in practice for more than seventy years we need not recite. (Senate Rep. *supra*, at 3–4)

15. Walter Dellinger, In Defense of the Electoral College, Slate, http://slate.msn.com/id/2108991 (last visited 11/01/04). *See* Lucius Wilmerding, Jr., The Electoral College xi, 22 ("the Founding Fathers meant to invite but not to compel a popular appointment of Electors. . . . [W]e must look upon them as a medium for ascertaining the public will") (Beacon Press 1958). Robert M. Hardaway, The Electoral College and the Constitution: The Case for Preserving Federalism 9 (Praeger 1994) writes of "[m]yths and folklore, such as that the framers intended that an elite group of privileged electors would make

a choice independent of the will of the people," but the citation he provides for the proposition does not seem to lead anywhere. Hardaway also provides an account of the array of opinions on the role of electors, but it is nothing short of bizarre for him to conclude that "the strongest evidence [is] that the framers did not intend electors to exercise independent judgment." Hardaway, *supra*, at 86. This is particularly so in light of the fact that he also insists that faithless votes would have to be counted as cast regardless of state law that might have outlawed faithlessness, and that a court order before the vote that required faithfulness "would clearly violate the Constitution." Hardaway, *supra*, at 50. *Cf.* Martin Diamond, The Electoral College and the American Idea of Democracy, in After the People Vote 44, 47–50 (Walter Berns, ed., AEI Press 1992). Kuroda, *supra* note 1, at 15 presents a more nuanced view.

16. Dellinger, *supra* note 15. There is, of course, no necessary connection between belief that there has been no essential change in the electoral college and approval of its contemporary operation. Thus Alexander Bickel, one of the most ardent, articulate, and sage defenders of the electoral college, recognized that it long ago ceased to operate as those who fashioned it envisaged. Alexander Bickel, Reform and Continuity: The Electoral College, The Convention, and the Party System 4 (Harper & Row 1971). We will return to Bickel's views in Chapter Four.

17. Diamond, *supra* note 15, at 47–48.

18. *See also* Madison's Federalist 39, where he defines a "republic" as "a government which derives all its powers directly or indirectly from the great body of the people."

19. James Wilson's Summation and Final Rebuttal, Dec. 11, 1787, in 1 The Debate on the Constitution 850 (Bernard Bailyn, ed., The Library of America 1993).

20. Federalist 39, where Madison seems to express the opinion common among convention delegates that the House of Representatives fallback procedure, to which the text will turn shortly, would quite often be necessary, so that the eventual presidential selection would be made by "national representatives." *See also, e.g.*, Federalist 44; Federalist 45.

21. Particularly nice summaries of the various views presented in the convention on selecting the president—drawing on James Madison's notes on the convention proceedings—are provided in Paul Boudreaux, The Electoral College and Its Meager Federalism, 88 Marq. L. Rev. 195, 199–206 (2004); and Paul Finkelman, The Proslavery Origins of the Electoral College, 23 Cardozo L. Rev. 1145, 1151–56 (2002).

22. *See* James Madison, Notes of Debates in the Federal Convention of 1787 524 (Bicentennial ed., W. W. Norton & Co. 1987) (Aug. 24).

23. In 1892, for instance, the distinguished Nineteenth-Century jurist and constitutional scholar Thomas Cooley put it this way:

It was supposed that by . . . [use of the electoral college system], the highest wisdom of the country would be best expressed in the choice finally made; each state selecting its most trusted citizens for electors, and these being left entirely free in the exercise of their judgment as to the persons most worthy to be elevated to the two offices respectively. Thomas M. Cooley, Methods of Appointing Presidential Electors, 1 Mich. L. J. 1 (1892).

Earlier Cooley's revision of Joseph Story's Commentaries says that

It has been observed with much point, that in no respect have the enlarged and liberal views of the framers of the Constitution, and the expectations of the public, when it was adopted, been so completely frustrated as in the practical operation of the system, so far as relates to the independence of the electors in the electoral colleges. It is notorious that the electors are now chosen wholly with reference to particular candidates, and are silently pledged to vote for them. Nay, upon some occasions the electors publicly pledge themselves to vote for a particular person; and thus, in effect, the whole foundation of the system, so elaborately constructed, is subverted. Joseph Story, 2 Commentaries on the Constitution of the United States §1463 (4th ed., Thomas Cooley, ed., Little Brown & Co. 1873).

More recently, U.S. Supreme Court Justice Robert Jackson made much the same point: the electors were to "be free agents, to exercise an independent and nonpartisan judgment as to the men best qualified for the Nation's highest offices." Ray v. Blair, 343 U.S. 214, 232 (1952) (Jackson, J., dissenting). While Jackson's assessment comes in dissent, the majority effectively concedes his historical point, while upholding a state-authorized political party pledge of support for the eventual party nominee for president that was to be extracted from candidates for elector in party primaries. Thus the majority sets forth and then does not dispute the following "argument against the party's power to exclude as candidates in the primary those unwilling to . . . support the national nominees":

The intention of the Founders was that those electors should exercise their judgment in voting for President and Vice-President. Therefore this requirement of a pledge is a restriction in substance, if not in form, that interferes with the constitutional duty to select the proper persons to head the Nation, according to the best judgment of the elector. 343 U.S. at 225.

Later the majority quotes 1802 and 1826 congressional reports that reflect this understanding. Annals of Congress 1289–1290, 7th Cong., 1st Sess. (1802); S. Rep. No. 22, 19th Cong., 1st Sess. 4 (1826) ("Electors, therefore, have not answered the design of their institution. They are not the independent body and superior characters which they were intended to be"), *cited at* 343 U.S. at 228 n.15.

A similar understanding of the original conception of how the electoral college was to operate is reflected in the Supreme Court's other major—and much earlier—decision about the college. McPherson v. Blacker, 146 U.S. 1, 36 (1892) ("[d]oubtless it was supposed that the electors would exercise a reasonable independence and fair judgment in the selection of the chief executive"). In addition *see* Williams v. Rhodes, 393 U.S. 23, 41, 43–44 (1968) (Harlan, J. concurring) ("[t]he [Electoral] College was [in its essence] created to permit the most knowledgeable members of the community to choose the executive of a nation whose continental dimensions were thought to preclude an informed choice by the citizenry at large"). *See also* Albert J. Rosenthal, The Constitution, Congress, and Presidential Elections, 67 Mich. L. Rev. 1, 19–20 (1968); Beverly J. Ross & William Josephson, The Electoral College and the Popular Vote, XII J. L. & Pol. 665, 675 (1996) ("[c]ourts and scholars agree that when the Framers drafted and urged adoption of the Constitution, they assumed that the presidential electors would be citizens who would exercise discretion and judgment in casting their votes for President"); William Josephson & Beverly J. Ross, Repairing the Electoral College, 22 J. Legis. 145, 156 (1996); Robert G. Dixon, Jr., Electoral College Procedure 3 Western Pol. Q. 214 (1950); Note, State Power to Bind Presidential Electors, 65 Colum. L. Rev. 697, 697 (1965); George C. Edwards III, Why the Electoral College Is Bad for America 82–84 (Yale University Press 2004); Michael J. Glennon, When No Majority Rules 8–9, 13 (quoting Rufus King and Joseph Story) (Congressional Quarterly, Inc., 1992); Birch Bayh, Foreword to Lawrence D. Longley & Alan G. Braun, The Politics of Electoral College Reform vii (Yale University Press 1972); *cf.* Karl N. Llewellyn, The Constitution as an Institution, 34 Colum. L. Rev. 1, 12 (1934).

24. U.S. Const., Art. II, § 1, cls. 3, 4.

25. U.S. Const., Art. II, § 1, cl. 3.

26. U.S. Const., Art. II, § 1, cl. 3.

27. Kuroda, *supra* note 1, at 11 says that the experience with absenteeism in the Continental Congress may have affected the Framers' hesitance about a single national meeting.

28. Federalist 10.

29. *See* Robert W. Bennett, Talking It Through: Puzzles of American Democracy 19–21 & n.3, 159–60 (Cornell University Press 2003). Wilmerding, *supra* note 15, at 106–9 draws on the distinctions of this paragraph (without using its terminology) to argue against a nationwide popular vote for president.

30. *Cf.* Federalist 76; Edmonds v. United States, 520 U.S. 651, 659 (1997) ("the Framers anticipated that the President would be less vulnerable to interest-group pressure and personal favoritism than would a collective body").

31. *See* Kuroda, *supra* note 1, at 21–22.

32. U.S. Const., Art. II, § 1, cl. 3.

33. For instance, if there were one hundred electors, there would be two hundred

votes, but a majority would be fifty-one, and three persons could garner as many as sixty-six votes apiece.

34. The constitutional language is that "a majority of all the states shall be necessary to a choice." U.S. Const., Art. II, § 1, cl. 3. Thus John Ferling errs when he asserts that abstentions by some states would affect the number necessary to prevail. *See* John Ferling, Adams vs. Jefferson 176, 189, 193 (Oxford University Press 2004). This is, I should say, an exceedingly minor blemish in a superb treatment of the election of 1800.

35. *See* Festa, *supra* note 4, at 2116.

36. U.S. Const., Art. II, § 1, cl. 3.

37. If the appeal of the House was grounded in the popular election of its members, however, that appeal would seem to be compromised to a degree by giving each state— rather than each member—one vote.

38. Tara Ross says that under those original Article II procedures, if the choice of president went to the House "the person who placed second in this House election would be Vice President." Tara Ross, Enlightened Democracy: The Case for the Electoral College 129 (World Ahead Publishing, Inc. 2004). This is in error. The constitutional provision was that "after the choice of the president, the person having the greatest number of votes of electors shall be the vice president." U.S. Const., Art. II, § 1, cl. 3. Somewhat more ambiguously, the same error can be found in David W. Abbott & James P. Levine, Wrong Winner: The Coming Debacle in the Electoral College 11 (Praeger 1991).

39. U.S. Const., Art. II, § 1, cl. 3. The original provisions were ambiguous about whether the vice president could break a Senate tie in his capacity as president of the Senate (in case of an electoral college tie for vice president, "the Senate shall choose from them by ballot"). The question was never tested, and the Twelfth Amendment is now explicit that "a majority of the whole number [of Senators] shall be necessary to a choice."

40. Madison, Notes, *supra* note 22, at 578 (proceedings of Sept. 4).

41. *See supra* note 20 for an indication of Madison's view; Lawrence D. Longley & Neal R. Peirce, The Electoral College Primer 2000 21 (Yale University Press 1999) (discussing views of George Mason of Virginia); *see also* Note, State Power to Bind Presidential Electors, 65 Colum. L. Rev. 696, 697 & n.15, 707–8 & ns.99, 100 (1965). In Federalist 66 Hamilton said that recourse to the House "will sometimes, if not frequently, happen." The differences of opinion are nicely summarized in Kuroda, *supra* note 1, at 19.

42. Tara Ross, *supra* note 38, at 51. The same commentator later says that "it is hard to see how [the] independent deliberation . . . [originally contemplated for] electors in this day and age will do anything to advance the goals of the Electoral College." Tara Ross, *supra*, at 119.

43. *See* Lawrence D. Longley & Alan G. Braun, The Politics of Electoral College Reform 26 (Yale University Press 1972).

44. *See* the passage from Joseph Story's Commentaries set out in *supra* note 23.

45. "[T]he formation of political parties was still in its infancy at the time of the Constitutional Convention, and the subsequent rise of the importance of political parties was not envisioned." Hardaway, *supra* note 15, at 40. "By 1800 partisanship in appointment of electors had become the absolute rule and consequently electors had become the pawns of political parties." Dixon, *supra* note 23, at 214.

46. No formal way, at least. This apparently did not stop the Rhode Island electors in the 1792 election. *See supra* note 11.

47. The story is related in Ron Chernow, Alexander Hamilton 271–73 (Penguin Press 2004). As it turned out, Washington received a vote from each elector and easily beat Adams 69-34. *See* Longley & Peirce, *supra* note 41, at 178. By some accounts at least Hamilton returned to scheming around the two-vote feature of the process in the 1796 election. *Compare* Kuroda, *supra* note 1, at 65 *with* Ferling, *supra* note 34, at 88.

48. I will use the informal designation of "Jeffersonian Party," because it went by various names (combinations of "Democratic" and "Republican") before the contemporary name of "Democratic Party" finally stuck.

49. Ferling, *supra* note 34, at 91.

50. *See* Kuroda, *supra* note 1, at 99.

51. Thus Chief Justice Rehnquist misstepped when he said that "the chosen electors did not give a majority of their votes to a single candidate . . . in 1800, when Thomas Jefferson and Aaron Burr each received the same number of votes." William H. Rehnquist, Centennial Crisis: The Disputed Election of 1876 4 (Alfred A. Knopf 2004); for a similar error *see* Hardaway, *supra* note 15, at 123 ("[s]ince no candidate [in 1800] received a majority of electoral votes, the election was referred to the House").

52. *See* Ferling, *supra* note 34, at 164–66.

53. *See* Ferling, *supra* note 34, at 176.

54. At least one commentator suggests that Burr would have won had each House member had one vote. Norman J. Ornstein, Three Disputed Elections, in After the People Vote, *supra* note 15, at 35, 37; After the People Vote 31 (3d ed., John C. Fortier ed., AEI Press 2004)

55. *See* Neal R. Peirce, The People's President 69 (Simon & Schuster 1968) (quoting letter to Albert Gallatin). Relations between Hamilton and Burr, of course, deteriorated over the time of Burr's vice presidency, and Burr killed Hamilton in a duel on July 11, 1804. *See* New York Times, July 5, 2004, at A19.

56. *See* James Roger Sharp, American Politics in the Early Republic 271 (Yale University Press 1993).

57. *See* Noble E. Cunningham, Jr., In Pursuit of Reason: The Life of Thomas Jefferson 221–37 (Louisiana State University Press 1987); Joanne B. Freeman, Corruption and

Compromise in the Election of 1800, in The Revolution of 1800 87–114 (James Horn, *et al.*, eds., University of Virginia Press 2002); Kuroda, *supra* note 1, at 83–105. One trenchant analysis of the evidence concludes that there was a deal. *See* Ferling, *supra* note 34, at 184–85, 191–94.

58. *See generally* Kuroda, *supra* note 1. Lucius Wilmerding argues instead that "this amendment looked forward to the election of 1804 rather than, as is commonly supposed, backward to the election of 1800." Wilmerding, *supra* note 15, at 38. It appears that as the 1804 election approached, the opposition Federalists were considering using their electoral votes strategically to provide a presidential victory to the Republican choice for vice president, rather than to Jefferson. Even if concern about this possibility contributed to the move for an amendment, it is hard to believe that the experience of 1800 and 1801 was not a very important contributor to the cause as well.

59. *See* Kuroda, *supra* note 1, at 129. Chief Justice Rehnquist seemed not to appreciate that the Twelfth Amendment had changed the number of candidates from which the House would choose the president from five to three. In his recent book on the contentious 1876 election (to which we will turn in Chapter Three), Rehnquist asserted that if the House had been called upon to decide in the 1876 election, it would have been governed by the Article II provision that the choice would be from the five candidates with the highest number of votes. Rehnquist, *supra* note 51, at 100–101. As it happened, only two candidates received electoral votes in the 1876 election.

60. *Cf.* Jack N. Rakove, The E-College in the E-Age, in The Unfinished Election of 2000 201, 207 (Jack N. Rakove, ed., Basic Books 2001).

61. As early as the 1792 election, for instance, only five persons received electoral votes. And "[b]y 1800 . . . . [p]ersons were chosen electors because they could be counted on to represent the wishes of those who appointed them." *See* Kuroda, *supra* note 1, at 60, 107. The same commentator opines that even in the first presidential election, the Massachusetts electors "[c]learly . . . had gathered to perform the sole duty of casting a predetermined vote; they had not come to discuss, deliberate and negotiate." Kuroda, *supra*, at 31. *See* Albert J. Rosenthal, The Constitution, Congress, and Presidential Elections, 67 Mich. L. Rev. 1, 17 (1968); Edwards, *supra* note 23, at 19.

62. *Cf.* Wilmerding, *supra* note 15, at x. "It is a supreme irony that the framers made a Constitution which sought to minimize the influence of political parties but actually required parties to make it work." Kuroda, *supra* note 1, at 27. "[There was] a glaring deficiency of the original 1787 Constitution—the assumption that there would be no party system and, therefore, that a 'politics of virtue' would determine the presidential and vice-presidential selections rather than a 'politics of party.'" Sanford A. Levinson & Ernest A. Young, Who's Afraid of the Twelfth Amendment?, 29 Fla. St. U. L. Rev. 925, 928 (2001).

63. Jules Witcover argues strenuously that vice-presidential candidates' qualifica-

tions to be president are not routinely made central considerations in the selection process. *See generally* Witcover, *supra* note 8; *see also* David P. Currie, The Twelfth Amendment, in Unintended Consequences of Constitutional Amendment 73, 75–77 (David E. Kyvig, ed., University of Georgia Press 2000).

64. David P. Currie, The Constitution in Congress: The Jeffersonians 1801–1829 41 (University of Chicago Press 2001). An objection on this ground was actually voiced in opposition to the Twelfth Amendment when it was under consideration. Currie, *supra* note 63, at 75.

65. *See* U.S. Senate Rep. No. 395, 43rd Cong., 1st Sess. 12–13 (1874); *see also* Bruce Ackerman & David Fontana, How Jefferson Counted Himself In, Atlantic Monthly, Mar. 2004, at 84; Ferling, *supra* note 34, at 186–87; Fortier ed., *supra* note 54, at 30. Presumably in recognition of this conflict Vice President Humphrey declined to preside at the joint meeting when the votes from the 1968 election—in which Humphrey was a candidate for president—were counted. *See* Congressional Research Service, Memorandum of Nov. 17, 2000, at 5.

66. With three candidates a bargain might occasionally be easier to strike, but that is at best a subtle point and even a successful bargain between two of the three candidates would still leave the possibility of the kinds of difficulties that two candidates pose.

67. *See* Sharp, *supra* note 56, at 243–44; Kuroda, *supra* note 1, at 84–87.

68. Rosenthal, *supra* note 61, at 4.

Chapter Three

1. *See* Neal R. Peirce, The Peoples' President 82–86 (Simon & Schuster 1968).

2. For summaries of the early variety of ways in which electors were chosen, *see* McPherson v. Blacker, 146 U.S. 1, 29–33 (1892); Matthew J. Festa, The Origins and Constitutionality of State Unit Voting in the Electoral College, 54 Vand. L. Rev. 2099, 2123–26 (2001).

3. Peirce, *supra* note 1, at 83–84.

4. *See* Norman J. Ornstein, Three Disputed Elections, in After the People Vote 35, 38 (Walter Berns, ed., AEI Press 1992); Lucius Wilmerding, Jr., The Electoral College 188–89 (Beacon Press 1958).

5. *See* Peirce, *supra* note 1, at 82–86. Peirce relates an alternative story of the causes at work that has gained some currency. Stephen Van Rensselaer of the New York delegation cast a decisive vote, relying, it is said, on the sign he received through spotting a piece of paper with Adams's name on it as he was seeking divine guidance through prayer. Peirce, *supra*, at 85. *See also* Ornstein, *supra* note 4, at 39–40.

6. U.S. Const., Art. I, § 2 cl. 1, § 3, cl. 1; Art. II, § 1, cl. 1. The provisions for the Senate and the executive are more explicit than are those for members of the House.

7. Explanation of the types of Sessions of Congress, p. 2, http://thegreenpapers.com/

Hx/SessionsExplanation (last visited 01/15/04); *see generally* S. Rep. No. 26, 72d Cong., 1st Sess. (1932).

8. U.S. Const., Art. II, § 1, cl. 4.

9. The only guidance on meeting times in the original Constitution was that "[t]he Congress shall assemble at least once in every year, and such meeting shall be on the first Monday in December, unless they shall by law appoint a different day." U.S. Const., Art. I, § 4, cl. 2.

10. 3 U.S.C § 15 (2000).

11. We will return in Chapter Five to some other provisions of the Twentieth Amendment. Robert Hardaway points out, quite correctly, that selection of the president by the new House rather than the old is not constitutionally required, and he argues strenuously that the outgoing House would be preferable. Robert M. Hardaway, The Electoral College and the Constitution: The Case for Preserving Federalism 64–65 (Praeger 1994).

12. U.S. Const., Am. XIV, § 2. The mention of "crime" was cited by the U.S. Supreme Court in rebuffing a constitutional challenge to the disenfranchisement of ex-felons. *See* Richardson v. Ramirez, 418 U.S. 24 (1974).

13. U.S. Const., Am. XIV, § 2.

14. *See* Wilmerding, *supra* note 4, at 72. The Fifteenth Amendment guarantees the right of citizens to vote against denial or abridgement "on account of race, color, or previous condition of servitude," and gives Congress the authority to enforce that guarantee by "appropriate legislation." U.S. Const., Am. XV, §§ 1, 2.

15. *E.g.*, Williams v. Rhodes, 393 U.S. 23 (1968).

16. Bush v. Gore, 531 U.S. 98 (2000).

17. U.S. Const., Ams. XIX, cl. 1; XXVI § 1.

18. U.S. Const., Am. XXIV § 1. While the Twenty-Fourth Amendment by its terms reaches only federal elections, elections for federal and state offices are typically conducted in tandem, and the integrated process makes it difficult for a state to apply the restriction only in the federal part of the whole.

19. U.S. Const., Am. XXIII § 1, cl. 2.

20. U.S. Const., Art. I, § 2, cl. 3.

21. *See* Peirce, *supra* note 1, at 86–92.

22. *See* note 96, *infra* for mention of some controversy about this proposition.

23. *See* U.S. Senate Rep. No. 395, 43rd Cong., 1st Sess. 10 (1874); Stephen A. Siegel, The Conscientious Congressman's Guide to the Electoral Count Act of 1887, 56 Fla. L. Rev. 541, 573 (2004); Ornstein, *supra* note 4, at 41.

24. *See* Roy Morris, Jr., Fraud of the Century 164–99 (Simon & Schuster 2003).

25. *See* Morris, *supra* note 24, at 183–85.

26. U.S. Const., Art. II, § 1, cl. 2. Controversies about the applicability of this consti-

tutional provision also played relatively minor roles in the disputes over Louisiana's and Florida's electors. *See* Paul Leland Haworth, The Hayes-Tilden Disputed Presidential Election of 1876 114 (Burrows Brothers Company 1906); William H. Rehnquist, Centennial Crisis: The Disputed Election of 1876 174–75 (Alfred A. Knopf 2004). Rehnquist also mentions a similar point being raised about a Wisconsin elector. Rehnquist, *supra*, at 178. Indeed a version of the issue had surfaced in an earlier election. *See* Siegel, *supra* note 23, at 580 n.237.

27. The story is engagingly told in Rehnquist, *supra* note 26, at 109–12.

28. *See* Morris, *supra* note 24, at 197–98. The Oregon statute on replacing ineligible electors is discussed in Charles Fairman, Five Justices and the Electoral Commission of 1877, Supplement to Volume VII of the Oliver Wendell Holmes Devise History of the Supreme Court of the United States 117 (Macmillan 1988).

29. Senator George F. Hoar of Massachusetts, a member of the House at the time and a prominent figure in the election controversy, wrote the following in an autobiography published in 1903:

> Threats of civil war were heard in many quarters. When I went to Washington for the session of December, 1876, while I did not believe there would be a civil war, and supposed there would be some method of escape devised, I confess I saw no such method. I now believe that but for the bitter experience of a few years before, with its terrible lesson, there would have been a resort to arms. It would have been a worse civil war than that of the Rebellion, because the country would have been divided not by sections, but by parties. George F. Hoar, I Autobiography of Seventy Years 369–70 (Charles Scribner's Sons 1903).

Apparently Civil War General and Democrat George McClellan gave serious consideration to doing armed battle. *See* Rehnquist, *supra* note 26, at 210.

30. *See* Peirce, *supra* note 1, at 89.

31. *See* House Special Committee, Counting Electoral Votes, H.R. Misc. Doc. No. 13 148, 44th Cong., 2d Sess. (1877); U.S. Senate Rep. No. 395, 43rd Cong., 1st Sess. 13–15 (1874).

32. *See* Siegel, *supra* note 23, at 553–54; Vasan Kesavan, Is the Electoral Count Act Unconstitutional?, 80 N.C. L. Rev. 1653, 1675 (2002).

33. *See* Siegel, *supra* note 23, at 554.

34. *See* Peirce, *supra* note 1, at 89–91. I do not mean to suggest that Bradley's votes were questionable. They were certainly very contentious at the time, and echoes of doubt about the independence of his judgments are still heard today. *See, e.g.,* George C. Edwards III, Why the Electoral College Is Bad for America 47 (Yale University Press 2004). But many historians have defended Bradley against charges of bias. *See* Fairman, *supra* note 28; Haworth, *supra* note 26, at 337–42; *see also* Rehnquist, *supra* note 26, at

185–200. Siegel, *supra* note 23, at 573–78 helpfully places Bradley's decisions within the context of administrative law principles at the time.

35. Ornstein, *supra* note 4, at 42.

36. *See* Rehnquist, *supra* note 26, at 209. There was perhaps a more plausible scenario through which the selection process could have reached the House. In his capacity as a member of the commission, Justice Field took the position that the Oregon Republican electors acted beyond their authority in naming the formerly ineligible elector to the vacancy created by his ineligibility, but also that the governor had no authority to fill the vacancy. Had that position prevailed, there would have been an electoral college tie (with neither candidate obtaining a majority of the electors appointed), and the process would have gone to the House. *See* Siegel, *supra* note 23, at 578 & n.227.

37. Michael J. Glennon, When No Majority Rules 17 (Congressional Quarterly 1992).

38. Actually the damping down had begun while Grant remained in office. For different perspectives on the dispute about the causal connection, *see* Eric Foner, Reconstruction 1863–1877 581–82 (Harper & Row 1988); Peirce, *supra* note 1, at 91; Edwards, *supra* note 34, at 47.

39. *See* Foner, *supra* note 38, at 566–80; Rehnquist, *supra* note 26, at 177–78, 203.

40. "It seems to have been taken for granted, that no question could ever arise on the subject; and that nothing more was necessary, than to open the certificates, which were produced, in the presence of both houses, and to count the names and numbers, as returned." Joseph Story, 3 Commentaries on the Constitution of the United States § 1464 (Boston, Hilliard, Gray & Co. 1833). *See* U.S. Senate Rep. No. 395, 43rd Cong., 1st. Sess. 12–13 (1874).

41. One storied instance was in Rhode Island in the 1840s. The tale, which gave rise to the U.S. Supreme Court decision in Luther v. Borden, 48 U.S. (7 How.) 1 (1849), is told briefly in Alexander Keyssar, The Right to Vote 71–76 (Basic Books 2000).

42. West Virginia was formed out of a portion of Virginia, after rival governments emerged, divided by attitudes toward secession. *See generally* Michael Stokes Paulson & Vasan Kesavan, Is West Virginia Constitutional?, 90 Calif. L. Rev. 291 (2002). Then during the Civil War, Missouri and Kentucky each had rival governments in the United States and the Confederacy. *See* James M. McPherson, Battle Cry of Freedom: The Civil War Era 291–97 (Oxford University Press 1988).

43. *See* Fairman, *supra* note 28, at 80 n.33; Siegel, *supra* note 23, at 580–81 n.240.

44. For reference to some instances of disputes about elector qualifications other than those mentioned in note 26, *supra*, *see* Siegel, *supra* note 23, at 559 & n.100.

45. U.S. Const., Art. II, § 1, cl. 5. The Constitution was initially silent on vice-presidential qualifications, but there is now a provision tagged on at the end of the Twelfth Amendment that "no person constitutionally ineligible to the office of President shall be eligible to that of Vice-President of the United States."

46. *See* Lawrence D. Longley & Neal R. Peirce, The Electoral College Primer 2000 130 (Yale University Press 1999).

47. *See* Peirce, *supra* note 1, at 131; Beverly J. Ross & William Josephson, The Electoral College and the Popular Vote, XII J. L. & Pol. 665, 706 n.232 (1996); Siegel, *supra* note 23, at 559 & n.98.

48. Art. II, § 1, cl. 4.

49. *See* Peirce, *supra* note 1, at 131; U.S. Senate Rep 395, 43rd Cong., 1st. Sess. 11–12 (1874). There is also a suggestion in the electoral college literature that in 1880 Georgia votes were cast on the wrong day and not counted for that reason. *See* Michael J. Glennon, When No Majority Rules 36–37 (Congressional Quarterly 1992) (the identification of the state, and contrary evidence, is mentioned in Ross & Josephson, *supra* note 47, at 706 n.232 (1996)). A Michigan provision that had become outdated and hence conflicted with the congressionally established date for the meeting of electors played a minor role in the litigation that yielded the Supreme Court's decision in McPherson v. Blacker, 146 U.S. 1, 41 (1892).

50. *See* Chapter Seven. In the counting for the 1872 election, a question was raised about Mississippi's failure to certify that its electors had voted by "ballot." *See* Kesavan, *supra* note 32, at 1687.

51. For instance, by some accounts at least there was controversy about whether the Arkansas electoral votes from the 1872 election had the appropriate state seal affixed. *See* Peirce, *supra* note 1, at 131. For reference to other disputes about procedural irregularity, *see* Siegel, *supra* note 23, at 559 & ns.101 & 102.

52. An objection on inhabitancy grounds was ruled untimely in the count for the 1872 election. *See* Kesavan, *supra* note 32, at 1688.

53. The Electoral Count Act is codified at 3 U.S.C. § 1 *et seq* (2000). In an effort to avoid confusion, I will use section numbers in the present codification of the act in Title 3 of the United States Code.

54. 3 U.S.C. § 1 (2000), originally enacted as Act of Jan. 23, 1845, ch. 1, 5 Stat. 721.

55. As it had been for the 1872 Louisiana dispute. *See* Siegel, *supra* note 23, at 580–81.

56. 3 U.S.C. § 7 (2000). *See* Siegel, *supra* note 23, at 584 & n.271.

57. In Chapter Nine I will return briefly to the question of the constitutionality of the ECA. And in Chapter Seven I will discuss the constitutionality of laws restricting elector discretion in casting their votes. Basically for the reasons explored there it seems to me that the ECA should be upheld as an attempt to bring order to a process that raises serious danger of uncertain and inconsistent outcomes. Abraham Lincoln, for one, seems to have thought that there was ample congressional power to exclude electoral votes upon a conclusion that they were illegal. *See* Berns, ed., *supra* note 4, at 19.

58. U.S. Const., Am. XII.

59. An Act Relative to the Election of a President and Vice President of the United

States, ch. 8, §§ 2, 3, 1 Stat. 239–40 (1792). *See* Tadahisa Kuroda, The Origins of the Twelfth Amendment 53 (Greenwood Press 1994); Kesavan, *supra* note 32, at 1664–69.

60. 3 U.S.C. § 6 (2000).

61. In Chapter Ten we will return to the relatively minor continuing problems in calculating nationwide vote totals for presidential (and vice presidential) candidates.

62. *See* 3 U.S.C. §§ 9–11 (2000). Other copies are sent to the national archivist, the state's secretary of state, and the chief judge of the local federal district court.

63. 531 U.S. 98 (2000).

64. 3 U.S.C. § 5 (2000). In the case of such a "final determination," Section Six of the ECA charges the state's governor with preparing a "certificate of such determination" for the U.S. secretary of state, who in turn is to provide copies to each house of Congress. 3 U.S.C. § 6 (2000). Siegel says that the "origin of the six-day limitation is mysterious." Siegel, *supra* note 23, at 591.

65. Siegel, *supra* note 23, at 544, 593 & n.319, 605 n.385.

66. *See* Siegel, *supra* note 23, at 606–8.

67. The Michael Moore film *Fahrenheit 911* that received some attention in the period leading up to the 2004 election shows a parade of black congressmen raising objections to the counting of the 2000 Florida electoral votes, but being told by the presiding Senate president Albert Gore that their objections are out of order for want of a supporting senator. At the January 6, 2005, count of the 2004 electoral votes, in contrast, a member of Congress from Ohio was joined in objection to the Ohio votes by California's Senator Barbara Boxer and thus able to force consideration of the objections. *See* Sheryl Gay Stolberg & James Dao, Congress Ratifies Bush Victory After a Rare Challenge, N.Y. Times, Jan. 7, 2005, at A19.

68. *See* Siegel, *supra* note 23, at 619–20.

69. *See* Glennon, *supra* note 49, at 37–40; Edwards, *supra* note 34, at 17–18.

70. The section goes on to provide that in the case of vacancies in the positions of one more electors who have passed the Section Five hurdle, "successors or substitutes" for those electors "appointed . . . in the mode provided by the laws of the State" can also cast effective votes. 3 U.S.C. § 15 (2000).

71. *See* Siegel, *supra* note 23, at 626 & n.519.

72. Here Section Fifteen sinks to dizzying redundancy, providing that both Houses must "concurrently decide" that the votes "were cast by lawful electors appointed in accordance with the laws of the State, unless the two Houses . . . shall concurrently decide such votes not to be the lawful votes of . . . legally appointed electors." 3 U.S.C. § 15 (2000).

73. Coming as it does near the end of a very long section, it is not entirely clear that this favoritism for governor-certified electors extends to all cases of competing slates that were earlier delineated. That, however, seems to be the best reading of the section,

if for no other reason than that it provides a default rule when the two houses disagree, save for complications about governor certification to which the text now turns.

74. *See* Siegel, *supra* note 23, at 610 n.420.

75. *See* note 67, *supra*.

76. *See* Longley & Peirce, *supra* note 46, at 46–52; Note, State Power to Bind Presidential Electors, 65 Colum. L. Rev. 696, 700 (1965); Edwards, *supra* note 34, at 48–51.

77. *See* William Josephson & Beverly J. Ross, Repairing the Electoral College, 22 J. Legis. 145, 166 n.154 (1996).

78. *See* Longley & Peirce, *supra* note 46, at 46–59. The story of the 1960 controversies is told briefly and compellingly in Todd J. Zywicki, The Law of Presidential Transitions and the 2000 Election, 2001 B.Y.U. L. Rev. 1573, 1606–1614.

79. *See* Siegel, *supra* note 23, at 544 n.13 ("Viewed empirically, the ECA seems to be a complete success"). Siegel rightly cautions that the 2000 election is suggestive of problems beneath "the surface." Siegel, *supra*.

80. *See* Kuroda, *supra* note 59, at 27–38.

81. *See* Noble E. Cunningham, Jr., In Pursuit of Reason: The Life of Thomas Jefferson 227 (Louisiana State University Press 1987). This is not unlike what happened before passage of the Seventeenth Amendment, when the state legislatures chose the U.S. senators. *See* Robert W. Bennett, Talking It Through: Puzzles of American Democracy 60–61 (Cornell University Press 2003).

82. *See* Longley & Peirce, *supra* note 46, at 102.

83. A few states apparently have a mix of designation vehicles. *See* Edwards *supra* note 34, at 2–3; Hardaway, *supra* note 11, at 45.

84. Edwards, *supra* note 34, at 4.

85. *See* Chapter Four.

86. McPherson v. Blacker, 146 U.S. 1, 35 (1892). More recently the Supreme Court summarily affirmed a lower court decision rebuffing a challenge to the winner-take-all approach. *See* Williams v. Virginia Board of Elections, 288 F. Supp. 622 (E.D. Va. 1968), *aff'd*, 393 U.S. 320 (1969) (*per curiam*).

87. Madison had been urged on by Charles Pinckney. Massachusetts, in the control of Federalists, then responded in kind with a "winner-take-all" approach, but employing legislative selection. *See* Kuroda, *supra* note 59, at 49, 73–74. The machinations around the country in juggling winner-take-all and districted elections for political advantage in the 1800 election are recounted in John Ferling, Adams vs. Jefferson 156–57 (Oxford University Press 2004).

88. *See* Wilmerding, *supra* note 4, at 60–61. Even in the era of winner-take-all, however, there have been a few states that, while displaying the electors on the ballots divided into slates, allow votes for individual electors across slates. Wilmerding, *supra*, at 73–74. We will return in Chapter Ten to the question of whether such individualized votes for

electors remain possible in any state. It is also important to appreciate that a general ticket does not necessarily imply that the entire elected slate will vote for a single set of candidates, or even that it is committed to do so. In early elections, there were instances where an elected slate split its electoral votes without a taint of faithlessness. *See* Kuroda, *supra* note 59, at 68.

89. In somewhat parallel fashion, Alexander Hamilton had unsuccessfully urged popular election through a districting system on New York's governor John Jay for the 1800 election in an attempt to ensure that the entire New York electoral college delegation did not go to the Jeffersonian slate that included, of course, the New Yorker Aaron Burr. *See* Ferling, *supra* note 87, at 131.

90. This was apparent as early as the 1800 when Jeffersonian ascendancy in Pennsylvania brought forth Jeffersonian espousal of winner-take-all. *See* Kuroda, *supra* note 59, at 90.

91. *See* Edwards, *supra* note 34, at 10.

92. This is not to say that the motivation for districting need be "democratic" in this sense, as the 1892 Michigan experience demonstrated.

93. Contemporary commentators who favor the electoral college, however, tend to favor the winner-take-all approach as well. One, for instance, depicts the winner-take-all approach as "crucial" to the modern version of the electoral college system, because it provides "a federal element," which "sends a federalizing impulse throughout our whole political process." Martin Diamond, The Electoral College and the American Idea of Democracy, in Berns, ed., *supra* note 4, at 51–52. We will take up that claim in Chapter Four as well.

94. The qualification "arguably" is required because candidates respond to the rules that are in place. With winner-take-all being one of those, there is often no telling how elections would have come out if different rules had prompted different campaign strategies. *See* Chapter Four.

95. *See* Longley & Peirce, *supra* note 46, at 182.

96. In addition to 2000 (assuming that Bush was appropriately declared the electoral college winner in that election) and 1888, the election of 1876 is usually put in the "clear" column, *see, e.g.*, Rehnquist, *supra* note 26, at 99; Hardaway, *supra* note 11, at 4, though doubt on that score is sometimes expressed on the ground that numbers of committed Hayes supporters were intimidated into not voting or voting for Tilden. *See, e.g.*, Tara Ross, Enlightened Democracy: The Case for the Electoral College 169 (World Ahead Publishing 2004), *citing* Haworth, *supra* note 26. As we saw earlier, the 1960 election is a debatable example, because it is impossible to know who won the popular vote. The Alabama ballots listed only the electors, and, due to the political situation in Alabama, it is unclear how to ascribe votes for the various Democratic electors to John Kennedy, the national Democratic candidate and electoral college winner by 84 votes.

97. *See* Diamond, *supra* note 93, at 63; Harrison Came in Second but Won the White House; Indiana Native Was Last President to Win with Lower Popular Vote due to Electoral College, Indianapolis Star, Nov. 9, 2000, at 10A.

98. *See* George Will, Foreword, in Tara Ross, *supra* note 96, at x.

99. *See* Wilmerding, *supra* note 4, at 198. We will return in Chapter Ten to the subject of comparative state influence in the electoral college.

100. Robert G. Dixon, Jr., Electoral College Procedure 3 Western Pol. Q. 214, 215 (1950).

101. Wilmerding, *supra* note 4, at xi.

Chapter Four

1. Federalist 68.

2. *But cf.* George Will's remark quoted at the front of After the People Vote (Walter Berns, ed., AEI Press 1992) ("The United States has the world's most successful system for selecting a chief executive").

3. *See* William Josephson & Beverly J. Ross, Repairing the Electoral College, 22 J. Legis. 145, 150–51 (1996).

4. "The electoral college needs only to be rid of the specter of the 'faithless elector,' who takes it in his head to act independently, and of the anachronism of election in the House of Representatives." Alexander Bickel, Reform and Continuity: The Electoral College, The Convention, and The Party System 34 (Harper & Row 1971). "[I]t is hard to find anyone who approves of the current contingency procedure . . . [through which i]f no presidential candidate wins a majority of the electoral votes, the House of Representatives must choose from among the top three winners of electoral votes." Judith Best, The Choice of the People? 13 (Rowman & Littlefield 1996). "[F]aithless elector[s] . . . seem anachronistic and potentially dangerous. There are virtually no defenders of this aspect of the electoral college." Best, *supra* at xiv. "[T]he present method for contingent election [of the President in the House] is unsatisfactory—indeed it is dangerous. . . . But it does not follow that the entire electoral system must be overhauled merely to eliminate this one undesirable feature." Albert J. Rosenthal, The Constitution, Congress, and Presidential Elections, 67 Mich. L. Rev. 1, 15 (1968). "[I]t is hard to see what positive purpose the role of elector plays in today's society." Tara Ross, Enlightened Democracy: The Case For the Electoral College 114 (World Ahead Publishing 2004). "[R]eforms are necessary to address . . . the 'faithless elector.'" Robert M. Hardaway, The Electoral College and the Constitution: The Case for Preserving Federalism 21 (Praeger 1994). "An amendment making the casting of electoral votes automatic would dispel [possible abuses]." Nelson W. Polsby & Aaron Wildavsky, Presidential Elections 254 (5th ed., Charles Scribner's Sons 1980). "Perhaps the only aspect of the electoral college system that has come under more universal contemporary criticism than the existence of individual electors is the House

contingent procedure for electing the president." Lawrence D. Longley & Alan G. Braun, The Politics of Electoral College Reform 44 (Yale University Press 1972). "[I]t is virtually impossible to find anyone who will defend the selection of the president by the House of Representatives, with each state having one vote." George C. Edwards III, Why the Electoral College Is Bad for America 89 (Yale University Press 2004).

5. *See* Akhil Reed Amar, The Electoral College, Unfair from Day One, N.Y. Times, Nov. 9, 2000, at A23; Dean B. Murphy, In Upstate Victory Tour, Mrs. Clinton Says Electoral College Should Go, N.Y. Times, Nov. 11, 2000, at B1; *see also* Lawrence D. Longley & Neal R. Peirce, The Electoral College Primer 2000 162–75 (Yale University Press 1999); Beverly J. Ross & William Josephson, The Electoral College and the Popular Vote, XII J. Law & Pol. 665, 667 (1996) ("In 1979, Senator Birch Bayh (D. Ind.) became another in a long line of lawmakers to propose a constitutional amendment providing for the direct popular election of the President and Vice President."); Chapter One, note 30.

6. Note, Rethinking the Electoral College Debate: The Framers, Federalism, and One Person, One Vote, 114 Harv. L. Rev. 2526 (2001).

7. Judith Best, Weighing the Alternatives: Reform or Deform?, in The Longest Night: Polemics and Perspectives on Election 2000 347 (Arthur J. Jacobson & Michel Rosenfeld eds., University of California Press 2002).

8. U.S. Const., Art. V. The state ratification can be effected either through legislative action at the state level or by state conventions, if Congress provides for them. Only the Twenty-First Amendment was ratified in this latter way. Similarly in addition to a two-thirds vote of each house of Congress, the proposal stage can be pursued by calls for amendment by two-thirds of the states, which is then to be followed by a national convention. This approach has never been employed.

9. *See* Lucius Wilmerding, Jr., The Electoral College 97–101 (Beacon Press 1958).

10. In a recent book, George Edwards makes each of these "errors," if such they be, in the space of two pages. Edwards, *supra* note 4, at 152–53.

11. The phrase seems to have been coined by David Abbott and James Levine in a book published in 1991. David W. Abbott & James P. Levine, Wrong Winner: The Coming Debacle in the Electoral College (Praeger 1991).

12. *See* in particular Chapter Three, note 96. In addition, the election of 1824 is occasionally cited as an instance where the eventual winner—John Quincy Adams—obtained fewer popular votes than his rival Andrew Jackson. But that choice was made in the House of Representatives, when four candidates garnered electoral votes and none had the required electoral college majority. In addition, only some states' electors were chosen by popular voting at the time, so even on its own term the "wrong winner" conclusion is questionable.

13. *See* Daron R. Shaw, The Methods Behind the Madness: Presidential Electoral College Strategies, 1988–96, 61 J. Pol. 893 (1999).

14. Neil R. Peirce, Foreword, in Edwards, *supra* note 4, at x. Edwards marshals other authority and pursues the point in chapter two of the same work. Edwards, *supra*, at 31–34. In reviewing Edwards's book, Alexander Keyssar embraces the same point. Alexander Keyssar, The Electoral College Flunks, New York Rev. of Books, Mar. 24, 2005, at 16. *See* Longley & Braun, *supra* note 4, at 82–83.

15. A bonus proposal was first advanced in 1978 by a task force of the Twentieth Century Fund. The proposed bonus was 102 electoral votes, which would have brought the total of electoral votes to 640, with 321 required to win. With the 102 vote bonus going to the winner of the nationwide vote, it would still have been possible to win without prevailing in the popular vote. A still larger bonus would, of course, have made it even more difficult, and a bonus the size of the existing electoral college would make victory without the popular vote mathematically impossible. *See* Winner Take All: Report of the Twentieth Century Fund Task Force on Reform of the Presidential Election Process (Holmes & Meier Publishers 1978).

16. *See, e.g.*, Peirce, *supra* note 14, at xiii.

17. Edwards, *supra* note 4, at 154.

18. If we assume that only whole electoral votes would be allowed, *see* note 28, *infra*, proportionality must come to grips with the problem of fractions, for the statewide popular vote will be exceedingly unlikely to divide evenly into fractions of the form y/x where "x" is the number of electoral votes to which the state is entitled. A similar problem of fractions is presented after each decennial census in distributing the total number of seats in the House of Representatives among the various states, and there is no one method that commands universal assent in that context. *See* Chapter Six.

In the 2004 election, a proportionality initiative appeared on the Colorado ballot, which specified the following approach for dealing with fractions:

(3) The allocation of a presidential ticket's popular proportion of this state's electoral votes shall be in whole numbers and shall be made in the following manner:

(a) The total number of ballots cast in this state for each presidential ticket at a general election shall be divided by the total number of ballots cast for all presidential tickets that receive votes at that general election; and

(b) The proportion of a presidential ticket's popular vote, as determined in paragraph (a) of this subsection, shall be multiplied by the number of electoral votes to which Colorado is entitled.

(4) The number of electoral votes that is attributable to the ballots cast for any presidential ticket, as determined in subsection (3) of this section, shall be rounded to the nearest whole number, subject to the following limitations.

(a) No presidential ticket shall receive any electoral votes from this state if its proportion of the total ballots cast for all presidential tickets would reflect less than a full electoral vote after rounding to the nearest whole number.

(b) If the sum of electoral votes allocated pursuant to paragraph (a) of this sub-section is greater than the number of electoral votes to which Colorado is entitled:

(I) The allocation of electoral votes to the presidential ticket receiving at least one electoral vote and the fewest numbers of ballots cast shall be reduced by whole electoral votes until only that number of electoral votes to which Colorado is entitled have been allocated; and

(II) The process set forth in subparagraph (I) of this paragraph shall be repeated if . . . [necessary].

(c) If the sum of all electoral votes allocated would be less than the number of electoral votes to which Colorado is entitled, the presidential ticket receiving the greatest number of ballots shall receive any unallocated electoral votes until all of the electoral votes to which Colorado is entitled have been allocated. Amendment 36: Colorado Electoral College Reform, http://www.makeyourvotecount.net/content.jsp?content_KEY=68 (last visited 11/18/04); *see* Neal R. Peirce, The People's President 164–65 (Simon & Schuster 1968).

The Colorado initiative was defeated.

19. Though not in the District of Columbia, judging by recent results. The respective popular votes of the Democratic and Republican slates in the 2004 election in the District were 171,923 and 18,073. Since the District has only three electors, it seems likely that the Democratic candidate would command all three under virtually any proportionality proposal. *See, e.g.*, the Colorado proposal in note 18, *supra*.

20. In some states at least it is theoretically possible to have a slate on the ballot that is either uncommitted to any candidate or split in its commitments. State laws discourage this, however, and, aside from the possibility of "faithless electors," *see* Chapter Seven, split slates seem to be a thing of the past in American presidential elections. In contrast, districting certainly could lead to a split in a state's electoral college delegation, but this did not in fact happen in either the 2000 or 2004 election in either Maine or Nebraska, the two states that continue to select some of their electors from districts. In each of the two elections Maine chose all Democratic electors and Nebraska all Republican ones.

21. By one count, in the elections between 1789 and 1892 "there were 52 instances in which states used some form of the district system." Peirce, *supra* note 18, at 161 (characterizing a 1961 memorandum prepared by James C. Kirby, Jr., chief counsel of the Senate Judiciary Committee). James Madison once opined that popular voting in districts was the method of selection "mostly, if not exclusively, in view when the Constitution was framed and adopted." *Quoted in* Note, State Power to Bind Presidential Electors, 65 Colum. L. Rev. 696, 698 (1965).

22. 146 U.S. 1 (1892).

23. *See* Note, *supra* note 21, at 700.

24. U.S. Const., Art. II, § 1, cl. 2.

25. We saw in Chapter Three that both Madison and Jefferson preferred a district-ing system in principle. That preference was, of course, expressed at a time when inde-pendence of elector judgment still had a measure of respectability in the electoral col-lege system. In that environment, districting could be thought to foster a relationship between elector and electorate that might help both to shape that exercise of judgment and to foster a sense of involvement by the electorate in the presidential election system. *See* Robert W. Bennett, Talking It Through: Puzzles of American Democracy 61–63 (Cor-nell University Press 2003). But even after elector discretion had largely passed from the scene, one of the classic works on the electoral college came down on the side of single-elector districts within states. *See* Wilmerding, *supra* note 9, at 128–68. And Michael Glennon is a contemporary champion. *See* Michael J. Glennon, When No Majority Rules 74–75 (Congressional Quarterly 1992); *see also* Peirce, *supra* note 18, at 152–64; Rosenthal, *supra* note 4, at 8–9.

26. And more litigated. *See* Vieth v. Jubelirer, 541 U.S. 267 (2004).

27. Jack N. Rakove, The E-College in the E-Age, in The Unfinished Election of 2000 201, 229 (Jack N. Rakove, ed., Basic Books 2001); Tara Ross, *supra* note 4, at 152–53; Hard-away, *supra* note 4, at 9; Longley & Braun, *supra* note 4, at 63.

28. The electoral college provisions now found in the Twelfth Amendment suggest the use of individual electors who cast ballots which are then toted up. This implicitly assumes that each elector casts a single integrated vote, so that allowing fractions of elec-toral votes would almost surely be unconstitutional. *See* Wilmerding, *supra* note 9, at 40. During the 1960s there were proposals for a constitutional amendment to do away with the office of elector and simply award the present state allocations of electoral votes di-rectly to the presidential candidates. They contemplated no fractionation of the electoral votes. *See* Rosenthal, *supra* note 4, at 31.

29. Part of the text of the initiative is set forth in note 18, *supra*. *See* John Harwood, Challenge to Electoral College in Colorado Could Have Big Impact, Wall St. Journal, Sept. 13, 2004, at A1.

30. Section Eight provided that it should "be liberally construed to achieve popular proportional allocation of presidential electors at the 2004 general election." http://www.makeyourvotecount.net/content.jsp?content_KEY=68 (last visited 11/18/04).

31. The most likely unfairness would seem to have been to potential third party vot-ers, who could not fairly assess their chances of electing an elector from their party if they did not know whether the initiative would be in effect. *See* Karen Abbott, Amend-ment 36 Suit Brings Out Lawyers, Rocky Mountain News [Denver], Oct. 15, 2004.

32. U.S. Const., Art. II, § 1, cl. 2. Section 1(b) of the initiative provided that "[t]he Colorado constitution reserves to the people of this state the right to act in the place of the state legislature in any legislative matter, and through enactment of this section, the people do hereby act as the legislature of Colorado for the purpose of changing the

manner of electing presidential electors in accordance with the provisions of article II, section 1 of the United States constitution." http://www.makeyourvotecount.net/content.jsp?content_KEY=68 (last visited 11/18/04).

33. This was an argument used in opposition to the Colorado initiative by the state's Republican governor, Bill Owens. *See* Harwood, *supra* note 29.

34. *Compare* U.S. Term Limits v. Thornton, 514 U.S. 779 (1975).

35. *See* Akhil Reed Amar & Vik Amar, President Quale?, 78 Va. L. Rev. 913, 928 n.57 (1992).

36. *See generally* Alexander Keyssar, The Right to Vote (Basic Books 2000).

37. U.S. Const., Art. I, § 3, cl.1.

38. The Supreme Court first used the phrase in Gray v. Sanders, 372 U.S. 368, 381 (1963).

39. In Chapter Ten we will discuss some minor complications that might make calculation of the nationwide popular vote totals somewhat less "simple."

40. *See* Paul Finkelman, The Proslavery Origins of the Electoral College, 23 Cardozo L. Rev. 1145, 1151–56 (2002).

41. Commission on Electoral College Reform, Electing the President (American Bar Association 1967) (hereinafter "Commission Report"). In the wake of the Commission Report, the House of Representatives proposed a constitutional amendment that tracked the commission's recommendations in important respects. The amendment actually passed overwhelmingly in the House in 1969, but then died in the Senate, where the opposition was aided by a filibuster. *See* Judith Best, The Case Against Direct Election of the President: A Defense of the Electoral College 16 (Cornell University Press 1975); Peirce, *supra* note 14, at xi; Martin Diamond, The Electoral College and the American Idea of Democracy, in Berns, ed., *supra* note 2, at 44. Much of the history through the 1960s is recounted in Peirce, *supra* note 18, at 181–94.

42. *See* Commission Report, *supra* note 41, at 3–13.

43. Commission Report, *supra* note 41, at 7–8; *see* David W. Abbott & James P. Levine, Wrong Winner: The Coming Debacle in the Electoral College 46, 152–53 (Praeger 1991) ("[T]he electoral college is morally wrong. It is undemocratic and therefore indefensible.")

44. *See, e.g.,* Best, *supra* note 7, at 352; Diamond, *supra* note 41, at 50–52.

45. Though just what population is to be distributed equally is far from clear. Some of the possibilities are total population, voting population, and citizen voting age population. *See* Bennett, *supra* note 25, at 66–71.

46. *See* Bennett, *supra* note 25, at 27.

47. *See* Federalist 51; Federalist 62; Bennett, *supra* note 25, at 27.

48. *See generally* Dennis C. Mueller, Public Choice II 217–28 (Cambridge University Press 1989).

49. *See* Chapter One. For a description of the early variation in state law and prac-

tice on voting qualifications, *see* John Ferling, Adams vs. Jefferson 86 (Oxford University Press 2004).

50. *See* U. S. Const., Ams. XV, XIX, XXIV, XXVI; Dunn v. Blumstein, 405 U.S. 330 (1972); Katzenbach v. Morgan, 384 U.S. 641(1966). In addition, as we saw in Chapter Three, the Fourteenth Amendment provides that a state's apportionment of members of the House of Representatives is to be proportionately reduced when the right to vote "is [with limited exceptions] denied to any of the male inhabitants of such State." U.S. Const., Am. XIV, § 2. This provision is expressly made applicable, *inter alia*, to an "election for the choice of electors for President and Vice-President of the United States."

51. We touched on this in Chapter One. *See* Note, The Disenfranchisement of Ex-Felons: Citizenship, Criminality, and the "Purity of the Ballot Box," 102 Harv. L. Rev. 1300 (1989).

52. "[I]n parliamentary democracies such as Great Britain, it is not uncommon for the country's leader to be chosen by party members receiving a minority of popular votes in the national election." Hardaway, *supra* note 4, at 9.

53. *See* Longley & Braun, *supra* note 4, at 194 n.7 (discussing views of Alexander Bickel).

54. Indeed even staunch majoritarians come to appreciate that what happens after selection of the president is fully as important as the choice of one or another candidate where two of them have close to the same measure of popular support. Any well-functioning democracy requires accommodation among competing interests. The mechanisms of accommodation are complex, and vary with varying forms of democracy. But a two-party "democratic" system with a bare majority that gives no quarter to the other party is courting a short stay in power at best and at worst serious ongoing societal tension, or even more encompassing failure. Of course, this is not to say that victory brings no rewards, that accommodation after a close two-party election will bring the same results regardless of which party won. But it is to say that in successful democracies, the winner cannot by any means take all.

55. *See, e.g.*, Best, *supra* note 7, at 352–53; Diamond, *supra* note 41, at 51–53.

56. *See* Edwards, *supra* note 4, at 123; Longley & Braun, *supra* note 4, 85–86; Abbott & Levine, *supra* note 43, at 136; Wilmerding, *supra* note 9, at 85, 134; *but see* Wilmerding, *supra*, at 115–16.

57. *See* Best, *supra* note 4, at 65–72; Best, *supra* note 7, at 349; Hardaway, *supra* note 4, at 1, 9, 63, 154, 158; Tara Ross, *supra* note 4, at 94–95, 128, 134. The solar system metaphor originated with John F. Kennedy who as senator from Massachusetts was a staunch defender of the electoral college in debates that took place in the 1950s. *See* Peirce, *supra* note 18, at 159 (quoting Kennedy's reference to "a whole solar system of governmental power. If it is proposed to change the balance of power of one of the elements of the solar system, [Kennedy continued,] it is necessary to consider the others"). Note that

Kennedy's insistence that one would have to "consider" other elements of the system presents a much less dire picture than the one that Best paints of a system where reverberations of change will almost necessarily be felt throughout the system. Albert Rosenthal turns the solar system metaphor to a normative point in Rosenthal, *supra* note 4, at 11. Robert Hardaway seems to have some point of political morality in mind when he says that if "advocates of direct election" count the electoral college as "wrong," they "must . . . open up the whole question of the federalist compact." Hardaway, *supra* note 4, at 30.

58. *See, e.g.*, Keith E. Whittington, The Electoral College: A Modest Contribution, in Jacobson & Rosenfeld, *supra* note 7, at 374; George Will, Foreword, in Tara Ross, *supra* note 4, at x. Martin Diamond's defense of the electoral college also makes the point (with characteristically excessive zeal): "[n]ot only is . . . [the electoral college] not at all archaic, but one might say that it is the very model of up-to-date constitutional flexibility. Perhaps no other feature of the Constitution has had a greater capacity for dynamic historical adaptiveness." Diamond, *supra* note 41, at 46. If this were advanced as a pure description of historical developments, a case could be made for its accuracy, though the case is far from clear and in any event does ignore the dangers to which we will turn in later chapters. But Diamond seems to be suggesting an element of deliberateness on the part of the constitutional framers in coming up with an adaptable system, and on that point please count me as exceedingly dubious.

59. Martin Diamond does not use the metaphor, but he nonetheless gets carried away in flights of rhetoric. Diamond, *supra* note 41, at 53 ("the abhorrence of the federal aspect of the Electoral College . . . rests upon premises that necessitate abhorrence of any and all *district* forms of election.") (emphasis in original), 55 (suggesting that if the president were elected by a nationwide popular vote he would not be responsive "to local needs, interests, and opinions"), 56 (suggesting that a nationwide popular vote would yield a "democracy" that was an "entirely untrammeled and undifferentiated national self"). Hardaway also seems to get carried away when he characterizes "the American system of electing a president" as "the envy of the world." Hardaway, *supra* note 4, at 5. Tara Ross is particularly given to overheated rhetoric, as when she claims that the electoral college is a "brilliant constitutional device," and "an ingenious method whereby the will of the people can be expressed while the freedom of Americans is protected." Tara Ross, *supra* note 4, at 9, 13.

60. Best, *supra* note 4, at 24; *see* Tara Ross, *supra* note 4, at 12.

61. Tara Ross, *supra* note 4, at 41.

62. Hardaway, *supra* note 4, at 22–23.

63. U.S. Const., Art. II, § 1, cl. 1.

64. U.S. Const., Art. I, § 1 (italics supplied).

65. Bickel, *supra* note 4, at 5.

66. Tara Ross, *supra* note 4, at 41.

67. United States v. Carolene Products Co., 304 U.S. 144, 152 n.4 (1938).

68. *See* Frontiero v. Richardson, 411 U.S. 677 (1973); *compare* Graham v. Richardson, 403 U.S. 365 (1971), *with* Foley v. Connelie, 435 U.S. 291 (1978).

69. *See* Tara Ross, *supra* note 4, at 163, 165 (discussing eleven most populous states).

70. Perhaps this is what Joy McAfee means when she says that "[c]apturing almost two-thirds of the smaller states and almost half of the larger states, the electoral votes of Bush were distributed more evenly throughout the states than that [*sic*] of Gore, thus capturing the federal plurality." Joy McAfee, 2001: Should the College Electors Finally Graduate? The Electoral College: An American Compromise from Its Inception to Election 2000, 32 Cumb. L . Rev. 643, 662 (2001–2).

71. Ross sometimes seems to suggest that states have interests apart from those of their citizens. "American states," she writes, "retain unique interests that should be protected in a free society." At another point she contrasts the voting power of individuals within a state with the "advantage given to the state as a whole." And then she disparages those "who continue to value individual votes over the good of the states and their voters as a whole." Tara Ross, *supra* note 4, at 75–76, 86, 121. *See* Walter Berns, Let's Hear It for the Electoral College, in After the People Vote 52 (3d ed., John C. Fortier, ed., AEI Press 2004). The notion of state interests may well be useful as a figure of speech, but surely the values of federalism are to be found not in some interests of the states as such, but in the succor they give to individuals through the dispersal of power and through attachments they can provide for the individuals within them. *See* New York v. United States, 505 U.S. 144 (1992); Sanford Levinson & Ernest A. Young, Who's Afraid of the Twelfth Amendment, 29 Fla. St. U. L. Rev. 925, 953 (2001). This may in the end be all that Ross means by her encomiums to states, for at other times she seems to appreciate that the assignment of power to states as entities is instrumental, a means to the end of protecting the interests of the individuals within a state. "The Electoral College protects the interests of the states," she writes at one point, "and thus their voters." Ross, *supra*, at 87. For another example of the instrumental view, *see* Ross, *supra*, at 76.

72. *See* Ann N. Crigler, Marion R. Just, & Edward J. McCaffery, Rethinking the Vote: The Politics and Prospects of American Election Reform 154 (Oxford University Press 2004); Edwin D. Dover, The Disputed Presidential Election of 2000 10 (Greenwood Press 2003); Timothy Egan, One Nation Indivisible, But Some of It Invisible, N.Y. Times, Sept. 29, 2004, at A18. Apparently the perception—erroneous as it turned out—of a late Bush surge in California in 2000 brought some late campaigning to the state. Ken Foskett & Jena Heath, Question Marks Dot Electoral College Map, Atlanta Journal and Constitution, Oct. 29, 2000, at 14A.

Not surprisingly then voter turnout in competitive states seems to be higher than in politically one-sided ones. *See* Scott L. Althaus, How Exceptional Was Turnout in 2004,

Political Communication Report, Winter 2005, http://www.ou.edu./policom/1501_2005_
winter/commentary.htm (last visited 03/18/05); Michael McDonald, Voter Turnout: The
Numbers Prove That 2004 May Signal More Voter Interest, Milwaukee Journal Sentinel,
Nov. 27, 2004, http://www.brookings.edu/views/op-ed/mcdonald20041127.htm (last vis-
ited 03/18/05); Alexander Keyssar, The Electoral College Flunks, New York Rev. of Books,
Mar. 24, 2005, at 18, n.10.

73. I qualify the point to make it a matter of degree, because it might be that efficient campaigning would cause candidates to focus to some degree on portions of a minority populations within one state or another.

74. James Madison made a similar point in the Constitutional Convention. Speech
in the Federal Convention on Relations Among the States, in James Madison, Writings
113 (The Library of America 1999) ("In point of manners, Religion, and the other circumstances which sometimes beget affection between different communities, [the more
populous states at the time, Virginia, Massachusetts, and Pennsylvania] . . . were not
more assimilated than the other States"). Thus I do not know what one defender of the
electoral college means when she characterizes the "small states" as "the country's most
permanent minority constituency." Tara Ross, *supra* note 4, at 33. One prominent commentator turned the argument back on defenders of the electoral college, urging that the
electoral college—at least as shaped by the prevalence of the winner-take-all approach
to choosing electors—turns states against one another, while abandonment of mono-
lithic state delegations would allow people in different regions of the country to better
appreciate their commonalities. Wilmerding, *supra* note 9, at 89–91.

75. In the 2004 election in the Carolinas, for instance, the Republicans captured the
south by 937,974 to 661,699, and the north by 1,961,166 to 1,525,849.

76. While there were three other candidates who secured electoral votes that year, it
seems likely that Lincoln would have won had he faced only one of them. For he would
have commanded a majority of the electoral college "even if the popular vote of all three
of his rivals had been concentrated on one candidate." Mark Neely, The Last Best Hope
of Earth: Abraham Lincoln and the Promise of America 57 (Harvard University Press
1993). *See* Longley & Peirce, *supra* note 5, at 181.

77. U.S. Const., Am. XII.

78. *See* Longley & Braun, *supra* note 4, at 192 n.40.

79. *See* Longley & Peirce, *supra* note 5, at 184.

80. *See* Longley & Peirce, *supra* note 5, at 60–65.

81. *See* Longley & Braun, *supra* note 4, at 132.

82. Best, *supra* note 7, at 353.

83. This point has been made by one ardent proponent of the electoral college.
Hardaway, *supra* note 4, at 29.

84. *See, e.g.*, Best, *supra* note 7, at 351.

85. This is the argument of Abbott & Levine, *supra* note 43, at 108–9.

86. Alexander Bickel argues that in making presidential selection more like our legislative selection process, a nationwide popular vote would "create a presidency with little or no incentive to act as a counterweight to Congress." Bickel, *supra* note 4, at 12. In today's environment, this strikes me as the least of our worries.

87. *See* Whittington, *supra* note 58, at 388–89; Diamond, *supra* note 41, at 61–62; Best, *supra* note 4, at 14, 57; Will, *supra* note 58, at x; Tara Ross, *supra* note 4, at 106–9; Hardaway, *supra* note 4, at 136–37.

88. As I write this, controversy about an extraordinarily close gubernatorial race in 2004 in the state of Washington had been resolved after a protracted period of time. *See* Sarah Kershaw, Democrat Wins by 130 in Latest Washington Count, N.Y. Times, Dec. 24, 2004, at A14; Eli Sanders, Judge Dismisses Lawsuit Over Washington Election, N.Y. Times, June 7, 2005, at A16.

89. *See* John Schwartz, Mostly Good Reviews for Electronic Voting, N.Y. Times, Nov. 12, 2004, at A20.

90. The general point has caused a number of commentators to argue that it is actually the winner-take-all approach to choosing electors within individual states that provides the inducement for fraud. *See* Edwards, *supra* note 4, at 123; Longley & Braun, *supra* note 4, 85–86; Abbott & Levine, *supra* note 43, at 136; Wilmerding, *supra* note 9, at 85, 134; *but see* Wilmerding, *supra*, at 115–16.

91. *Cf.* Edwards, *supra* note 4, at 124.

92. Tara Ross, *supra* note 4, at 108.

93. Another point that is made repeatedly by defenders of the electoral college is that where the nationwide popular vote is close, the electoral college tally most frequently is less close, replacing "the numerical uncertainty [of the popular vote] with an unambiguously visible constitutional majority that sustains the legitimacy of the electoral result." Diamond, *supra* note 41, at 61; Will, *supra* note 58, at x; Tara Ross, *supra* note 4, at 102–6; Berns, *supra* note 71, at 51. This may well be true if a close popular vote is accompanied by an "unambiguously" decisive electoral college vote, whether the latter is close or not so close. When as in 2000, however, the electoral college tally is close and the popular vote in decisive states is also close, controversy is likely, no matter who has won the popular vote, and no matter the margin of that nationwide popular vote.

94. Commission Report, *supra* note 41, at 8.

95. Judith Best makes an argument to this effect, as does Robert Hardaway. *See* Best, *supra* note 7, at 351; Hardaway, *supra* note 4, at 19. For a formal treatment of strategic voting, *see* Robin Farquharson, Theory of Voting 17–27 (Yale University Press 1969). The insight that single member legislative districting fosters a two-party system is usually traced to the French political theorist Maurice Duverger. *See* Maurice Duverger, Political Parties: Their Organization and Activity in the Modern State 217–18, 239 (Wiley 1954).

96. *See* Longley & Braun, *supra* note 4, at 90, 196 n.25.

97. *See* Diamond, *supra* note 41, at 64–66; Polsby & Wildavsky, *supra* note 4, at 249–50.

98. Commission Report, *supra* note 41, at 10.

99. George Edwards mentions other arguments against a runoff requirement:

A runoff at the end of an already lengthy campaign would also place added burdens on the presidential candidates and on their depleted campaign treasuries. It would require a more rapid count and certification of ballots, including the resolution of disputes, than would otherwise be necessary. It is possible that a runoff would also result in a considerable vote drop-off from the initial ballot. By definition, a second ballot would delay the selection of the winner. Edwards, *supra* note 4, at 155.

100. *See* John F. Bibby & L. Sandy Maisel, Two Parties or More: The American Party System 75 (2d ed., Westview Press 2003).

101. I discuss this literature in Bennett, *supra* note 25, at 106–15.

102. *Cf.* Abbott & Levine, *supra* note 43, at 135 (invoking "the weight of opinion").

103. *See* Chapter Eight.

104. *See* Longley & Braun, *supra* note 4, at 87–88.

105. *See* Polsby & Wildavsky, *supra* note 4, at 245.

106. The commission generalizes the point to include selection of the vice president by Senate as well, *see* Commission Report, *supra* note 41, at 9, but the vice-presidential selection seems much less problematic, if only because the likelihood of a Senate stand-off is much less substantial than that of a House standoff. *See* Chapter Five.

107. Even in a political system dominated by two political parties, the joinder of the presidential and vice-presidential selections is potentially complicated not only by the use of the two different houses for a fallback selection procedure, but by the "inhabitancy" limitation that we discussed in Chapters One and Two. In theory that limitation might require the electoral college itself to choose a president and vice president of different parties. But for reasons we will discuss in Chapter Nine, the provision that an elector can vote for an "inhabitant" of his own state only for one of the two offices should not be allowed to pose a problem in the electoral vote tally.

108. Michael Glennon characterizes the problem as "serious," but does not provide much explanation of why that is so. Glennon, *supra* note 25, at 56–57. Similarly David Abbott and James Levine call the possibility of the two officers coming from different parties "political madness," but they offer no explanation of the damage it might do. Abbott & Levine, *supra* note 43, at 67. *See* Hardaway, *supra* note 4, at 21, 62.

Chapter Five

1. U.S. Const., Am. XII.

2. Chief Justice William Rehnquist mistakenly asserted that the Article II provision

for choice among five survived passage of the Twelfth Amendment. *See* William H. Rehnquist, Centennial Crisis: The Disputed Election of 1876 100–101 (Alfred A. Knopf 2004).

3. 10 The Writings of Thomas Jefferson 1816–26 264 (Paul Liecester Ford ed., G. P. Putnam's Sons 1899) (letter to George Hay, Aug. 17, 1823).

4. Just a smattering of more recent disparaging comments can be found in Lawrence D. Longley & Neal R. Peirce, The Electoral College Primer 2000 126 (Yale University Press 1999). *See* U.S. Senate Rep. No. 395, 43rd Cong., 1st Sess. 19 (1874).

5. Indeed, many commentators who approve of the electoral college in general are critical of the House contingent procedure. *See* remarks collected in Chapter Four, note 4; Tara Ross, Enlightened Democracy: The Case for the Electoral College 127–38 (World Ahead Publishing 2004). In sharp contrast is Robert Hardaway who not only approves of the House contingent procedure but urges that it "be retained even if reformers are successful in amending the Constitution to provide for direct popular election." Robert M. Hardaway, The Electoral College and the Constitution: The Case for Preserving Federalism 62 (Praeger 1994).

6. The eventual vote was 271-266. One elector, Barbara Lett-Simmons of the District of Columbia, abstained, but it seems likely that she would have voted had her vote (for Gore) made a difference, so that the vote would have been 271-267, the closest since 1876. *See* George C. Edwards III, Why the Electoral College Is Bad for America 24 (Yale University Press 2004).

7. A collection of some of the warnings is provided in Chapter Six, note 14.

8. *See* Birch Bayh, Foreword to Lawrence D. Longley & Alan G. Braun, The Politics of Electoral College Reform vii (Yale University Press 1972).

9. *See* Chapter Two.

10. *See* Chapter Four.

11. On those few occasions when the popular vote "winner" has lost in the electoral college, the popular vote margin has been relatively small. Martin Diamond, The Electoral College and the American Idea of Democracy, in After the People Vote 44, 56–57 (Walter Berns, ed., AEI Press 1992).

12. *See* Chapter Four.

13. In 1992 H. Ross Perot, running as an independent, came away with almost nineteen percent of the popular vote, while winning no electoral votes. *See* Chapter Eight. It is certainly plausible to imagine that he would have won a sizable electoral vote bloc and then gone down to defeat in the House, but even then he would presumably have lost to another candidate with a sizable popular vote total.

14. Albert J. Rosenthal, The Constitution, Congress, and Presidential Elections, 67 Mich. L. Rev. 1, 14–15 (1968).

15. As the 1968 election was nearing and promised to be close, some members of the

House of Representatives sought support for a proposal that if recourse to the House became necessary the House would give the nod to the nationwide popular vote winner. *See* Longley & Peirce, *supra* note 4, at 215 n.27. Some House members, on the other hand, had publicly indicated that in the case of House selection of the president, they would vote as their districts had voted. *See* Edwards, *supra* note 6, at 70; *cf.* Lucius Wilmerding, Jr., The Electoral College 186 (Beacon Press 1958).

16. Edwards, *supra* note 6, at 70.

17. *See* After the People Vote 18 (3d ed., John C. Fortier ed., AEI Press 2004). It is not clear to me why Tara Ross thinks that the possibility of a standoff in the House is so remote, Tara Ross, *supra* note 5, at 137, apart, of course, from the unlikelihood of having to resort to the House at all.

18. *See* John Ferling, Adams vs. Jefferson 176 (Oxford University Press 2004). The breakdown is sometimes reported as 63-43. James Roger Sharp, American Politics in the Early Republic: The New Nation in Crisis 248 (Yale University Press 1993). In any event, remember that it was not the newly elected House but the outgoing one that made the presidential selection at that time. *See* Chapter Three.

19. *See* Sharp, *supra* note 18, at 253.

20. *See* Wilmerding, *supra* note 15, at 201.

21. U.S. Const., Am. XX, §§ 1, 3.

22. There could theoretically be a divergence, caused, for instance, by the "inhabitancy" limitation discussed in Chapters One and Two.

23. U.S. Const., Am. XII.

24. U.S. Const., Am. XII.

25. U.S. Const., Am. XX, § 3.

26. *See* 3 U.S.C. § 19 (2000).

27. U.S. Const., Art. I, § 6, cl. 2.

28. 3 U.S.C. § 19(d)(1) (2000).

29. *See* Wilmerding, *supra* note 15, at 190. While the vice-presidential backup was not available at the time, in the 1800 House selection, some Federalists apparently considered the possibility that the then-prevailing—statutory—backup possibilities might make ongoing deadlock in the House an attractive option. *See* Ferling, *supra* note 18, at 178.

30. Michael Bellesiles displays confusion about this (as well as a number of other things) in his essay, "The Soil Will Be Soaked with Blood," a contribution to The Revolution of 1800 (James Horn *et al.*, eds., University of Virginia Press 2002). Bellesiles incorrectly asserts that in the 1800 contest "[n]either Burr nor Jefferson had a majority [of the electoral college]." Bellesiles, *supra,* at 78. If that had been the case, then the House would have chosen the new president from those receiving the five highest number of electoral votes. U.S. Const., Art. II, § 1, cl. 3. Perhaps it is for that reason that Bellesiles asserts that "the House could have felt justified in going further down the list, say to John

Adams [who had also received a sizable number of electoral votes, though fewer than Jefferson and Burr had received]." Bellesiles, *supra*. Since both Jefferson and Burr had received a majority of the number of electors—and the same majority—(73 out of 138, *see* Longley & Peirce, *supra* note 4, at 179, 188), the House's choice was limited to the two of them. U.S. Const., Art. II, § 1, cl. 3.

31. U.S. Senate Rep., *supra* note 4, at 19. As a more recent report put it, selection of the president in the House "is likely to involve political deals and pressures and to place the President in a position of indebtedness to those who voted for him." Commission on Electoral College Reform, Electing the President 9 (American Bar Association 1967). *Cf.* Norman J. Ornstein, Three Disputed Elections, in After the People Vote, *supra* note 11, at 35, 37.

32. *See* Chapters Two and Three.

33. U.S. Const., Am. XII.

34. *See* Eric Foner, Reconstruction: 1863–1877 566–80 (Harper & Row 1988); Rehnquist, *supra* note 2, at 107–8.

35. Perhaps this is what a Virginian taking part in the debates about ratification of the Constitution meant when he said of the House procedure that "[i]t seemed rather founded on accident than any principle of government I ever heard of." *See* Tadahisa Kuroda, The Origins of the Twelfth Amendment 18 (Greenwood Press 1994); *cf.* David W. Abbott & James P. Levine, Wrong Winner: The Coming Debacle in the Electoral College 66 (Praeger 1991).

36. *Cf.* Edwards, *supra* note 6, at 27, 72 ("electors seeking personal recognition or attention to a pet cause").

37. *See* Chapter Nine.

38. In 2004 one of the Minnesota electors voted for John Edwards for president. This may have been a mistake, but the identity of the aberrant elector is not known, because the Minnesota balloting is a secret one. *See* MN Elector Votes for Edwards, http://wcco.com/topstories/local_story_348135504.html (last visited 01/06/05); Bush Carries Electoral College After Delay, http://www.cnn.com/2005/ALLPOLITICS (last visited 01/07/05).

39. U.S. Const., Art. II, § 1, cl. 2.

40. *See* Chapter Four.

Chapter Six

1. The technical trigger for recourse to the House is not a tie as such, but a failure of any candidate to obtain an electoral college majority. U.S. Const., Am. XII. The required majority, moreover, is not of the allocated electors, but of those "appointed." In recent years, no states have failed to "appoint" their full complement of electors, but that has happened—as early as the nation's first election. And it is not farfetched to believe that Florida might have failed to appoint its electors in 2000. I discuss both of these matters in Chapter Nine.

Even with an odd number of electors, a tie between the only two candidates to garner electoral votes could come about if an elector (or three, or five, or some other odd number) abstained. Abstentions could obviously also create ties with an even number of electors. As we will see shortly, there was an abstention in the 2000 election, though it did not result in a tie. Abstention might be by an uncommitted elector, but also by an elector who breaks faith with a commitment to vote for the candidate of a particular political party. We take up the problem of such "faithless electors" in Chapter Seven.

2. With an odd number of members of the electoral college and all of them casting votes, the final tally in the 1876 election was 185-184. *See* Lawrence D. Longley & Neal R. Peirce, The Electoral College Primer 2000 181 (Yale University Press 1999).

3. There have been relatively brief periods without much party competition, and also ones with third parties that provided a good measure of competitiveness. In retrospect at least, the quick reversion to two-party competition, even after the displacement of one party by another, seems much more remarkable than the temporary deviations from the pattern. We will touch on these matters in Chapter Eight, but both here and there I hold back from delving into the complex history in any depth, since it could take us far afield from the central project of this book.

4. Longley & Peirce, *supra* note 2, at 3.

5. This is not to say that uncompetitive candidates do not change the outcome of races between the two principal parties. Running under the banner of the Green Party in 2000, for instance, Ralph Nader received close to three million votes across the nation, including more votes in eight states than the margin of victory in those states between the candidates of the two major parties. At the same time, Nader never seriously threatened to win any electoral votes in the 2000 election.

6. *See* Longley & Peirce, *supra* note 2, at 211, n.20 ("In 1972, Roger MacBride, a Virginia Nixon elector, cast an unexpected vote—for Libertarian Party candidate John Hospers. Similarly, in 1976, Republican elector Mike Padden of the state of Washington declined to vote for Republican nominee Gerald Ford, and instead voted for Ronald Reagan. Finally, Margaret Leach, a West Virginia Democratic elector in 1988, for unexplained reasons cast her *president* [*sic*] vote for *vice presidential* nominee Lloyd Bentsen and her *vice presidential* electoral vote for *presidential* candidate Michale Dukakis") (emphasis in original). In addition, one of the Minnesota Democratic electors cast a presidential vote for the party's vice-presidential candidate in 2004. Whether this was deliberate or not is not known as of this writing. *See* note 12, *infra*.

7. *See* Chapter Five, note 6.

8. For a report of political insider speculation about the possibility of a tie in the days leading up to the 2000 election, *see* John M. Broder, Lessons of 2000 Shape Strategy of Today, N.Y. Times, Oct. 30, 2004, at A13.

9. *See* Vieth v. Jubelirer, 541 U.S. 267 (2004).

10. Not surprisingly, Pennsylvania remained a "battleground," or swing, state in the 2004 election. *See, e.g.*, The Electoral Map, N.Y. Times, Oct. 24, 2004, at 24.

11. Just a few other possibilities were switches in Ohio, New Hampshire, and Pennsylvania, or Ohio, Nevada, and Pennsylvania, or West Virginia and Vermont, or Arizona, Louisiana, Minnesota, and New Mexico.

12. Somewhat mysteriously a Minnesota elector pledged to the Democratic Party nominees voted for John Edwards for president, rather than for John Kerry, the party's presidential nominee. Had it not been for this (possibly inadvertent) misstep, Bush would have beaten Kerry in the electoral college by thirty-four votes, 286-252. *See* MN Elector Votes for Edwards, http://wcco.com/topstories/local_story_348135504.html (last visited 01/06/05); Bush Carries Electoral College After Delay, http://www.cnn.com/2005/ALLPOLITICS (last visited 01/07/05).

13. *See, e.g.*, Marjorie Connelly, Other Polls Are Also Tight, N.Y. Times, Nov. 1, 2004, at A16.

14. *See* William Saletan, David Kenner, & Louisa Herron Thomas, Where the Presidential Race Stands Today, Slate, http://slate.msn.com/id/2108751/ (last visited 11/01/04). Writing before the 2000 election, and admittedly using a sterilized mathematization of the possibilities, two commentators came up with a 1.5 percent chance of an electoral college tie. Paul Sracic & Nathan P. Ritchey, All Tied Up in Presidential What-Ifs, Wash. Post, Aug. 23, 2004, at B02. No doubt sensitized by the 2000 election, others began to notice the possibility as the 2004 election approached. *See, e.g.*, Susan Page, Remember the Mess in 2000? How About a tie?, USA Today, Sept. 3, 2004, at 1A; Stephen J. Marmon, President Edwards?, N.Y. Times, Oct. 29, 2004, at A23; Dana Milbank, Electoral College Calculus: Computer Analysis Shows 33 Ways to End in a Tie, Wash. Post, Oct. 27, 2004, at A01; Alexander Keyssar, The Electoral College Flunks, New York Rev. of Books, March 24, 2005, at 16; *see also* Robert W. Bennett, The Peril that Lurks in Even Numbers: Selecting the President, 7 The Green Bag 2d ser. 113 (2004) (hereinafter "The Peril"); Robert Bennett, Fit to be Tied, N.Y. Times, Aug. 11, 2004, at A19.

15. *See* The Electoral Map, *supra* note 10.

16. "[I]n 1976[,] had Ford received 11,950 extra votes in Delaware and Ohio[,] . . . he and Carter would both have wound up with 269 votes!" David W. Abbott & James P. Levine, Wrong Winner: The Coming Debacle in the Electoral College 134 (Praeger 1991).

17. *See, e.g.*, Paul Farhi, Parties Square Off in a Database Duel; Voter Information Shapes Strategies, Wash. Post, July 20, 2004, at A01; Alexander Keyssar, The Right to Vote and Election 2000, in The Unfinished Election of 2000 75, 96 (Jack N. Rakove, ed., Basic Books 2001).

18. U.S. Const., Art. II, § 1, cl. 2.

19. Under the Davis proposal to which we will turn shortly, the size of the electoral college would actually differ from the sum of these three components.

20. The number is "in no event [to be] more than the least populous State." U.S. Const., Am. XXIII, § 1, cl. 2. Even if the size of the House were to remain constant at its present 435, it is conceivable—albeit only barely—that the distribution of the nation's population would lead to the smallest House delegation being two or more (rather than one, as at the present time), and hence to the smallest electoral college delegation being four, or some larger even number. This would come about only if the relative size of the populations of the states narrowed quite substantially—a remote possibility that might safely be ignored. Another possibility is that the House could be increased in size so substantially that even without population shifts the least populous states would have larger delegations than they do at present. I am assuming that we can safely ignore that possibility as well, and I turn in the text to the more realistic possibilities for altering the size of the electoral college.

21. U.S. Const., Art. I, § 2, cl. 3.

22. *See* Act of Aug. 8, 1911, c. 5, §§ 1, 2, 37 Stats. 13, 14. The size has remained constant since that time, except for temporary increases to accommodate the admission to the union of Hawaii and Alaska. *See* David A. Crockett, Dodging the Bullet: Election Mechanics and the Problem of the Twenty-Third Amendment, XXXVI PS Online No. 3, at 423 (July 2003).

23. *See* Bennett, The Peril, *supra* note 14.

24. Adam Graham-Silverman, Initiative to Ensure Congress Carries on After a Catastrophe Get Cool Receptions, CQ Weekly, June 7, 2003.

25. *See* U.S. Const., Art. I, § 2, cl. 5.

26. Professor David Crockett reports that during a one-hundred-and-fifty-eight-week period over three years from 1999 to 2001 deaths and resignations resulted in eighty-eight weeks of a House with an odd number of members and seventy weeks of a House with an even number. A House of the allotted size of 435 was the exception rather than the rule during that period. Crockett, *supra* note 22, at 426.

27. U.S. Const., Art. I, § 8, cl. 17. *See* James Dao, Bill to Give Washington a House Vote Is Proposed, N.Y. Times, May 4, 2005, at A19. There surely would be a question of Congress's power to provide District representation, since the Constitution also says that representatives are to be "chosen . . . by the People of the several States." U.S. Const., Art. I, § 2, cl. 1.

28. *See* U.S. Const., Art. I, § 2, cl. 2.

29. *See* Wesberry v. Sanders, 376 U.S. 1 (1964); Chapter Four, note 45.

30. Aside from the complication mentioned in note 22, *supra*.

31. *See, e.g.*, Christopher St. John Yates, A House of Our Own or a House We've Outgrown? An Argument for Increasing the Size of the House of Representatives, 25 Colum. J. L. & Soc. Probs. 157 (1992); Charles A. Kromkowski & John A. Kromkowski, Why 435? A Question of Political Arithmetic, 24 Polity 129 (1991).

32. I do not seriously treat the possibility of a reduction in the size of the House, because the political considerations would seem to make that essentially impossible.

33. *See* Michel L. Balinski & H. Peyton Young, Fair Representation: Meeting the Ideal of One Man, One Vote 10–22 (Yale University Press 1982).

34. U.S. Const., Art. I, § 2, cl. 3.

35. *See* note 22, *supra*.

36. Different results will also be produced depending upon whether, on the one hand, each state is first allocated the one representative to which it is minimally entitled, and the remaining representatives are then assigned by the selected method, or instead the chosen method is first applied, and then each state is assured its minimum entitlement. *See generally*, Paul H. Edelman & Suzanna Sherry, Pick a Number, Any Number: State Representatives in Congress after the 2000 Census, 90 Calif. L. Rev. 211 (2002).

37. *See generally* Edelman & Sherry, *supra* note 36; *see also* Kromkowski & Kromkowski, *supra* note 31.

38. *See* United States Department of Commerce v. Montana, 503 U.S. 442 (1992).

39. *See* Utah v. Evans, 536 U.S. 452 (2002).

40. For reasons suggested in Chapters Two and Four, the office of vice president is not nearly as important as that of president, and the possibility of a tie in the Senate backup process for choosing a vice president is considerably less serious than for choosing a president in the House. For those reasons I do not feel obliged to discuss the Senate backup procedure at any length. Should that process be deemed a matter of concern, however, I have no feasible solution to offer to the possibility of a Senate tie vote if the choice of a vice president does fall to that body.

Chapter Seven

1. U.S. Const., Am. XII.

2. U.S. Const., Art. II, § 1, cl. 3.

3. *See* Ray v. Blair, 343 U.S. 214 (1952).

4. *See* Lawrence D. Longley & Alan G. Braun, The Politics of Electoral College Reform 4-6 (Yale University Press 1972) (1960 election).

5. *See* Chapter Six, note 12.

6. Neal R. Peirce, The People's President 64 (Simon & Schuster 1968). By the end of Washington's second term, the expectation that electors would hew to the line of the political party that had advanced them had already taken hold, but it was only over time that it became a firm commitment in the way it is generally understood today. In that sense the notion of "faithlessness" has come into focus only gradually. Thus one commentator, noting that in the 1820 election Samuel Plumer did not vote as expected for James Monroe (thus depriving him of a unanimous vote in the electoral college), says rather blandly that this was "contrary to the expectations of his constituents." Albert J.

Rosenthal, The Constitution, Congress, and Presidential Elections, 67 Mich. L. Rev. 1, 17 (1968). *See* Note, State Power to Bind Presidential Electors, 65 Colum. L. Rev. 696, 698 (1965); George C. Edwards III, Why the Electoral College Is Bad for America 21 (Yale University Press 2004).

7. *See* CNN.com, Electoral College Explainer, http://www.cnn.com/ELECTION/ 2004/special/president (last visited 11/03/04).

8. *See* Kris Wise, Robb Defends Position, Charleston Daily Mail, Sept. 14, 2004, at A1. In a subsequent story in the *New York Times*, Robb was quoted as saying that according to his research "an elector had 'qualified discretion' when it came to casting a vote." Campaign Briefing, West Virginia: Elector May Not Vote for Bush, N.Y. Times, Oct. 22, 2004, at A18.

9. Robb signed the (unanimous) certificate of vote that was submitted by the West Virginia electors. *See* Certificate of Vote, http://www.freerepublic.com/focus/f-news/ 1309528/posts/ (last visited 01/06/05).

10. *See, e.g.*, Lawrence D. Longley & Neal R. Peirce, The Electoral College Primer 2000 110–16 (Yale University Press 1999); Beverly J. Ross & William Josephson, The Electoral College and the Popular Vote, XII J. L. & Pol. 665 (1996).

11. *E.g.*, Me. Rev. Stat. Ann. Tit. 21-A § 805(2) (2004); *see generally* Note, *supra* note 6, at 703; Edwards, *supra* note 6, at 25.

12. N.C. Gen. Stat. Ann. § 163–212 (2001); N.M. Stat. Ann. § 1–15–9(B) (2004).

13. *Compare* AK Stat. § 15.30.040 (2003) ("party shall require . . . a pledge"), *with* Mass. Gen. L. Ann. ch. 53 § 8 (2004) ("acceptance [of nomination for post of elector] . . . signed by each candidate . . . on a form to be provided by the state secretary . . . . [which] form shall include a pledge").

14. *See, e.g.*, Mich. Comp. Laws Ann. § 168.47 (2004); N.C. Gen. Stat. § 163–212 (2001); Utah Code Ann. § 20A–13–304(3)(2004).

15. *See* Edwards, *supra* note 6, at 152.

16. *See* Ross & Josephson, *supra* note 10, at 690. On the basis of a research assistant's compilation, I counted twenty-two such states in mid-2005.

17. In at least one case—the 1960 votes of an Oklahoma Republican elector named Henry Irwin for Senators Harry Byrd and Barry Goldwater, rather than for the party's nominees, Richard Nixon and Henry Cabot Lodge—the votes were cast in the face of state law that required an oath by electors to vote as pledged. *See* Note, *supra* note 6, at 696, 703; Peirce, *supra* note 6, at 18, 26 n.1.

18. *See* Longley & Peirce, *supra* note 10, at 113.

19. *Cf.* Lucius Wilmerding, Jr., The Electoral College 179 (Beacon Press 1958). One commentator insists, probably correctly as an historical matter, that "never once has a 'faithless' ballot been cast with the intention of influencing the outcome of an election. They have all been cast for symbolic purposes only." Martin Diamond, The Electoral

College and the American Idea of Democracy, in After the People Vote 100 n.17 (Walter
Berns, ed., AEI Press 1992). More questionable is the same commentator's confidence
about the future: "it is about as likely that 'faithless electors' will usurp an election as it is
that the English Crown will reassume the regal power of, say, Henry VIII." Diamond,
supra, at 100 n.17. As we will see shortly, there seems to have been at least one presidential campaign which thought the possibilities were good enough to give it a try.

   20. *See, e.g.,* Ross & Josephson, *supra* note 10, at 676; Berns, ed., *supra* note 19, at 13
("electors . . . constitutional status of free agents"); After the People Vote 8 (3d ed., John
C. Fortier, ed., AEI Press 2004); Edwards, *supra* note 6, at 20, 25–26; Akhil Reed Amar,
Presidents, Vice Presidents, and Death: Closing the Constitution's Succession Gap, 48
Ark. L. Rev. 215, 219, 230 (1995); David W. Abbott & James P. Levine, Wrong Winner: The
Coming Debacle in the Electoral College 57, 118 (Praeger 1991); Robert M. Hardaway,
The Electoral College and the Constitution 164 (Praeger 1994); Lawrence D. Longley &
Alan G. Braun, The Politics of Electoral College Reform 29 (Yale University Press 1972);
Alexander Keyssar, The Electoral College Flunks, N.Y. Rev. of Books, March 24, 2005, at
16; *cf.* Tara Ross, Enlightened Democracy: The Case For the Electoral College 114, 116
(World Ahead Publishing 2004).

   21. *See* Chapter Two. This was apparently the view of many in Congress who decided in the 1968 electoral vote count to allow the faithless vote of North Carolina elector Lloyd Bailey to stand as cast. *See* Lawrence D. Longley & Alan G. Braun, The Politics
of Electoral College Reform 140 (Yale University Press 1972).

   22. A Virginia Republican ballot from the 1824 election is reproduced in Appendix
K of Peirce, *supra* note 6, at 342. It contains the name of the presidential candidate, John
Quincy Adams, and the slate of electors committed to his candidacy, but apparently no
vice-presidential running mate had been designated, and the ballot refers only to
"[s]ome tried and approved Patriot" for vice president. Johnson was the designated vice-
presidential candidate in 1836, and I would assume that the ballot recited his name. But
I cannot be sure of that, nor that the names of the Republican electors appeared on the
ballot.

   23. Interestingly, Virginia's two senators voted for Johnson. *See* Leland Winfield
Meyer, The Life and Times of Colonel Richard M. Johnson of Kentucky 428 (Columbia
University Press 1932). Robert M. Hardaway identifies Robert Richardson as the candidate who went through this tortured process, but I believe he simply got the name
wrong. *Compare* Hardaway, *supra* note 20, at 61 *with* Longley & Peirce, *supra* note 10, at
127–28 and Democratic Ticket for the 1836 Presidential Election, http://search.netscape.
com/ns/boomframe.jsp?query=1836+presidential+election&page=1&offset=0&result_
url=re (last visited 02/25/05).

   24. *See* Note, *supra* note 6, at 701; Tara Ross, *supra* note 20, at 114.

   25. After the 1976 election, one Robert Brewster of New Mexico is reported to have

sent a letter to each member of the electoral college urging them to elect him as president. In all likelihood Brewster had not received any popular votes for president (since there would seem to be no way to cast them, unless there were slates of electors committed to him), but he also was apparently unpersuasive, and did not receive any electoral votes. *See* Longley & Peirce, *supra* note 10, at 78, 185. Almost surely, however, individual electoral votes have been cast for persons who received no popular votes for president. *See, e.g.*, Edwards, *supra* note 6, at 21–22 (vote for Walter E. Jones).

26. Tara Ross, *supra* note 20, at 118. In Fortier, ed., *supra* note 20, at 8 it is reported that "[d]uring the 2000 election controversy, Bob Beckel, a Democratic consultant, claimed to head an effort to persuade Bush electors to vote for Al Gore, using the argument that Gore had won the popular vote."

27. At least one commentator confessed to having thought it was a real possibility. *See* Timothy Noah, Faithless Elector Watch, Slate, http://c.msn.com/c.gif?NA=1132&NC=1262&DI=4098&PI=7315&PS=61736 (last visited 12/07/04)

28. *See* Tara Ross, *supra* note 20, at 144. Such a prediction had earlier been generalized in Abbott & Levine, *supra* note 20, at 5, 42. Their prediction was that the "electoral system . . . [will] produce an electoral college majority for a Democratic candidate who was defeated at the polls by a plurality of over a million votes." Abbott & Levine, *supra*, at 41–42. This should give pause not only about electoral college predictions more narrowly but about our ability to foresee what is going to happen with American democracy just a few years out.

29. Edwards, *supra* note 6, at 158.

30. The allegations of any plan by the Bush campaign to "discredit" the electoral college were denied by highly placed officials in the campaign. *See* Tara Ross, *supra* note 20, at 217 n.34.

31. In 1977 Robert Dole, who had been the Republican vice-presidential candidate in the close 1976 election, testified that after the election—and before the electoral college vote—the Republican ticket was "looking around for electors." Dole remarked that "the temptation is there for that elector in a very tight race to really negotiate quite a bunch." *See* Longley & Peirce, *supra* note 10, at 78. A casual remark to the same effect is reported in T. R. Reid, Direct Presidential Election Again Sought by Sen. Bayh, Wash. Post, Jan. 28, 1977, at A2.

32. In the 1968 election third-party candidate George Wallace captured forty-six electoral votes. This was not enough to deprive Richard Nixon of an electoral college majority, but before the election it seemed entirely possible that no candidate would obtain the required majority and the election would be thrown into the House of Representatives. *See* Longley & Peirce, *supra* note 10, at 59–69. In that context, James Michener, who became a Democratic elector, reported that before the election he and another Democratic elector "decided that if the vote was as close as some predicted, and if the re-

sults in the electoral college were such that a President was not elected, [they] would rather decide who the next President should be than to have that choice left in the hands of Governor Wallace [presumably in the electoral college balloting], or to the chicanery of a log-rolling session in the House of Representatives." *See* Direct Popular Election of the President and Vice President of the United States: Hearings on S.J. Res. 28 before the Subcommittee on the Constitution of the Senate Committee on the Judiciary, 96th Cong., 1st Sess. 74–75 (1979). *See also* James A. Michener, Presidential Lottery: The Reckless Gamble in Our Electoral System 16, 56 (Random House 1969).

33. *See* Edwards, *supra* note 6, at 23 (1960 faithless Oklahoma Republican elector Henry Irwin reporting on his reasoning); note 32, *supra*.

34. *See* Chapter Three.

35. *See* Chapter Two.

36. *See* Chapter Three. One account is provided in the late Chief Justice William Rehnquist's recent book on the 1876 election. William H. Rehnquist, Centennial Crisis: The Disputed Election of 1876 107–8 (Alfred A. Knopf 2004).

37. *See* Abbott & Levine, *supra* note 20, at 17–18, 119; *cf.* Hardaway, *supra* note 20, at 51.

38. There is no good way to measure the degree of social discontent caused by the 2000 election, and if I am right that there does not seem to be a great deal of it, that may well be a function in part of the extraordinary events of September 11, 2001, which diverted attention from the way in which the executive is chosen to how he deals with things that happen while he is in office. *See* Chapter One. We saw in Chapter Three that little social turmoil accompanied the divergence in the 1888 election between the electoral college winner and the candidate with the most popular votes.

39. The comment appeared in the newspaper, United States Gazette. *See* Longley & Peirce, *supra* note 10, at 24. For a defense of Miles, *see* Wilmerding, *supra* note 19, at 177.

40. Horace Elisha Scudder, James Russell Lowell: A Biography 216–17 (Houghton Mifflin 1901).

41. One ardent defender of the electoral college—particularly against proposals for a nationwide popular vote discussed in Chapter Four—praises its demonstrated flexibility over the years, including the fact that the "electors became nullities." Martin Diamond, The Electoral College and the American Idea of Democracy, in Berns, ed., *supra* note 19, at 46. Compare this with Berns's own words in the same volume: "electors . . . constitutional status of free agents." Berns, ed., *supra* at 13.

42. Rosenthal, *supra* note 6, at 17. Another, with elector faithlessness largely in view, says that "[t]he legitimacy of the electoral process would shatter if the American electorate were suddenly confronted with a fully revitalized electoral college." Michael J. Glennon, When No Majority Rules 67 (Congressional Quarterly 1992).

43. Ray v. Blair, 343 U.S. 214 (1952). The court did, however, explicitly reserve the

possibility that the pledge was "legally unenforceable because of an assumed constitutional freedom." 343 U.S. at 230. The Supreme Court's decision is discussed in Glennon, *supra* note 42, at 33–34.

44. Peirce, *supra* note 6, at 129–30; Rosenthal, *supra* note 6 at 20 n.72; Wilmerding, *supra* note 19, at 172–73; *see* Ray v. Blair, 343 U.S. 214, 228 (1952).

45. "1. a. a small ball dropped into a box or urn in secret voting; b. a ticket or sheet of paper . . . used to cast a secret ballot." Webster's New International Dictionary 168 (3d ed. 1993).

46. Among current members of the Supreme Court, Justice Scalia is most closely associated with this position. *See* Johnson v. Transportation Agency, 480 U.S. 616, 657 (1987) (Scalia, J., dissenting).

47. "An indirect and limited means of promoting a literate electorate was the adoption of the secret or Australian ballot. . . . For much of the nineteenth century, voters had obtained their ballots from political parties: since the ballots generally contained only the names of an individual party's candidates, literacy was not required. . . . Since ballots tended to be different sizes, shapes, and colors, a man's vote was hardly a secret." Alexander Keyssar, The Right to Vote: The Contested History of Democracy in the United States 142 (Basic Books 2000). Several of the state laws that restrict or forbid elector faithlessness use the word "ballot" without any suggestion of secretiveness. *See, e.g.,* Mich. Comp. Laws Ann. § 168.47 (2004) ("[t]he ballot used by the elector shall bear the name of the elector"); 21-A Me. Rev. Stat. Ann. § 805(2) (2004) ("electors . . . shall cast their ballots for the presidential and vice-presidential candidates who received the largest number of votes").

48. *See, e.g.,* Green v. Bock Laundry Machine Co., 490 U.S. 504, 527 (1989).

49. The term seems to have originated with Paul Brest. *See* Paul Brest, The Misconceived Quest for the Original Understanding, 60 Bos. U. L. Rev. 204 (1980). A classic statement of the idea is that of Justice George Sutherland, dissenting in Home Bldg & Loan Ass'n v. Blaisdell, 290 U.S. 398, 453 (1934): "The whole aim of construction, as applied to a provision of the Constitution, is to discover the meaning, to ascertain and give effect to the intent, of its framers and the people who adopted it."

50. *See generally* Appendix: Originalism and the Enduring Need for Conversation, in Robert W. Bennett, Talking It Through: Puzzles of American Democracy 147 (Cornell University Press 2003).

51. *See* Robert W. Bennett, Justifying Dynamism, Issues in Legal Scholarship, Dynamic Statutory Interpretation (2002): Article 4, http://www.bepress.com/ils/Iss3/art4.

52. The electoral college is governed to a great extent by the Twelfth Amendment and, on a particular specialized matter, by the Twenty-Third Amendment. Amendments typically require the involvement of even more people than did the original Constitution. Both houses of Congress must normally approve amendments—by two-thirds

votes—and then ratification in three-fourths of the states is required, typically through the agency of state legislatures, most of which have two chambers and many members. *See* U.S. Const., Art. V. And needless to say, there were more states in being at the time of the relevant constitutional amendments than at the time of the original Constitution. In any event, whether the question of elector discretion is thought to be governed by a provision in the body of the Constitution, by one of both of these amendments, or by some combination of them all, an "intention" or "understanding" can be ascribed to it only by ascribing to the provision intentions, understandings, or purposes of the multiplicity of persons involved, distilled in the way suggested in the text.

53. The closest judicial articulation of this dilemma in thinking about contemporary constitutional questions is in Justice Robert Jackson's justly storied concurrence in the Steel Seizure Case, Youngstown Sheet & Tube Co. v. Sawyer, 343 U.S. 579, 634 (1952): "Just what our forefathers did envision, or would have envisioned had they foreseen modern conditions, must be divined from materials almost as enigmatic as the dreams Joseph was called upon to interpret for Pharaoh."

54. *See* Abbott & Levine, *supra* note 20, at 11.

55. *See* U.S. Senate Report No. 395, 43rd Cong., 1st Sess. 3–4 (1874).

56. *See* Robert G. Dixon, Jr., Electoral College Procedure, 3 Western Pol. Q. 214, 220–21 (1950).

57. Edwards, *supra* note 6, at 8. Edwards reports that only "[o]ne state—Mississippi—uniquely prints the names of the electors but makes no mention of the presidential candidates they favor—unless the electors are pledged and wish to indicate their preference." Edwards, *supra*, at 8. If that was true when Edwards was writing only a couple of years ago, Mississippi has since fallen into line. Its election code provides that the ballots are to say " 'PRESIDENTIAL ELECTORS FOR (here insert the name of the candidate for President [etc.] . . .)' in lieu of placing the names of such presidential electors on such official ballots." Miss. Code Ann. § 23-15-785(4) (2004). I have on file an "official" Mississippi sample presidential ballot that contains no names of electors, though it does say "Presidential Electors For" in bolder print than the names of the presidential candidates that immediately follow.

58. The form and wording of ballots vary enormously from state to state, and sometimes even within states. Jim McMasters of the Northwestern Law Library collected sample ballots for the 2000 election from fourteen states for me. Those from California, Wisconsin, Washington, West Virginia, Texas, North Carolina, Nevada, and Maine contain neither the names of the elector candidates, nor any hint of a role for such an officer. Instead, the ballots indicate that a vote is to be cast for one or another candidate for president and vice president. The Oregon ballot indicates at the top of a column of "national" candidates listed by party that in voting for president and vice president "[y]our vote for the candidates for President and Vice President shall be a vote for the electors

supporting those candidates." The ballots from Tennessee, Colorado, and Florida indicate that the vote is for "electors," but does not name them. The voter then casts a vote for a named presidential candidate. The Leon County Florida ballot has a column headed by the word "electors," and then instructs the voter to "vote for group," designated by the names of presidential candidates in large type and their running mates in smaller type. The Clay and Palm Beach County Florida ballots, on the other hand, add a parenthetical explanation that "[a] vote for the candidates will actually be a vote for their electors." And finally, ballots from Georgia and Idaho list the electors in fine print underneath the names of the presidential and vice-presidential candidates.

59. *See* Longley & Peirce, *supra* note 10, at 107–9. As of 1999, Longley and Peirce counted a mere eleven states where the electors' names actually appear on the ballot. The number is, however, a moving—and no doubt somewhat uncertain—target, in part because there may be intrastate variation. *See* note 58, *supra*. Writing in 1992, for instance, Walter Berns counted only eight states where the electors' names appeared on the ballot. Berns, ed., *supra* note 19, at 11. In all but three of the nonshort ballot states in Longley and Peirce's 1999 count, the voter was required to choose an entire slate. Alone among the states, Mississippi, Louisiana, and South Carolina allowed the voter to pick and choose among the individuals listed on slates of electors and indeed allowed the voter to write in an elector not listed. Only in Mississippi, however, were the names of the presidential candidates omitted unless the electors chose to include their commitments. Longley & Peirce, *supra*, at 107–9. As noted above, *see* note 57, *supra*, Mississippi no longer requires that the presidential candidates' names be omitted, nor that the name of the candidates for elector be listed.

60. *See* Note, *supra* note 6, at 699; Abbott & Levine, *supra* note 20, at 18. One prominent commentator describes the present—short ballot—system as "artificial and delusive." Wilmerding, *supra* note 19, at viii. For a discussion of the short ballot, and more generally of "contract" theories for holding electors bound to their commitments—including some surprising conclusions of some politicians over the years that the short ballot carried with it no particular implication that the office of elector came with some commitment to vote for the only person named on short ballots—*see* Ross & Josephson, *supra* note 10, at 701–4. Others have recognized the argument that omission of the electors' names from the ballot implies that they are bound to vote as pledged. *See, e.g.,* Rosenthal, *supra* note 6, at 23. On the other hand, an argument has been advanced, at least impliedly, that the constitutional provision for state decision about the "manner" of choosing electors leaves room for omitting elector names from the ballot while leaving them discretion in the choices they then make. *See* State *ex rel.* Hawke v. Myers, 132 Ohio St. 18, 4 N.E. 2d 397 (1936). The decision is far from explicit about the point, however, and in the modern day of constitutional sensitivity to the right to vote, I would find it difficult to take such an argument seriously. *See generally* Erwin Chemerinsky, Consti-

tutional Law: Principles and Policies 842–77 (2d ed., Aspen Law & Business 2002). In the 1968 election, North Carolina employed a short ballot, so that the name of Lloyd Bailey, the eventually faithless elector discussed in Chapter Three, nowhere appeared on the ballot. *See* Longley & Braun, *supra* note 21, at 139.

61.   U.S. Const., Art. I, § 2, cl. 1.

62.   "The Congress may determine the time of choosing the electors." U.S. Const., Art. II, § 1, cl. 4.

63.   "History [already] abounds with examples of spoiled ballots resulting from voter confusion over how to vote for electors." Longley & Peirce, *supra* note 10, at 108. *Cf.* Edwards, *supra* note 6, at 8–9.

64.   "[C]learly the electoral college cannot exercise the role originally contemplated by the Framers. In an era of party slates—following 200 years of evolution of political parties—the electoral college cannot be composed of unpledged electors, all of them free to exercise full discretion in examining issues and all of them independent in se-lecting a candidate for president. It cannot uproot political parties from the civic soil; it cannot exclude electors who have run and been elected on promises to vote for a speci-fied major-party candidate. The clock cannot be turned back." Glennon, *supra* note 42, at 67.

65.   Karl Llewellyn captured the point, albeit hyperbolically, when he wrote:

[I]t is only the practice which can legitimatize . . . words as being still part of our going Constitution. . . . This is the first principle of a sane theory of our constitutional law. Its necessity is patent wherever practice has flatly abrogated a portion of this "supreme law of the land." Discretion in the electoral college is the classic instance; can any doubt that if that college should today disregard their mandate, such action would be contrary to our Constitution? Yet "vote by ballot"—the original language repeated in the Twelfth Amendment—is a strange way of saying "act as rubber stamps." Karl N. Llewellyn, The Constitution as an Institution, 34 Colum. L. Rev. 1, 12 (1934) (emphasis in original).

66.   *See* Note, *supra* note 6, at 703–4.

67.   Ray v. Blair, 343 U.S. 214, 229 (1952).

68.   The oath is now mandatory and is administered by public officials. D.C. Code Ann. § 1–1001.08(g) (Supp. 2004).

69.   Support for this proposition goes back to McCulloch v. Maryland, 17 U.S. (4 Wheat.) 316, 401 (1819). *See* Myers v. United States, 272 U.S. 52, 136 (1926)

70.   If I am reading him correctly, Rosenthal, *supra* note 6, at 23–24, concludes that there is at least a "respectable argument" that where elector names do not appear on the ballot state legislation restricting elector discretion is permissible, or even that the Con-stitution by its own force forbids the exercise of elector discretion. *See* Ross & Josephson, *supra* note 10, at 697–98.

71. *See, e.g.*, Antonin Scalia, A Matter of Interpretation: Federal Courts and the Law 17 (Princeton University Press 1997).

72. When push comes to shove Justice Scalia embraces the absurd result "exception." *See* Green v. Bock Laundry Machine Co., 490 U.S. 504, 527 (1989). Apparently the first caution against the "suicide pact" possibility was in Justice Robert Jackson's dissent in Terminiello v. City of Chicago, 337 U.S. 1, 37 (1949), where Jackson more colorfully also recited the "old proverb [that] warns us to take heed lest we 'walk into a well from looking at the stars.'" 337 U.S. at 14. George Fletcher discusses the use of the suicide pact analogy in George P. Fletcher, The Cliche that "The Constitution Is Not a Suicide Pact': Why It Is Actually Pro-, not Anti-, Civil Liberties, Find Law's Legal Commentary, http://writ.news.findlaw.com/commentary/20030107_fle (last visited 11/30/04).

73. 345 U.S. 461 (1953).

74. *See* Nixon v. Herndon, 273 U.S. 536 (1927); Nixon v. Condon, 286 U.S. 73 (1932).

75. *See* Nixon v. Condon, 286 U.S. 73 (1932).

76. *See* Smith v. Alwright, 321 U.S. 649 (1944).

77. Terry v. Adams, 345 U.S. 461 (1953).

78. *See* authorities collected in Chemerinsky, *supra* note 60, at 491 n.25.

79. *See also* Shelley v. Kraemer, 334 U.S. 1 (1948).

80. Adjustment in this fashion is not particularly rare. *See, e.g.*, Home Bldg & Loan Ass'n v. Blaisdell, 290 U.S. 398, 453 (1934); Downes v. Bidwell, 182 U.S. 244 (1901); Knox v. Lee, 79 U.S (12 Wall.) 457 (1871); Sanford Levinson & Ernest A. Young, Who's Afraid of the Twelfth Amendment, 29 Fla. St. U.L. Rev. 925, 971 (2001) ("the practical irrelevance of the Declaration of War Clause is surely evidence of a widespread belief that the country can no longer afford to pay the price of a full executive/congressional partnership with regard to . . . the use of American armed force"); Richard Pildes, Foreword: The Constitutionalization of Democratic Politics, 118 Harv. L. Rev. 29, 45 (2004) ("the Court's recognition of the right to vote as a fundamental equal protection right" even though not justified by "textual or originalist grounds").

81. McCulloch v. Maryland, 17 U.S. (4 Wheat.) 316, 401 (1819); *see also, e.g.*, The Pocket Veto Case, 279 U.S. 655, 689 (1929); Eldred v. Ashcroft, 537 U.S. 186, 200–201 (2003); Walz v. Tax Commission of New York, 397 U.S. 664, 678 (1970).

82. *See* Chapter Nine.

83. That seems to be the implicit message of Chief Justice Rehnquist's recent book on the 1876 election. *See* Rehnquist, *supra* note 36.

84. Ray v. Blair, 343 U.S. 214 (1952).

85. *Cf.* Longley & Braun, *supra* note 21, at 43, 130.

86. *See, e.g.*, Federal Maritime Commission v. South Carolina State Ports Authority, 535 U.S. 743 (2002); Florida Prepaid Postsecondary Education Expense Bd. v. College Savings Bank, 527 U.S. 627 (1999).

87. *See* Ross & Josephson, *supra* note 10, at 690 & n.131.

88. U.S. Const., Art. I, § 8, cl. 1.

89. *See* South Dakota v. Dole, 483 U.S. 203 (1987).

90. *Cf.* Matthew J. Festa, The Origins and Constitutionality of State Unit Voting in the Electoral College, 54 Vand. L. Rev. 2099, 2148 (2001) ("In the wake of the controversy over the 2000 election, politicians of all stripes are calling for legislation to provide massive grants to states in order to support modernized and standardized voting equipment. . . . Congress could try to condition these grants on state legislatures implementing the 'manner' of selecting electors favored by Congress.") Michael Glennon urges use of the spending power to induce the states to adopt districts for the election of electors. *See* Glennon, *supra* note 42, at 75.

91. Starting in 1992, Minnesota Commissioner Jack Davies repeatedly urged NC-CUSL to propose a uniform law on what he called the "renegade elector" problem. Correspondence on file with author.

92. I should acknowledge a possible fly in this ointment. It is conceivable that some of the least populous states might hesitate to corral faithless votes because that would decrease the chances of recourse to the House contingent procedure. In the House procedure the least populous states would have a larger proportionate say (1/50) than they do in the electoral college (3/538). But the immediate benefit from House selection would inure to the representative(s) from a state, not the state legislators who would have to decide whether or not to adopt a uniform law. And faithless voting followed by presidential selection in the House is only one very small part of the faithless voting problem, and, moreover, the least likely part to trouble the process. For these reasons, this obstacle might not loom very large.

93. I would thus resist Michael Glennon's inclination to adapt the elector pledge mechanism that the Supreme Court approved in Ray v. Blair, 343 U.S. 214 (1952). In the case of a victorious elector pledged to a third-party candidate, Glennon argues that the candidate rather than the elector should be allowed to determine to whom the elector's vote should go if the candidate decides to withdraw. Glennon, *supra* note 42, at 35. In general, I think that it would be much preferable to rely on state law, rather than either elector pledges or candidate decisions, to dictate the electors' votes. In Chapter Eight I will suggest the possibility of state law that will deal with the problem of electoral votes secured by minor party candidates.

94. The analysis would seem similar for even less likely eventualities like serious illness short of death, or withdrawal by a candidate that comes between the popular election and the meetings of electors.

95. *See* Longley & Peirce, *supra* note 10, at 130.

96. *See* Longley & Peirce, *supra* note 10, at 129.

97. *See* William Josephson & Beverly J. Ross, Repairing the Electoral College, 22 J. Legis. 145, 189 (1996); *cf.* Wilmerding, *supra* note 19, at 180–82; Fortier, ed., *supra* note 20, at 24.

98. Tenn. Code Ann. § 2–15–104(c)(2) (2004) (in case of death of a candidate to whom the electors are pledged, they "may cast their ballots in the electoral college as they see fit"); Wis. Stat. § 7.75(2) (2004) ("[a] presidential elector is not required to vote for a candidate who is deceased at the time of the meeting").

99. U.S. Const., Am. XX, § 3.

100. Walter Berns suggests a distinction, on the one hand, between the period between the meetings of electors in mid-December and January 6, when the electoral votes are counted in the joint meeting of the Senate and House of Representatives, and, on the other hand, between the joint meeting and inauguration day. Berns, ed., *supra* note 19, at 26. The Twentieth Amendment deals with the death of the president elect, and Berns raises the question of whether there is a president elect after the electors have voted, or only after their votes have been counted. Equivocating a bit, Berns seems to conclude that there can be no president elect until after the votes have been counted, so that the loss of a "victorious" candidate before that time will force the selection into the House.

In the third edition of After the People Vote, Fortier, ed., *supra* note 20 at 25-26, it is said that the joint meeting could either count the votes for the dead man, thereby making him president elect, so that the vice-president elect would then be sworn in on inauguration day, or not count the votes for the dead man, thereby likely throwing the election into the House. *See also* Amar, *supra* note 20, at 217; Tara Ross, Enlightened Democracy: The Case for the Electoral College 122 (World Ahead Publishing 2004). These seem to me to be bad solutions to questions in this area that have reasonably clear right ones. It is the vote of electors that should make a candidate the president elect, not their later counting. *Cf.* Stephen A. Siegel, The Conscientious Congressman's Guide to the Electoral Count Act of 1887, 56 Fla. L. Rev. 541, 569 & n.164 (2004) (discussing Nineteenth-Century election law, where it was "the voters' ballots," not some later certification, that "entitled someone to elective office"). If there has been a death of someone who is determined to have won, then the Twentieth Amendment's contingency would come into play and the vice-president elect would succeed to the presidency on inauguration day. Since this is precisely what would happen after the votes had been counted, there is no reason to strain for a different solution if the death were to occur a few days earlier.

There is no specific provision for filling the vice-presidential position in this time frame. After the president is in office, however, there would presumably be a vacancy in the office of vice president, and the Twenty-Fifth Amendment provides for filling that vacancy with a nomination by the president and confirmation by both houses of the Congress.

101. Writing in 1992, Walter Berns reported that South Carolina permitted a state party executive committee to "release an elector from . . . [his] pledge, if, in its judgment, it would not be in the best interest of the state for the elector to cast the vote as pledged." Berns, ed., *supra* note 19, at 12.

102. That was provided in the original Constitution, U.S. Const., Art. II, § 1, cl. 6, and is now found in the Twenty-Fifth Amendment.

103. If the vice-presidential candidate receives the votes originally cast for the presidential candidate of the same party, he should not also receive the votes for vice president. *See* Amar, *supra* note 20, at 219–20. Again this dilemma cries out for uniform state treatment, probably to allow party choice of a vice-presidential substitute, who would then receive electoral votes associated with that party.

104. The temptation is on display in Berns, ed., *supra* note 19, at 26, and in Amar, *supra* note 20, at 232.

105. *See* Chapter Three.

Chapter Eight

1. Faithless votes—though not ones for minor party candidates—were cast in the elections of 1972, 1976, and 1988, as they were in 2000 and 2004. *See* Chapter Seven.

2. To avoid repetition, hereafter I will refer to both minor party and independent candidates as either "minor candidates," "third-party candidates" or "minor party candidates." Similarly I will refer to "third-party" or "minor party" command of electoral votes, without feeling obliged each time to add the "independent" possibility as well.

3. *See* George C. Edwards III, Why the Electoral College Is Bad for America 62–71 (Yale University Press 2004). In states other than Alabama, however, the national democratic ticket succeeded in securing places on the ballot under one name or another. *See, e.g.*, Compromise Reached on Louisiana Ballot; Legislature Moves to Let Truman Run, N.Y. Times, Sept. 24, 1948, at 22.

4. As we saw in Chapter Three, the electoral vote was split four ways in the 1824 election, but the four candidates were all associated with the same political party.

5. U.S. Const., Am. XII.

6. *See* David W. Abbott & James P. Levine, Wrong Winner: The Coming Debacle in the Electoral College 49 (Praeger 1991).

7. The picture could be more complicated in the unlikely event that there were faithless elector abstentions in large numbers. *See* Chapter Seven. It would then be conceivable that only one of the two candidates would have broad electoral support.

8. *See* U.S. Const., Art. II, § 1, cl. 2. A third-party candidate might have won just a single electoral vote if it came in a state that awarded some of its electoral votes to the popular vote winner in each congressional district in the state. *See* Chapter Three. At the present time there are two such states, Maine and Nebraska. Or it is possible that a faithless elector could cast a single vote for an unaffiliated candidate and thereby send a choice among three to the House. *See* Chapter Seven.

9. *See* Tadahisa Kuroda, The Origins of the Twelfth Amendment 173 (Greenwood Press 1994).

10. *See* Lawrence D. Longley & Neal R. Peirce, The Electoral College Primer 2000 44 (Yale University Press 1999).

11. Longley & Peirce, *supra* note 10, at 42–44.

12. Longley & Peirce, *supra* note 10, at 44. Longley and Peirce then continue with the possibility of a deadlock in the House:

> Had the House deadlock held . . . until inauguration day, January 20, the new vice president would have assumed the presidency under the terms of the Twentieth Amendment. . . . But who would have been the new vice president? If Truman had failed to win an electoral majority, his vice presidential running mate, Sen. Alben Barkley, would also have failed to win a majority. Under the Constitution the Senate would have had the task of electing the new vice president. The party lineup in the Senate was 54 Democrats, 42 Republicans. The senators would have had only two choices: Barkley or [Republican vice-presidential candidate Earl] Warren. Barkley was a highly respected senator and member of its inner club. Thus he could have expected solid backing from all the northern Democrats and probably from all but one or two of his colleagues and long-time associates from Dixiecrat states. The chances are very high that Barkley would have been chosen as vice president. And if the House had failed to break its deadlock by January 20, Barkley would have assumed the powers of the presidency—even though not a single American had voted to elect him to that position. But Barkley would have been only acting president and would have been obliged to relinquish the office at any time in the following four years that the House resolved its deadlock and chose a new president. Longley & Peirce, *supra* at 44–45.

13. *See* Chapter Seven, note 32. Running as the presidential candidate of the American Independent Party, Wallace had made no bones about an intention to trade electoral votes for "policy concessions" if he could win enough of them to hold the electoral college balance. *See* After the People Vote 4 (Walter Berns, ed., AEI Press 1992). Wallace is reported to have "obtained affidavits from all of his electors in which they promised to vote for Wallace 'or whomsoever he may direct' in the electoral college." After the People Vote 8 (3d ed., John C. Fortier, ed., AEI Press 2004).

14. *See* Lawrence D. Longley & Alan G. Braun, The Politics of Electoral College Reform 75 (Yale University Press 1972); Alexander Bickel, Reform and Continuity: The Electoral College, the Convention, and the Party System 79–80 (Harper and Row 1971).

15. *See* William Josephson & Beverly J. Ross, Repairing the Electoral College, 22 J. Legis. 145, 146 (1996).

16. The importance of geographic concentration in third-party efforts is also dramatized by the 1948 election mentioned above, when Strom Thurmond garnered thirty-nine electoral votes through a geographically concentrated effort, while Henry Wallace

got no electoral votes with almost as many popular votes as Thurmond, because Wallace's support was dispersed around the country. *See* Chapter Four.

17. Conventional wisdom is that Nader commanded more votes that might otherwise have been cast for Gore than for Bush. *See* Gerald M. Pomper, The Election of 2000 135 (Chatham House Publishers 2001); Edwards, *supra* note 3, at 140. The eight states are Florida, Iowa, Maine, Minnesota, New Hampshire, New Mexico, Oregon, and Wisconsin. Of the eight, Bush won only in Florida and New Hampshire, and hence it is only those states where the Green Party candidacy likely affected the electoral college outcome. The qualification "likely" is necessary, because if Nader had not been in the race, the Bush campaign strategy would no doubt have been different. In the 1948 election, in all likelihood Henry Wallace's third-party candidacy, *see* note 16, *supra*, similarly deprived Democratic candidate Harry Truman of the electoral votes in several states, but it did not change the election outcome, since Truman won in a close electoral college contest. *See* Abbott & Levine, *supra* note 6, at 70–71.

18. The Liberal, Free Soil, and other minor parties kept abolitionist pressure on in the years leading up to the Civil War, for instance, clearly presaging this as a major element of the program of the Republican Party which was soon to displace the Whigs as the country's second major party. In the 1890s, the Peoples Party likely affected policy stances of both the Republican and Democratic Parties. And at the end of the Nineteenth and beginning of the Twentieth Centuries the effect of the Progressive Party on policy positions of the major political parties, and indeed on the country as a whole, was very substantial. *See* James L. Sundquist, Dynamics of the Party System 74–82, 149–59, 170–81 (rev. ed., Brookings Institution 1983).

19. One very important example, the effects of which are still with us today, is the Progressive advocacy of forms of "direct democracy," principally the initiative and referendum, vehicles for bypassing or overruling the decisions of legislatures in a number of states. *See* Samuel Issacharoff *et al.*, The Law of Democracy 982–85 (rev. 2d ed., Foundation Press 2002). For an evaluation of the contemporary effects of these devices, *see* David B. Magleby, Governing by Initiative: Let the Voters Decide? An Assessment of the Initiative and Referendum Process, 66 U. Colo. L. Rev. 13 (1995).

20. This is probably a fair characterization of the relationship between the Whig Party and the Republican Party, which in the 1850s and 1860s displaced the Whigs as the second major party. *See* Sundquist, *supra* note 18, at 54–82.

21. *See, e.g.*, James Dao, The 2000 Campaign: The Green Party; Democrats Ask Nader to Back Gore in Swing States, N.Y. Times, Oct. 31, 2000, at A20; Alison Neumer, It's Time for Nader to take a Hint, Chi. Trib., May 21, 2004, at 2; Phil Reisman, Nader's Narcissism May Spur 2000 Rerun, White Plains Journal News, Feb. 24, 2004, at 1B.

22. *See* Josephson & Ross, *supra* note 15, at 147; George Will, Foreword, in Tara Ross, Enlightened Democracy: The Case for the Electoral College ix (World Ahead Publishing 2004); Tara Ross, *supra*, at 90.

23. *See, e.g.*, Nelson W. Polsby & Aaron Wildavsky, Presidential Elections 147 (5th ed., Charles Scribner & Sons 1980): Joy McAfee, 2001: Should the College Electors Finally Graduate? The Electoral College: An American Compromise from Its Inception to Election 2000, 32 Cumb. L. Rev. 643, 656 (2001–2); Davis v. Bandemer, 478 U.S. 109, 144–45 (1986) (O'Connor, J., concurring).

24. *See generally* Arend Lijphart, Patterns of Democracy 143–50 (Yale University Press 1999). For a discussion of proportional representation by one who is no fan, *see* Lucius Wilmerding, Jr., The Electoral College 118–25 (Beacon Press 1958).

25. *See generally* John F. Bibby & L. Sandy Maisel, Two Parties—or More?: The American Party System 61 (2d ed., Westview Press 2003). I have myself elsewhere discussed the stability enhancing effects of single-member legislative districts. *See* Robert W. Bennett, Talking It Through: Puzzles of American Democracy 34–36 (Cornell University Press 2003); *see also* Wilmerding, *supra* note 24, at 125. Obviously, as we also saw in Chapter Four, a significant number of voters apparently votes sincerely rather than strategically. That is perhaps one reason why third-party candidacies occasionally change the outcome of elections.

26. *See* Williams v. Rhodes, 393 U.S. 23 (1968).

27. *See* Storer v. Brown, 415 U.S. 724 (1974).

28. *See* Vieth v. Jubelirer, 541 U.S. 267 (2004).

29. *See* Buckley v. Valeo, 424 U.S. 1, 96, 98 (1976); Edwards, *supra* note 3, at 138; *see also* Justice Thomas's dissent in U.S. Term Limits, Inc. v. Thornton, 514 U.S. 779, 845, 922–23 (1995), where he discusses advantages provided for incumbents in current federal law.

30. *See* Edwards, *supra* note 3, at 136–37.

31. *See* Bibby & Maisel, *supra* note 25, at 68.

32. *See* Bibby & Maisel, *supra* note 25, at 63.

33. Timmons v. Twin Cities Area New Party, 520 U.S. 351, 366–67 (1997) (internal citations omitted).

34. Williams v. Rhodes, 393 U.S. 23, 32 (1968).

35. U.S. Const., Art. II, § 1, cl. 2.

36. *See* Chapter Three; McPherson v. Blacker, 146 U.S. 1 (1892).

37. *See* Chapter Four.

38. McPherson v. Blacker, 146 U.S. 1 (1892).

39. 146 U.S. at 35, 36.

40. Bush v. Gore, 531 U.S. 98, 104 (2000).

41. *See* Wilmerding, *supra* note 24, at 43. Apparently the state of Tennessee did delegate the selection of electors to a small number of designated individuals for the 1796 and 1800 elections. *See* Wilmerding, *supra*, at 45-46.

42. 146 U.S. at 37–41.

43. U.S. Const., Ams. XIX, XXVI.

44. U.S. Const., Am. XXIV. For some reason, the drafters of the Twenty-Fourth Amendment explicitly mentioned its coverage of "any primary or other election for President or Vice President," in addition to "election . . . for electors for President or Vice President."

45. Reynolds v. Sims, 377 U.S. 533 (1964); *see* Wesberry v. Sanders, 376 U.S. 1 (1964).

46. U.S. Const., Am. I, applicable to the states through the Fourteenth Amendment.

47. *See* Michael J. Glennon, When No Majority Rules 12 (Congressional Quarterly 1992).

48. Kuroda, *supra* note 9, at 54.

49. Massachusetts Resolves XX, June 13, 1796, at 12. *See* McPherson v. Blacker, 146 U.S. 1, 31 (1892). Tadahisa Kuroda says that the legislature chose from "the top two candidates." Kuroda, *supra* note 9, at 30; *see also* Tara Ross, *supra* note 22, at 23–24.

50. Wilmerding, *supra* note 24, at 47; Kuroda, *supra* note 9, at 28–29.

51. Georgia Code § 34–1514, 1964 Ga. Laws 26, 174–75 (extraordinary session).

52. Georgia Code § 34–103, 1964 Ga. Laws 26, 174–75 (extraordinary session).

53. Georgia Code § 34–1514, 1968 Ga. Laws 257, 258–59. *See* Albert J. Rosenthal, The Constitution, Congress, and Presidential Elections, 67 Mich. L. Rev. 1, 19 & n.19 (1968).

54. I add the qualification, because the result in the electoral college could become clear even though the results from a number of states were not yet in.

55. In most instances, the "first-cut" answer for the nation as a whole would be clear, even if there were states where disputes caused some lingering uncertainty about who had won in the state. On occasion, disputes in particular states might cause the national count to remain unclear for a period of time, in which case a state adopting the suggested contingency would be delayed in awarding its electoral votes.

56. For states where electoral votes are awarded to district, rather than statewide, winners, the awards would be adjusted accordingly.

I ignore the exceedingly remote possibility that neither of the two nationwide electoral vote leaders would have qualified to appear on the ballot of one or more states. In 1970 Senators Thomas Eagleton and Robert Dole introduced a proposal to replace the electoral college system with a complex approach grounded in a nationwide popular vote. It contained a fallback electoral vote procedure where neither of the two front runners satisfied the complex vote requirements. In the fallback, electoral votes for minor party candidates were allocated between the two front runners. *See* Longley & Braun, *supra* note 14, at 71.

While a version of the approach suggested in the text might be adapted to the vice-presidential context, there are shades of difference in that setting. Most importantly, misfiring in selection of the vice president is simply not a problem on the scale of misfiring in the selection of the president. *See* Chapters Two and Five. My present concern is thus with the presidential selection alone. For that reason my use of the terms "candidate," "winner," and the like in this discussion is meant to refer to the presidency.

57. *See* Chapter Seven.

58. *See* Dana Canedy, Contesting the Vote: The Florida Legislature; House Adopts Bush Electors, but Act May Be Moot, N.Y. Times, Dec. 13, 2000, at A26; Alexander Keyssar, The Right to Vote and Election 2000, in The Unfinished Election of 2000 75, 76 (Jack N. Rakove, ed., Basic Books 2001). In the wake of the 2000 election, the Texas and North Carolina legislatures moved to regularize an appointment procedure for electors in the event that no decisive election results were available before the "safe harbor" deadline that we discussed in Chapter Three. The Texas Constitution and North Carolina statutes were amended to include such provisions. *See* Tex. Const. Art. IV, § 8b (amended Nov. 6, 2001); N.C. Session L. 2001–289; Fortier, ed., *supra* note 13, at 11.

59. 146 U.S. at 29 (noting two different mechanisms of choice by legislatures adopting these contingent approaches, "joint ballot," and "a concurrent vote of the two houses [of bicameral legislatures]").

60. U.S. Senate Rep. No. 395, 43rd Cong., 1st Sess. 9 (1874).

61. 146 U.S. at 35.

62. Bush v. Gore, 531 U.S. 98, 104 (2000). The reason I qualify my characterization of the Court's approval is that in the Court's opinion the quoted passage is preceded by the Court's own assertion that after opting for an electoral process, "[t]he state . . . in the special context of Article II, can take back the power to appoint electors." 531 U.S. at 104. This omits the phrase "at any time" that might be thought to give particular expansiveness to the language from the Senate report and *McPherson*. The text turns now to ambiguity about just how expansive that language should be thought to be.

63. Even more clear in this regard was an apparent move in the Louisiana legislature in 1960 "to suspend the state's election laws and appoint independent electors after Kennedy electors had won." James C. Kirby, Jr., Limitations on the Power of State Legislatures over Presidential Elections, 27 Law & Contemp. Probs. 495, 497 n.24 (1962).

64. Reynolds v. Sims, 377 U.S. 533, 561–62 (1964); *see* Bush v. Gore, 531 U.S. 98, 104 (2000). For further development of the constitutional argument, *see* Chapter Ten, note 14.

65. U.S. Const., Art. II, § 1, cl. 4.

66. 3 U.S.C. § 2 (2000).

67. No such issue would have arisen in the Louisiana situation depicted in note 63, *supra*.

68. *See, e.g.,* Minneapolis Star Trib., Dec. 13, 2000, at 21A (quoting Charles Umbanhowar, Sr. of St. Olaf College as saying "The Florida election's a tie, and someone needs to break the tie").

69. Without using the term, Richard Posner discusses the count in terms of a margin of error in Richard Posner, Prolegomenon to an Assessment, in The Vote: Bush, Gore & the Supreme Court 165, 166 (Cass R. Sunstein & Richard A. Epstein, eds., University of Chicago Press 2001).

70. *See* David Barstow, Contesting the Vote: The Florida Legislature; Florida Lawmakers Moving to Bypass the Courts for Bush; Judge Bars a Quick Recount, N.Y. Times, Nov. 29, 2000, at A29 (quoting Professor Robert [*sic*] Yoo of Berkeley Law School as finding the section dealing with "failure" applicable because the election results were "in doubt" or because there was "an unresolved contest" or because of "counting procedures that were altered after election day").

71. *See, e.g.*, Frank J. Murray, Both Sides Agree Time Is Running Out; Electoral College Vote Drawing Closer, Wash. Times, Dec. 7, 2000, at A12 (characterizing views of Beverley J. Ross); Robert Kaise, Florida May Broach Sensitive Legal Issue; Limits on Choosing Electors Largely Untested, Wash. Post, Dec. 6, 2000, at A24 (reporting on position of Professor Bruce Ackerman and thirty-seven law professors led by Professor Stephen Griffin); John C. Roberts, Do Not Tread Here, Chicago Daily Law Bulletin, Dec. 13, 2000, at 5; Bruce Ackerman, As Florida Goes . . . , N.Y. Times, Dec. 12, at A33. In Chapter Nine, we will discuss the possibility that the U.S. Supreme Court might have concluded that the appropriate remedy was essentially to declare the election indecisive. That might have justified a conclusion of statutory "failure."

72. 531 U.S. at 111.

73. 531 U.S. at 112–13.

74. *See, e.g.*, Michel Rosenfeld, Bush v. Gore: Three Strikes for the Constitution, the Court, and Democracy, but There Is Always Next Season, in The Longest Night: Polemics and Perspectives on Election 2000 122–25 (Arthur J. Jacobson & Michel Rosenfeld, eds., California University Press 2002); Lawrence Tribe, Comment, 115 Harv. L. Rev. 170, 194–217 (2001).

75. *See* Lijphart, *supra* note 24, at 146–47. Runoff elections are quite common in Louisiana. *See* Landrieu's Victory, Wash. Times, Dec. 9, 2002, at A18.

76. *See* Longley & Braun, *supra* note 14, at 187 n.3.

77. *See* Bennett, *supra* note 25, at 34–35.

78. There is also nothing in the concurring opinion in Bush v. Gore, 531 U.S. 98, 111 (2000) that would cast a cloud over legislative adoption of the contingent selection procedure. Quite to the contrary, even more than the Court majority's rationale, the tenor of the concurring opinion is that state legislatures can do pretty much what they please in the selection of electors.

79. I am grateful to a gathering of stalwarts at NYU law school organized by Norman Dorsen and John Ferejohn for insisting that I take this possibility seriously.

80. *See* Chapter Three.

81. U.S. Const., Art. II, § 1, cl. 4.

82. U.S. Const., Am. XX, § 1.

83. *See* Lijphart, *supra* note 24, at 147. In 2002, San Francisco voters approved the use of an instant runoff system for local elections. *See* How San Francisco Voted, San Fran-

cisco Chron., March 7, 2002, at A21; Center for Voting and Democracy, www.fairvote. org/sf/robmessage.htm (last visited 02/15/05); Rachel Gordon, New Vote—It's a Go, San Francisco Chron., Nov. 3, 2004, at B1. The instant runoff is also used in a smattering of other localities around the country. *See* Ilene Lelchuk, Confusion Seen in Ranked Voting, San Francisco Chron., Oct. 29, 2004, at B1.

84. *See* Center for Voting and Democracy, www.instantrunoff.com/faq.asp (last visited 02/15/05).

Chapter Nine

1. A 1996 effort to survey the problems that might arise in the counting of electoral votes in the joint session of Congress came up with an array of them:

> whether an Elector has been appointed in a mode authorized by the Legislature of his state or not; (2) whether the time at which he was chosen, and the day on which he gave his vote were determined by Congress; (3) whether he was not at the time, a Senator or Representative of the United States, or held an office of trust or profit under the United States; (4) whether at least one of the persons for whom he has voted is an inhabitant of a state other than his own; (5) whether the Electors voted by ballot, and signed, certified and transmitted to the President of the Senate, a list of all the persons voted for, and the number of votes for each; (6) whether the persons voted for are natural born citizens, or were citizens of the United States, at the time of the adoption of the Constitution, were thirty five years old, and had been fourteen years resident within the United States. Yet it would be difficult in many cases to determine for whom an unqualified elector voted, since returns frequently listed only the candidates and the aggregated number of votes. In that case, should all the votes of the state be cast aside? Who should have this discretionary authority? Tadahisa Kuroda, The Origins of the Twelfth Amendment 79–80 (Greenwood Press 1996).

The possibilities for mishaps in the electoral college may well be limited, however, only by the human imagination. In any event, I will not try to be exhaustive in this chapter. I ignore, for instance, the problem of electoral votes cast by new states in the transition period to statehood, a set of problems that arose several times in the nation's history. *See, e.g.,* Stephen A. Siegel, The Conscientious Congressman's Guide to the Electoral Count Act of 1887, 56 Fla. L. Rev. 541, 559 n.98 (2004); U.S. Senate Rep. No. 395, 43rd Cong., 1st Sess. 13 (1874). For contemporary purposes, there seems to be little to be learned from these incidents. Similarly, I ignore the possibility that the electors might violate a secrecy requirement implied by the constitutional provision that electors are to "vote by ballot." U.S. Const., Am. XII. *See* William Josephson & Beverly J. Ross, Repairing the Electoral College, 22 J. Legis. 145, 172 (1996). The states have long appreciated the silliness of a secrecy requirement in the contemporary environment. It is so regularly ignored that there seems little danger that a violation of secrecy would be offered as justification for disregarding a state's electoral vote. *See, e.g.*, George C. Edwards III, Why the Electoral College Is Bad for America 12 (Yale University Press 2004). I will not go on, because, as suggested, the list of conceivable electoral college mishaps that this chapter does not cover could well be endless.

2. In addition, in 1912 the Republican vice-presidential candidate James S. Sherman died before the election.

3. Most recently in the 1972 election when Thomas Eagleton withdrew as the Democratic vice-presidential nominee after questions about his health emerged. The other times were in 1860 and 1912. *See* Lawrence D. Longley & Neal R. Peirce, The Electoral College Primer 2000 129 (Yale University Press 1999); After the People Vote 25 (Walter Berns, ed., AEI Press 1992); Edwards, *supra* note 1, at 27.

4. Current party rules are set out in Appendix E, in After the People Vote 88 (3d ed., John C. Fortier, ed., AEI Press 2004).

5. *See* Chapter Seven, note 100. In a 1994 article Akhil Amar offers a comprehensive solution to the problem of death of a candidate. I do not deal with the problem of death before the election, where Amar's solution is postponement of the election. Beyond that Amar's solutions seem close kin to those I suggest in the text. *See* Akhil Reed Amar, Presidents, Vice Presidents, and Death: Closing the Constitution's Succession Gap, 48 Ark. L. Rev. 215, 217, 222–24, 236 (1994).

6. Actually the vice-presidential candidate of a party has received a single electoral vote on at least two occasions, in 1988 and 2004. *See* Chapter Seven. There seems to be no reason to expect such votes with any regularity.

7. The Twentieth Amendment specifically authorizes Congress to pass legislation dealing with the case where on inauguration day "neither a President elect nor a Vice President elect shall have qualified," U.S. Const., Am. XX, § 4, *i.e.*, where neither the House nor the Senate would yet have chosen. To date Congress has not passed such legislation.

8. U.S. Const., Am. XII.

9. This might have resulted from action of the Florida legislature, *see* Chapter Eight, or of the Florida courts if the recount had been allowed to proceed.

10. *See* Chapter Three.

11. For a contemporary commentary that concludes that the act is unconstitutional for this reason, *see* Vasan Kesavan, Is the Electoral Count Act Unconstitutional?, 80 N.C.L. Rev. 1653 (2003). This position is seldom espoused these days, but is nonetheless often recognized by electoral college commentators. *See, e.g.*, Michael J. Glennon, Nine Ways to Avoid a Train Wreck: How Title 3 Should Be Changed, 23 Cardozo L. Rev. 1159, 1164 (2002). Constitutional debate entered into congressional consideration of the act. *See* Siegel, *supra* note 1, at 543–44 n.12.

12. U.S. Const., Art. II, § 1, cl. 2; Am. XII.

13. U.S. Const., Art. II § 1, cl. 4.

14. U.S. Const., Art. II, § 1, cls. 2, 5;

15. For accounts of two such incidents in American history, *see* Luther v. Borden, 48 U.S. (7 How.) 1 (1849) and Vasan Kesavan & Michael Stokes Paulsen, Is West Virginia Unconstitutional?, 90 Calif. L. Rev. 291 (2001); *see also* Georgia v. Stanton, 73 U.S. 50 (1867).

16. One example is the question of whether a popular initiative is action by the legislature. *See* Chapter Four for a discussion of just such a question raised by an initiative on the ballot in Colorado at the same time as the 2004 presidential election. That question became moot when the initiative went down to defeat.

17. *See* Siegel, *supra* note 1, at 544 n.13, 558 n.96. Siegel also collects commentary to that effect.

18. *See* U.S. Senate Rep. No. 395, 43rd Cong., 1st Sess. 16 (1874).

19. U.S. Const., Art. II, § 1, cl. 4.

20. *See* Edwards, *supra* note 1, at 7.

21. *See* Edwards, *supra* note 1, at 7. An obvious objection is that a midweek day in the middle of November depresses voter turnout. In the wake of the 2000 election, a privately supported commission on election reform with former presidents Ford and Carter serving as honorary co-chairs recommended that "Congress should enact legislation to hold presidential and congressional elections on a national holiday." The National Commission on Federal Election Reform, to Assure Pride and Confidence in the Electoral Process 7 (2001).

22. U.S. Const., Art. II, § 1, cl. 4.

23. U.S. Const., Am. XX, § 1.

24. 3 U.S.C. § 7 (2000).

25. U.S. Const., Am. XX, § 1.

26. 3 U.S.C. § 15 (2000). Set by statute, this date is sometimes changed by statute, when January 6 falls on a day thought inappropriate or inconvenient.

27. *See* Chapter Three.

28. Bush v. Gore, 531 U.S. 98 (2000).

29. Bush v. Gore, 531 U.S. 98, 110 (2000). The court's citation for this passage is confusing, but a version can be found at Palm Beach County Canvassing Board v. Harris, 772 So. 2d 1273, 1289 (Fla. Sup. Ct. 2000).

30. Palm Beach County Canvassing Board v. Harris, 772 So. 2d 1220, 1230, 1236 (Fla. Sup. Ct. 2000); Fla. Const., Art. I, § 1.

31. *See* Developments in the Law—Elections, 88 Harv. L. Rev. 1114, 1298, 1302 (1975).

32. *Cf.* Siegel, *supra* note 1, at 591.

33. Even under the safe harbor provision, the joint meeting reserves to itself questions of whether the safe harbor conditions are met. Among those conditions is that the dispute resolution laws must have been in place before election day, the dispute resolu-

tion must have been "final," and that it must have been made under "judicial or other methods or procedures." *See generally* Siegel, *supra* note 1 at 589–608. There seems to be no reason why the joint meeting could not make those self-same determinations in resolving tabulation disputes that took place after the meetings of electors. This is so whether or not there are rival slates.

34. I see no reason to believe that voting irregularities would require "months" to clear up, presenting the possibility of an "intolerable limbo" before installation of the new president. *See* Robert M. Hardaway, The Electoral College and the Constitution: The Case for Preserving Federalism 25 (Praeger 1994).

35. U.S. Const., Art. II, § 1, cl. 2 (comma omitted).

36. Casting the decisive vote on the special Electoral Commission, Justice Joseph Bradley had no trouble concluding that the offending elector had been properly selected to fill a vacancy. *See* Charles Fairman, Five Justices and the Electoral Commission of 1877, Supplement to Volume VII of the Oliver Wendell Holmes Devise History of the Supreme Court of the United States 120 (Macmillan 1988). With little choice because of the requirement of concurrence by both houses to overrule the special commission, the joint meeting then accepted the commission's decision. In the same election, a variation on the Oregon question arose with a Florida candidate for elector who before the election had held the federal post of shipping commissioner. He evidently attempted to resign that post before election day, but a dispute subsequently arose about whether his attempt had been successful. *See* Fairman, *supra*, at 112–14. A question of the qualifications of a Michigan elector was raised in the 1836 election. *See* Siegel, *supra* note 1, at 559 n.100; *see also* Hardaway, *supra* note 34, at 102–3. I have not attempted to trace down other similar cases, but one knowledgeable commentator suggests that elector disqualification on account of this constitutional requirement has been a recurrent problem. Robert G. Dixon, Jr., Electoral College Procedure, 3 Western Pol. Q. 214, 219 (1950).

37. A fuller version of the story is provided in William H. Rehnquist, Centennial Crisis 109–12 (Alfred A. Knopf 2004).

38. Indeed, the new president would then have been Samuel Tilden who was the nationwide popular vote winner in that election. It is true that at the time, Oregon voters cast individual votes for electors, and the substitution of a Democratic elector would have supplanted an elector who received a higher number of votes. But electors ran as slates, and the Democratic slate had won a very substantial minority of the popular vote, easily justifying one-third of the Oregon electors—the result if the governor's approach had prevailed—had the state, for instance, opted for proportionality.

39. *See* Chapter Three. Technically the infirmity would have been that no candidate had received a "majority . . . of the electors appointed." U.S. Const., Am. XII. Another member of the commission, Justice Stephen Field, took the position that neither the governor nor the other Republican electors had the authority to fill the vacancy. Had

this view prevailed, Oregon would similarly have cast one electoral vote fewer than its allotment, and again the contingent procedures would have been engaged, whether or not the missing elector was deemed to have been "appointed." *See* Siegel, *supra* note 1, at 578 & n.227.

40. *See* Neal R. Peirce, The Peoples's President 131 (Simon & Schuster 1968).

41. Peirce, *supra* note 40, at 131. Siegel concludes that this was a rationalization of "[l]ater Congresses," and that the real basis for rejecting the Arkansas votes was objection to the election in a state then under reconstruction. Siegel, *supra* note 1, at 553–54, 580–81 n.240, 586 n.284.

42. U.S. Const., Am. XII.

43. Lucius Wilmerding, Jr., The Electoral College 18 (Beacon Press 1958). In the count after the 1872 election, the joint meeting refused to count some contentious electoral votes but then the two Houses appear to have treated the rejected votes differently in calculating the total of which a majority was required to win. *See* Siegel, *supra* note 1, at 654 n.680.

44. Kuroda, *supra* note 1, at 39–49; Peirce, *supra* note 40, at 60. North Carolina and Rhode Island also cast no votes, but that was because they had not yet ratified the Constitution. Peirce, *supra*, at 61.

45. *See* Jack N. Rakove, Introduction: Dangling Questions, in The Unfinished Election of 2000 xi, xiii–xiv (Jack N. Rakove, ed., Basic Books 2001); Richard Posner, Breaking the Deadlock: The 2000 Election, the Constitution, and the Courts 49 (Princeton University Press 2001); *cf.* Tara Ross, Enlightened Democracy: The Case for the Electoral College 182 (World Ahead Publishing 2004). To my mind Einer Elhauge is being rather perverse when he insists that it would be "perverse" if Florida's votes had not been counted at all. Einer Elhauge, The Lessons of Florida 2000, 110 Pol. Rev. 15, 35 (2002).

46. In Florida in 2000 this might then have opened the way—had sufficient time remained—for legislative appointment of electors on account of a federal statutory "failure" of the state to make a choice. *See* Chapter Eight. This could, of course, itself be productive of controversy and resentment.

47. Or there might have been procedural infirmities, such as those mentioned in the text that ostensibly bedeviled the 1872 Arkansas electors. It also seems that in 1821 no votes were counted when electors from three different states died before the meetings of electors. *See* Siegel, *supra* note 1, at 102; Beverly J. Ross & William Josephson, The Electoral College and the Popular Vote, XII J. L. & Pol. 706 n.232 (1996). It is, of course, even possible that an elector might be absent from a meeting, because he missed a train. Issue has been joined on several occasions over the years on just what it takes to reduce the number necessary for the required majority when Congress refuses to count an electoral vote. *See* Siegel, *supra*, at 559.

48. U.S. Const., Art. II, § 1, cl. 2.

49. U.S. Const., Am. XII.

50. Behind the scenes, of course, it might have caused the rejection of some otherwise sterling vice-presidential candidates.

51. A lawsuit urging the infirmity was rebuffed both on standing grounds and also after finding that plaintiffs were unlikely to prevail in the claim that Cheney remained an "inhabitant" of Texas. Jones v. Bush, 122 F. Supp. 2d 713 (N.D. Tex. 2002), *aff'd without opinion*, 244 F.3d 134 (5th Cir. 2000), *cert. denied*, 531 U.S. 1062 (2001). *See generally* Sanford Levinson & Ernest A. Young, Who's Afraid of the Twelfth Amendment, 29 Fla. St. U. L. Rev. 925 (2001).

52. Ross & Josephson, *supra* note 47, at 711, assert that "[t]he . . . qualifications for electors . . . lie at the heart of their constitutional function." It is pretty clear that they mean the "constitutional function" as conceived by the constitutional framers, including those responsible for the Twelfth Amendment, but much mischief is worked by assertions like this. In fact the qualifications of electors are supremely irrelevant to the "constitutional" function they now serve. In the dispute over the 1876 election, *see* Chapter Three, Justice Bradley took the position that the vote of an elector who was constitutionally ineligible to serve should nonetheless be counted, as he was a "de facto" elector. *See* Rehnquist, *supra* note 37, at 175.

53. Siegel, *supra* note 1, at 559 n.102, makes note of a colloquy concerning the death before the balloting of three electors in 1820.

54. *See* Chapter Two.

55. Even this gives too much credit to the formalities of the system. In recent times, vice-presidential candidates have typically been selected by the party's presidential candidate, who in turn was chosen largely through popular primary elections.

56. This can be traced to the earliest elections. *See* Kuroda, *supra* note 1, at 64. The claim is made in After the People Vote 11 (3d ed., John C. Fortier, ed., AEI Press 2004) that the constitutional limitation was the cause of "political parties . . . nominating a candidate for president from one state and a candidate for vice president for another." Whatever the historical basis for that claim, it seems likely that the party practice would have developed in any event.

57. *See* Fortier, ed., *supra* note 56, at 12.

58. *See* Jack N. Rakove, The E-College in the E-Age, in The Unfinished Election of 2000 201, 204 (Jack N. Rakove, ed., Basic Books 2001); Levinson & Young, *supra* note 51, at 938–39. More generally, one commentator notes that "in this era of residential mobility and multiple residences, . . . it is a simple matter to change one's legal residence." Berns ed., *supra* note 3, at 16. To be sure, as argued by Levinson & Young, *supra*, at 940–41, a person might be an inhabitant of more than one state. Cheney then might have been an "inhabitant" of Texas even if he had managed also to become an inhabitant of Wyoming. The possibility does not, of course, add any particular contemporary force to the inhabitancy requirement. *But cf.* Levinson & Young, *supra*, at 950–52.

59. There is ambiguous evidence of some other potentially "mishandled" exclusion of votes collected in Ross & Josephson, *supra* note 47, at 706 n.232.

60. This is assuming that the Supreme Court does not make a habit of resolving electoral college disputes before they reach the joint meeting.

61. *See* Bruce Ackerman & David Fontana, How Jefferson Counted Himself In, Atlantic Monthly, March 2004, at 86. Jefferson was, of course, a candidate for president at the time, and the sentiment was expressed against his own electoral interest. Ackerman & Fontana, *supra*, at 86. Four years later, when Jefferson was vice president and thus the presiding officer at the joint meeting, he similarly accepted votes from Georgia that might have been thought to be procedurally irregular. This raised a question of a conflict of interest for Jefferson, since he was a presidential candidate, indeed one whose victory—without recourse to the House contingent procedure—depended on his ruling. Ackerman & Fontana, *supra*, at 91–93.

62. "[T]he [Supreme] Court continuingly . . . perceive[s] distinctions in the imperative character of Constitutional provisions, since that character must be discerned from a particular provision's larger context." Poe v. Ullman, 367 U.S. 497, 522, 543 (Harlan, J., dissenting).

63. *See* note 1, *supra*.

Chapter Ten

1. For examples of just such an assumption, albeit in some instances from persons not deterred from the fight, *see* Lucius Wilmerding, Jr., The Electoral College ix (Beacon Press 1958); Ronald Dworkin, A Badly Flawed Election, N.Y. Rev. of Books, Jan. 11, 2001, at 53, 55; Jack N. Rakove, The E-College in the E-Age, in The Unfinished Election of 2000 201, 228, 232 (Jack N. Rakove, ed., Basic Books 2001); Tara Ross, Enlightened Democracy: The Case for the Electoral College 124 (World Ahead Publishing 2004).

2. The three-fourths of the states can act through their legislatures or by special conventions "as the one or the other mode of ratification may be proposed by the Congress." It is also possible to have the initial proposal made by "application of the legislatures of two thirds of the several states," but that route has never been successfully employed. *See* U.S. Const., Art. V.

3. More precisely the District is given "[a] number of electors . . . equal to the whole number of Senators and Representatives in Congress to which the District would be entitled if it were a State, but in no event more than the least populous State" U.S. Const. Am. XXIII, § 1, cl. 2. For the foreseeable future, that number will be three. *See* Chapter Six, note 20.

4. *See, e.g.*, Abolish the Electoral College, N.Y. Times, Aug. 29, 2004, at 10; George C. Edwards III, Why the Electoral College Is Bad for America 39 (Yale University Press 2004); Jack N. Rakove, Introduction: Dangling Questions, in The Unfinished Election of 2000 xix (Jack N. Rakove, ed., Basic Books 2001) (hereinafter I will cite the book as

"Rakove"); Jack N. Rakove, The E-College in the E-Age, in Rakove, *supra*, at 201, 203, 222; Alexander Keyssar, The Right to Vote and Election 2000, in Rakove, *supra*, at 100; Michael J. Glennon, When No Majority Rules 76 (Congressional Quarterly 1992). The same "mistake," if such it be, was made by an earlier generation of distinguished scholars. *See* Lawrence D. Longley & Alan G. Braun, The Politics of Electoral College Reform 97 (Yale University Press 1972).

5. *See* Lawrence D. Longley & Neal R. Peirce, The Electoral College Primer 2000 149–54 (Yale University Press 1999) (based on the 1990 census apportionment of the electoral college); David W. Abbott & James P. Levine, Wrong Winner: The Coming Debacle in the Electoral College 78–82 (Praeger 1991). The point was originally demonstrated in mathematical terms in John Banzhaf, One Man, 3.312 Votes: A Mathematical Analysis of the Electoral College, 13 Vill. L. Rev. 304 (1968), though presidential scholars had earlier recognized the disproportionate importance of more populous states. We will turn shortly to qualifications based on the political makeup of states, but I know of no sustained challenge to Banzhaf's mathematical demonstration. *See* Longley & Braun, *supra* note 4, at 104–15; *but see* Robert J. Sickels, The Power Index and the Electoral College: A Challenge to Banzhaf's Analysis, 14 Vill. L. Rev. 92 (1968).

6. *See* Ann N. Crigler, Marion R. Just, & Edward J. McCaffery, Rethinking the Vote: The Politics and Prospects of American Election Reform 154 (Oxford University Press 2004); Edwin D. Dover, The Disputed Presidential Election of 2000 10 (Greenwood Press 2003); Rakove, E-College *supra*, note 4, at 201, 207; Abbott & Levine, *supra* note 5, at 84. A dramatic depiction of the varying use of campaign advertisements—and accompanying expenditures—in the 2004 election is provided in The Great Ad Wars of 2004, N.Y. Times, Nov. 1, 2004, at A19.

7. *See* Longley & Peirce, *supra* note 5, at 138, and sources cited.

8. Other changes that would be worked by a move to a nationwide popular vote can be identified, but seem less likely to be influential in determining a state's stance. For instance, the electoral college allocation favors states that are losing population, because reallocation only occurs once every ten years, after the decennial census.

9. U.S. Const., Art. I, § 3, cl. 1.

10. Paul Finkelman suggests an intriguingly close parallel between the way the 1858 choice of Illinois senator actually proceeded and the modern operation of the electoral college:

> Prior to the passage of the Seventeenth Amendment[, when] the state legislatures chose U.S. Senators . . . [the] scheme was similar to the electoral college, and it was quite possible for the candidate with the greatest voter support to lose. . . . [In] the 1858 senatorial election in Illinois[, i]t is likely that more Illinois voters supported state legislative candidates who favored Abraham Lincoln than his opponent Stephen A. Douglas. However, supporters of Douglas carried more legislative districts[, and

hence Douglas eventually got the senatorial position]. Paul Finkelman, The Proslavery Origins of the Electoral College, 23 Cardozo L. Rev. 1145, 1146 n.7 (2002).

Indeed, in some ways the electoral college had actually been a precursor of senatorial selection, rather than the other way around. For at least as early as the election of 1800, the choice of state legislators by the electorate often turned on the approach of legislative candidates to the selection of electors. *See* Tadahisa Kuroda, The Origins of the Twelfth Amendment 83–84 (Greenwood Press 1994).

11. *See* George H. Haynes, The Election of Senators 133–48 (Henry Holt 1906).

12. George H. Haynes, I The Senate of the United States 104 (Houghton Mifflin 1938) (citing Boston Herald of December 26, 1910).

13. The characterization comes from McPherson v. Blacker, 146 U.S. 1, 7, 10 (1892).

14. Section Two of the Fourteenth Amendment provides that "when the right to vote at any election for the choice of electors for President and Vice President of the United States . . . is denied to any of the male inhabitants of such state . . . or in any way abridged . . . the basis of representation therein shall be reduced [proportionally]." The impetus for this provision was clearly protection of the voting rights of then newly emancipated slaves, and it may well be that the provision has been impliedly repealed by the Fifteenth Amendment which protects those rights more fully. If the Fourteenth Amendment penalty is still effective, however, it would provide a good start to an argument against the preemptive move that the Florida legislature was contemplating. And even if the provision is no longer effective, it might still bolster an argument grounded in the importance that the Supreme Court has attributed to the individual citizen's "right to vote." *See* Chapter Eight. There is also a nonconstitutional argument that is suggested by the discussion in Chapter Eight. The Electoral Count Act provides that "[w]henever any State has held an election for the purpose of choosing electors, and has failed to make a choice on the day prescribed by law, the electors may be appointed on a subsequent day in such a manner as the legislature of such State may direct." 3 U.S.C. § 2 (2000). This might be taken impliedly to forbid the Florida legislature's preemptive move unless there had been a failure "to make a choice" on election day.

15. In descending order of electoral votes, these eleven states are: California, Texas, New York, Florida, Illinois, Pennsylvania, Ohio, Michigan, New Jersey, Georgia, and North Carolina. *See* Tara Ross, Enlightened Democracy: The Case for the Electoral College 235 n.25 (World Ahead Publishing 2004). The same group commanded a majority of the electoral votes after the 1990 census. *See* Longley & Peirce, *supra* note 5, at 188–92.

16. Under the 2000 census, Texas supplanted New York as the second most populous state.

17. *See* Tara Ross, *supra* note 15, at 235 n.25.

18. There have been at most four instances in our history—two clear and two not so

clear—where the outright winner in the electoral college lost the popular vote. *See* Chapter Three, note 96.

19. The effect would be similar to that of the "bonus" electoral college reform plan discussed in Chapter Four.

20. *See, e.g.,* the remarks of David Abbott in a discussion of the idea on a panel devoted to the electoral college at the conference. Election 2000: The Role of the Courts, the Role of the Media, the Roll of the Dice, Conference Transcript, Panel 2, p. 161, http://pubweb.nwu.edu/%7Ejsp381/Panel_2_Final.pdf (last visited 08/23/01); *see also* Tara Ross, *supra* note 15, at 156–58.

21. *See* Longley & Braun, *supra* note 4, at 115. In contrast, voters in Wyoming (three electoral votes), the least populous state, had over 1.3 times the voting power of Montana voters; and in the eight most populous states voters had 1.4 times the Montana voting power on up to California's 2.663. Longley & Peirce, *supra* note 5, at 151–52. While these calculations are based on the 1990 census, and hence are a bit out of date, none of the essential points are likely to be changed in the new calculations. By one calculation in the run-up to the 2004 election, a total of "44 states stand to gain power should the Electoral College be eliminated." *See* Timothy Noah, America's Worst College, Part 4, Slate, http://slate.msn.com/id/2108420/ (last visited 10/19/04).

22. A good representation of these states joined in a challenge a number of years ago to the winner-take-all approach in (unavailing) litigation before the U.S. Supreme Court. *See* Delaware v. New York, 385 U.S. 895 (1966); *see also* Williams v. Virginia State Board of Elections, 288 F. Supp. 622 (E.D. Va. 1968); Abbott & Levine, *supra* note 5, at 142–45.

23. *See* John M. Carey, Term Limits and Legislative Representation 9 (Cambridge University Press 1996). For a brief discussion of the role of private individuals, *see* Alan E. Peterson, Term Limits: The Law Review Article, Not the Movie, 31 Creighton L. Rev. 767 (1998). In 1995, the Supreme Court found term limits unconstitutional as applied to federal offices, U.S. Term Limits, Inc. v. Thornton, 514 U.S. 779 (1995), but that does not make the political lessons of the term limits movement any less applicable to the electoral college possibility.

24. *See* Carey, *supra* note 23, at 12–13.

25. Carey, *supra* note 23, at 65.

26. U.S. Const., Art. II, § 1, cl. 2.

27. *See* Napolitano v. Davidson, 2004 U.S. Dist. LEXIS 22133 (D.C. Colo., filed Oct. 13, 2004).

28. U.S. Const., Art. I § 10, cl. 3.

29. In Northeast Bancorp, Inc. v. Board of Governors of the Federal Reserve System, 472 U.S. 159 (1985), the Supreme Court listed "classic indicia of a compact" that were missing in the situation presented there. Among the reasons that no compact was in-

volved was that "each State [involved] is free to modify or repeal its law unilaterally." 472 U.S. at 175.

30. Virginia v. Tennessee, 148 U.S. 503, 519 (1893); New Hampshire v. Maine, 426 U.S. 363, 369 (1976); Northeast Bancorp, Inc. v. Board of Governors of the Federal Reserve System, 472 U.S. 159, 175–76 (1985).

31. Northeast Bancorp, Inc. v. Board of Governors of the Federal Reserve System, 472 U.S. 159, 176 (1985) (emphasis supplied).

32. *See* Joseph Story, 3 Commentaries on the Constitution of the United States § 1397 (Boston, Hilliard, Gray 1833); U.S. Senate Rep. No. 395, 43rd Cong., 1st. Sess. 12–13 (1874).

33. *See* United States Steel Corp. v. Multi-state Tax Commission, 434 U.S. 452 (1978); *cf.* Virginia v. Tennessee, 148 U.S. 503 (1893) (clause inapplicable to boundary adjustments which have no particular tendency to enhance political powers of contracting states).

34. *See* National Association of Secretaries of State, Fact Sheet: NASS Presidential Primary/Caucus Plan, http://www.nass.org (last visited 05/11/05).

35. I actually developed the approach first in the nationwide vote context, and only later applied it to the third-party problem. *See* Robert W. Bennett, Popular Election of the President Without a Constitutional Amendment, 4 The Green Bag, 2d ser. 241 (2001); Robert W. Bennett, State Coordination in Popular Election of the President Without a Constitutional Amendment, 5 The Green Bag, 2d ser. 141 (2002).

36. Board of Governors of the Federal Reserve System, 472 U.S. 159, 175 (1985).

37. Kane v. New Jersey, 242 U.S. 160, 167–68 (1916).

38. 3 U.S.C. § 6 (2000).

39. To be precise, election day is "the Tuesday . . . after the first Monday in November," and the electors meet and vote on "the first Monday after the second Wednesday in December." 3 U.S.C. §§ 1, 7 (2000).

40. *See* Chapter Four.

41. We touched on these restrictions in Chapter One.

42. *See* Trevor Potter & Marianne H. Viray, Barriers to Participation, 36 U. Mich. J. L. Reform 547, 572–73 (2003).

43. *See generally*, Alexander Keyssar, The Right to Vote: The Contested History of Democracy in the United States (Basic Books 2000).

44. Uniformed and Overseas Citizens Absentee Voting Act, 42 U.S.C. §§ 1973ff–1 to 1973ff–6 (1994). The doubt derives from the fact that the Constitution still defines eligibility to vote in federal elections in terms of the "qualifications requisite for electors of the most numerous branch of the state legislature." U.S. Const., Art. I, § 2, cl. 1; *see* Am. XVII, cl. 1. As we have seen there are several—large and important, but defined—limitations on this power, but nothing to suggest any general federal authority to extend voting rights when the states have not seen fit to do so.

Chapter Eleven

1. *See, e.g.*, Richard A. Posner, Breaking the Deadlock: The 2000 Election, the Constitution, and the Courts (Princeton University Press 2001); John C. Yoo, In Defense of the Court's Legitimacy, in The Vote: Bush, Gore & the Supreme Court 223 (Cass R. Sunstein & Richard A. Epstein, eds., University of Chicago Press 2001). This also seems to be the message of William H. Rehnquist, Centennial Crisis: The Disputed Election of 1876 (Alfred A. Knopf 2004). For a similar point made by a critic of the decision *see* Frank I. Michelman, Suspicion, or the New Prince, in The Vote, *supra*.

2. Help America Vote Act of 2002, Pub. L. 107–252, 116 Stat. 1666.

3. New State Ice Co. v. Liebmann,. 285 U.S. 262, 311 (1932) (Brandeis, J., dissenting).

4. *See* in particular Stephen A. Siegel, The Conscientious Congressman's Guide to the Electoral Count Act of 1887, 56 Fla. L. Rev. 541, 573 (2004).

5. Seth Barrett Tillman, The Federalist Papers as Reliable Historical Source Material for Constitutional Interpretation, 105 W. Va. L. Rev. 601 (2003) has footnotes filled with speculative possibilities for courting, using, or avoiding the House and Senate contingent procedures. For discussion of open procedural questions once the selection of the president has moved to the House, *see* Robert M. Hardaway, The Electoral College and the Constitution: The Case for Preserving Federalism 54–61 (Praeger 1994).

6. *See, e.g.*, Tara Ross, Enlightened Democracy: The Case for the Electoral College 12 (World Ahead Publishing 2004); Hardaway, *supra* note 5, at 5, 9, 14 ("vision and genius of the constitutional framers"), 87 ("the flexibility the Constitution so wisely provided").

7. *See* Adam Liptak, Voting Problems in Ohio Set Off an Alarm, N.Y. Times, Nov. 7, 2004, at 37; James Dao, Ford Fessenden, & Tom Zeller, Jr., Voting Problems in Ohio Spur Call for Overhaul, N.Y. Times, Dec. 24, 2004, at A1; *see generally* New Standards for Elections, N.Y. Times, Nov. 7, 2004, at 10.

8. This is, of course, part of a more general problem of what Rick Pildes calls "the structural cancer of political self-entrenchment." Richard H. Pildes, Foreword: The Constitutionalization of Democratic Politics, 118 Harv. L. Rev. 29, 44 (2004).

Index

ABA Commission on Electoral College Reform (1967): congressional response to, 215n41; on House contingent procedure, 71–73, 221nn106,107,108; overview of proposal, 54, 215n43; plurality requirement of, 56, 67–68, 69; runoff provision of, 68–71, 139–40; on state discretion for voter eligibility, 56–57

Abbott, David, x, 221n108

abstaining electors: as Florida possibility, in 2000 election, 155–56, 251nn45,46; in 2000 election, 97, 99, 222n6; and voting ties, 224–25n1. *See also* faithless electors

Adams, John, 21–22, 24–25, 86, 102

Adams, John Quincy, 28, 75, 102, 202n5, 211n12, 230n22

Agnew, Spiro, 39

Alabama, 40, 209n96

Alaska, 227n22

ALI (American Law Institute), 117–18

Amar, Akhil, 248n5

American Bar Association's Commission on Electoral College Reform. *See* ABA Commission on Electoral College Reform

American Independent Party, 122, 241n13

American Law Institute (ALI), 117–18

Anti-Mason Party, 122

Arizona, 87

Arkansas, 155, 159, 206n51, 251nn41,47, 253n59

Bailey, Lloyd, 38–39, 97–98, 230n21, 235–36n60

ballots: connotations of term, 104–5, 233nn45,47; different formats of, 44–45, 234n57, 235n59; in 2000 election, 7, 234–35n58; in originalist approach, 107–8, 235–36n60; short form of, 2, 191n5; third-party access to, 129–30

Banzhaf, John, 254n5

Barkley, Alben, 241n12

Bayard, James, 23

Beckel, Bob, 231n26

Bellesiles, Michael, 223–24n30

Bentsen, Lloyd, 225n6

Berns, Walter, 235n59, 239nn100,101

Best, Judith, x, 58, 216–17n57

bicameralism, 13, 55–56

Bickel, Alexander, 60, 61, 196n16, 220n86

Boxer, Barbara, 40, 207n67

Bradley, Joseph, 33, 204–5n34, 250n36, 252n52

Brandeis, Louis, 183

Brest, Paul, 233n49

Brewster, Robert, 230–31n25

Bryd, Harry, 229n17

Burr, Aaron, 4, 22–23, 25, 74, 82, 86, 200nn54,55, 209n89, 223–24n30

Bush, George W., 5, 8, 66–67, 87, 88, 97, 100–101, 127, 157, 218n70, 231n30

Bush, Jeb, 40

Bush v. Gore, 30, 37, 207n64, 246n78. *See also* Florida (election 2000)

Butler, Nicholas, 119

Calhoun, John, 102

California, 41, 80, 124, 166, 168, 256n21

campaigning for president: in electoral college system, 3–4, 49, 62, 218–19n72; face-to-face debates in, 129; in nationwide popular vote, 62–63, 166–69, 219nn73,74; technology of, 89; third-party strategies in, 63–64

Carter, Jimmy, 89, 193n25, 226n16, 249n21

census 2000: least populous states in, 76–77; most populous states in, 165–66, 255nn15,16

certificate of ascertainment, 37, 53–54, 174, 175, 207n62

certificate of vote, 37, 207n62

Cheney, Dick, 5, 157, 158, 159, 252nn51,58

Chernow, Ron, 200n47

Clay, Henry, 28

Cleveland, Grover, 4, 44

Clinton, Bill, 4

"co-inhabitancy" limitation, 4–5, 14, 157–58, 159, 221n107, 252n51,55, 252nn56,58

Colorado, 42, 166; proportionality initiative in, 51–52, 130, 170, 212–13n18, 214nn30,31,32, 215n33

Commission on Electoral College Reform. *See* ABA Commission on Electoral College Reform

Compact Clause, 170–71, 174, 256–57n29

compacts, 170–74, 256–57n29

congressional districting, 55, 92–93, 215n45

Conley, Patricia, x

Connecticut, 171, 174

constitutional amendments: electoral college reform without, 8–9, 10–11, 182–84, 185; requirements for passage of, 8, 48, 161–62, 211n8, 233–34n52, 253n2. *See also individual amendments*

Constitutional Convention (1787), 12–13, 54

constitutional language: on authority in

electoral vote count, 148–50; on elector discretion, 104–5, 116; originalist approach to interpretation of, 105–7, 233n49, 234n53; practical interpretation of, 109–11, 113–14, 236n65; subordination of, in white primary cases, 111–13; textualist approach to interpretation of, 105, 111, 233n46, 237n72

contingent nationwide popular vote legislation, 173–75

contingent selection of electors: and *Bush v. Gore,* 246n78; as constitutional issue, 141; as democratic process issue, 137–38; methodology/purpose of, 133–34, 183–84, 244nn55,56; prior use of, 132; runoff alternative to, 139–41; third party's impact on, 141–42; timing of, 138–39; as voter preferences issue, 139

contingent selection of president. *See* House selection of president

Cooley, Thomas, 196–98n23

Councils of State Governments, 172

Crawford, William, 28

Crockett, David, 227n26

Davies, Jack, 238n91

Davis, David, 33

Davis, Thomas M., III, 91–93

death/disability of candidate: and elector discretion, 118–19, 145, 238n94, 239nn98,101; for president, before electoral college vote, 119–20, 145, 239n100, 240nn102,103; for president, before term begins, 146–47, 248n7; for vice-president, before election, 145–46, 248nn2,3

Debs, Eugene, 126

Dellinger, Walter, 15

democratic legitimacy: and contingent selection of electors, 137–38; and electoral college system, 54–55, 215n43; and House selection procedure, 76–78, 84–85, 222nn11,13; majoritarianism and, 55–56, 57–58, 153–54, 216n54, 250n38; voter qualification issue of, 56–57

Democratic Party: in 1876 election, 31–32, 33–34; in 1892 Michigan districting dispute, 42–43; in 1948 election, 124, 241n12; in 108th Congress, 80; and white primary cases, 111–12

Dewey, Thomas, 124

Diamond, Martin, 217nn58,59, 229–30n19

disenfranchisement: of blacks in white primary cases, 111–13; of felons/ex-felons, 6–7, 176; of former slaves, 30, 203n14; limited state discretion on, 6–7, 30–31, 56–57, 193nn21,22, 203n18, 216n50; in nationwide popular vote, 176–78; of U.S. citizens abroad, 177, 257n44

disqualification of electoral vote: for "co-inhabitancy" transgression, 157–58, 252n51; in contemporary context, 158, 252n52; as Florida alternative, 155–56, 251nn45,46; impact of, 154–55, 156–57, 250–51n39, 251nn41,43; in Oregon, 1876 election, 32, 203–4n26, 205n36, 250n36

District of Columbia: electoral college votes of, 31, 90, 110, 162, 253n3; House status of, 78, 91–92, 227n27; selection of electors in, 43; in 2000 election, 87, 97, 99, 222n6; 2004 popular vote results in, 213n19

districts for choice of electors: disincentives for, 50–51; proposal for, 49; split slate implications of, 50, 213n20; states with, 43, 130; use of, 42–44, 130–31, 209nn89,92, 213n21, 214n25

Dixiecrat (States' Rights) Party, 122, 124, 240n3

Dole, Robert, 231n31, 244n56

Douglas, Stephen, 164, 254–55n9

Dukakis, Michael, 225n6

Durbin, Richard, 194n30

Duverger, Maurice, 220n95

Eagleton, Thomas, 244n56, 248n3

ECA. See Electoral Count Act

Edwards, George, 100–101, 221n99, 234n57

Edwards, John, 224n38, 226n12

election (1789), 21, 155, 251n44

election (1792), 132, 195n11, 201n61

election (1796), 21–22, 96, 102, 132, 137, 138, 159, 200n54, 243n41

election (1800), 47, 102; control of House delegations in, 80, 223n18; electoral college tie in, 22, 82, 86, 200n51, 223–24n30; House contingent procedure in, 4, 22–23, 74, 200n54, 223n29; selection of electors in, 41–42, 43, 208n87, 243n41

election (1820), 228–29n6

election (1824), 28, 75, 102, 125, 202n5, 211n12, 230n22

election (1832), 122

election (1836), 99, 230nn22,23

election (1856), 35, 154–55

election (1860), 63, 219n76

election (1872), 34–35, 155, 159, 206nn50,51,52, 251nn41,47

election (1876), 47, 159, 209n96; commission's resolution of, 33–34, 82–83, 192n17, 204–5n34, 205n36; electoral college vote in, 88, 225n2; elector controversies in, 4, 31–32, 102–3, 153–54, 203n26, 250nn36,38,39, 252n52; political climate during, 31, 204n29

election (1888), 4, 44

election (1892), 42–43

election (1912), 126

election (1916), 88

election (1948), 64, 122, 124, 240n3, 241nn12,16, 242n17

election (1960), 39, 40–41, 88–89, 191–92n8, 209n96, 245n63

election (1968): House proposal before, 222–23n15; joint meeting challenge in, 38–39, 97–98, 230n21; short ballot in, 235–36n60; third-party strategy in, 64, 125, 231–32n32, 241n13; third-party votes in, 122

election (1972), 225n6

election (1976), 89, 225n6, 230–31n25, 231n31

election (1988), 96, 97, 225n6

election (1992), 4, 126–27, 222n13

election (1996), 126

election (2000): abstaining elector in, 97, 99, 222n6; ballots used in, 7, 234–35n58; close popular-vote states in, 66–67, 229n93; "co-inhabancy" issue in, 5, 157–58, 159, 252nn51,58; disenfranchisement in, 6–7, 176–77; election reform after, 7, 193n27, 194n28, 238n90, 245n48; electoral college results in, 222n6; elector defection possibilities in, 100–101, 231nn26,30; joint meeting objections in, 207n67; jurisdictional issues in, 5–6, 180–81, 192n16; states' voting power in, 168, 256n21; third-party impact on, 127–28, 242n17; tie possibilities in, 87, 226nn10,11; "wrong winner" charge in, 3, 48–49, 102, 232n38. *See also* Florida (election 2000)

election (2004): Colorado's proportionality initiative in, 51–52, 170, 212–13n18, 214nn30,31,32, 215n33; faithless elector's vote in, 96, 224n38, 225n6, 226n12; joint meeting challenge in, 207n67; Richie Robb's vote in, 97, 229nn8,9; states' voting power in, 168; tie possibilities in, 88

election day: date selected for, 150, 249n21, 257n39; use of term, 2, 191n4

electoral college: backup procedure to, 19–20, 76, 198–99n33, 199nn34,37,38, 199nn39,41; and campaign incentives, 3–4, 49, 62, 166, 218–19n72; close contests in, 87–89, 226nn10,11,16; counting procedures of, 24–25, 29, 202n65; defenders' perspectives on, 15, 58–62, 185–86, 195–96n15, 196n16, 216–17n57, 217nn58,59, 218n70, 220n93; "democracy" issue of, 54–55, 215n43; Eagleton-Dole proposal to replace, 244n56; Fourteenth Amendment and, 29–30, 216n50; fraud oversight with, 65–66, 220n90; historical background of, 12–15, 195nn7,11, 195nn12,14; and presidential power, 64–65, 220n86; problems of, generally, 47, 144–45, 160, 179–80, 182–83, 210–11n4, 247–48n1;

proposal to increase size of, 90–94; scholarly neglect of, ix–x, 5; senatorial selection history's lessons for, 164, 254–55n9; state delegations to, 90, 162, 226n19, 227n20; states disadvantaged by, 168, 256n21; and third-party strategies, 63–64; tie in, 1800 election, 4, 22, 82, 86, 200n51, 223–24n30; tie in, from abstention, 224–25n1; timing issues of, 150–53, 249nn21,26,33, 250n34. *See also* electoral college reform; electors; joint meeting on electoral count

electoral college reform: ABA Commission, 54, 56–57, 67–68, 215nn41,43; districting proposal, 49, 50, 213nn20,21; Fourteenth Amendment effects on, 29–30; House selection and, 71–73; instant runoff, 139–41, 246–47n83; limiting state discretion, 31, 131–32, 244n44; motivation for, 163–64, 181; "national bonus" plan, 49–50, 212n15; nationwide popular vote, 165–69, 244n56, 255n15; nonconstitutional approach to, x, 8–9, 161, 182–84; popular vote focus of, 7–8, 53–54, 194n30; proportionality proposal, 49, 50, 51–52, 212–13n18, 213n19, 214nn28,30, 214nn31,32, 215n33; reasons for neglect of, 5–7, 47–48, 193n25; risk assessment of, 187; by Twelfth Amendment, 4–5, 23–26, 201n59, 202nn64,66; by Twentieth Amendment, 29, 203n11; by Twenty-Third Amendment, 31; uniform law proposal, 117–21, 238nn92,93,94, 240n103; "wrong winner" focus of, 48–49, 211n12. *See also* contingent selection of electors; Electoral Count Act; nationwide popular vote for president

electoral college tie: from abstentions, 224–25n1; in 1800 election, 22, 82, 86, 200n51, 223–24n30; House contingent procedure, 4, 22–23; justification for concern, 88–90; from plausible reversals, in 2000 and 2004, 87–88, 226nn10,11

Electoral Count Act (ECA, 1887), 47, 116,

184, 206n53; adoption of, 4; applied in 1960 election, 40–41; on competing slates, 39, 207nn70,72,73; dispute resolution provisions of, 37–38, 136, 207nn64,67; on gubernatorial certification, 37, 38, 39–40, 148, 207n62; proposed revision of, 152–53, 249–50n33; suspect constitutionality of, 148–49, 248n11; on timing and procedures, 36–37, 206n57, 255n14

electorate. *See* voters

elector discretion: candidate's death/disability and, 118–19, 145, 238n94, 239nn98,101; as constitutional issue, 98, 104, 230n21, 232–33n43; existing practice, lessons from, 113–15; federal statute proposal on, 116; historical treatment of, 14–17, 195nn12,14,15, 196nn18,20, 196–98n23; as posing originalist dilemma, 106–10, 113, 233–34n52, 234n53, 235–36n60, 236nn63,64,65; Twelfth Amendment on, 104–5; and Twenty-Third Amendment, 110–11; uniform law proposal on, 117–21, 182–83, 238nn91–94, 240n103. *See also* faithless electors

electors: ballots' indication of, 44–45, 108, 234nn57,58, 235nn59,60; as bargaining targets, 83–84; "co-inhabitancy" limitation, 5, 14, 157–58, 221n107, 252n51; contingent procedures to select, 132–34, 244nn55,56; date for meetings of, 36, 150–51, 257n39; in disqualification scenarios, 32, 153, 154–58, 203–4n26, 205n36, 250nn36,39, 251nn41,43, 251nn46,47, 252n52; gubernatorial certification of, 37, 38, 39–40, 53–54, 207n62; meetings of, 17, 18–19, 95–96, 198n27; original conception of, 14–17, 195nn12,14, 196nn16,23; pledge requirements for, 95–96, 97, 98, 104, 110–11, 115, 230n21, 232–33n43, 236nn68,69,70; publicly perceived role of, 1–3, 102–3, 232n41; qualifications to vote for, 6–7, 192–93n19, 193nn21,22; reform proposals linked to, 49–52; rival slates of,

ECA on, 39, 148, 207nn70,72,73; rival slates of, in 1876 election, 4, 32–34, 204–5n34; selection in districts, 42–44, 208n86, 209nn89,92, 213n21, 214n25; selection of, historically, 13–14, 41–42, 195n7, 208n81; smallest delegation of, 31; states' role in selection of, 43, 130–32, 134–35, 148–49, 165, 208n86, 243n41, 244n44, 245nn58,59, 245nn62,63; ties to political parties, 20–22, 23–24, 44–45, 186, 200n45, 201nn61,62; total number of, 1; unpledged category of, 96; winner-take-all designation of, 43–44, 162, 208nn87,88, 209nn90,93. *See also* contingent selection of electors; districts for choice of electors; elector discretion; faithless electors; winner-take-all elector selection

Elhauge, Einer, 251n45

Equal Protection Clause, 6, 111–12, 131

ex-felons and felons, 6–7, 176

Fahrenheit 911 (film), 207n67

faithless electors: as bargaining targets, 83–84; candidate's search for, 100–102, 231nn26,30,31; in 1836 vice-presidential selection, 98–99, 230nn22,23; federal statute proposal on, 116; joint meeting challenge to, 38–39; motives of, 96–97, 101, 229–30n19, 231–32n32; in past elections, 38–39, 96, 222n6, 224n38, 225n6, 226n12, 228–29n6; problematic implications of, 10, 99–100, 102, 103–4, 114–15, 186, 230–31n25, 232n42; states' handling of, 97–98; uniform law proposal on, 117–21, 182–83, 238n91–94, 240n103. *See also* elector discretion

"federalism" rhetoric, 58–59, 209n93, 216–17n57, 217n59

Federalist 10, 17

Federalist 39, 16, 196nn18,20

Federalist 66, 199n41

Federalist 68, 18

Federalist 78, 16
Federalist Party, 21–23, 28, 80, 201n58, 223n18
felons and ex-felons, 6–7, 176
Ferling, John, 199n34
Field, Stephen, 205n36, 250–51n39
Fifteenth Amendment, 30, 131, 203n14, 255n14
Finkelman, Paul, 254–55n9
Florida, 31–32, 88, 168, 250n36
Florida (election 2000): abstention alternative for, 155–56, 251nn45,46; disenfranchisement in, 6–7, 176; gubernatorial certification in, 39–40; in instant runoff scenario, 142–43; joint meeting objections to, 207n67; legislative preemption issues in, 134–37, 138–39, 165, 245nn62,69, 245nn70,71, 246n78, 255n14; safe harbor issue in, 37–38, 151–53, 207n64, 249–50n33, 250n34; Supreme Court involvement, 180–81; third-party impact in, 127, 142, 242n17; vote recount in, 6, 65, 67, 192n16
Florida Supreme Court, 136, 151–52
Ford, Gerald, 89, 193n25, 225n6, 226n16, 249n21
Fourteenth Amendment, 6, 29–30, 47, 111–12, 131, 203n12, 216n50, 255n14
framers: bicameralism, 55–56; contingent presidential selection, 19–20, 199nn34,37,38, 199nn39,41; on elector meetings, 17, 18, 198n27; on electors' role, 14–17, 195nn12,14, 196n20, 196–98n23; on legislature's role, 17–18, 198n29; presidential selection views of, 12–14, 15–16, 196n20. See also U.S. Constitution
freedmen, 30, 203n14
Free Soil Party, 242n18

Georgia, 132, 206n49
gerrymandering, 51
Glennon, Michael, 221n108, 238nn90,93
Goldwater, Barry, 229n17
Gore, Albert, 57, 66–67, 87, 96, 100, 127, 157, 207n67, 218n70, 231n26, 242n17

Governors' Associations, 172
Grant, Ulysses S., 31
Great Compromise, 13
Greeley, Horace, 34–35, 118–19, 145
Green Party, 127, 242n17
gubernatorial certification of electors, 37, 38, 39–40, 148, 207n62

Hamilton, Alexander, 16, 93; election scheming by, 21, 22, 200nn47,55; on electoral college system, 46; on elector discretion, 14, 18, 195n12; on House contingent procedure, 199n41; proposal for elector districts, 209n89
Hardaway, Robert M., 58, 195–96n15, 200nn45,51, 203n11, 216–17n57, 217n59, 222n5, 230n23
Harrison, Benjamin, 4, 44
Hawaii, 41, 151, 227n22
Hayes, Rutherford B., 32, 33, 34, 57, 83, 88, 103, 209n96
Help America Vote Act (2002), 193n27, 194n28
Hoar, George F., 204n29
Hospers, John, 225n6
House Committee on Government Reform, 91
House of Representatives: allocation of seats in, 55, 93, 215n45, 228n36; District of Columbia's status in, 78, 91–92, 227n27; elections by the people, 192–93n19; Fourteenth Amendment effects on, 30, 216n50; membership increase proposal for, 91–94, 182, 227n27, 228n32; resignation from, by acting president, 81; single-member districts, 128; size of, 90, 227n22; state delegations to, 78–80, 222–23n15, 223n17,18; tie vote prospects in, 91; vacancies in, 90–91, 227n26; vote requirement for constitutional amendments, 8. See also House selection of president
House selection of president: ABA Commission's criticism of, 71–73, 221nn106,107,108; after death of president-elect, 239n100; bargaining in,

82–85, 141–42, 224nn31,35; commentators' consensus on, 186, 210n4, 222n5; constitutional provision on, 19–20, 199nn34,37, 199nn38,41; constitutional trigger for, 94, 224–25n1; "democracy" issue of, 76–78, 222nn11,13; District of Columbia's status in, 78; in 1800 election, 4, 22–23, 74, 200n54; in 1824 election, 28, 75; Thomas Jefferson on, 75; least populous states' status in, 238n92; by old versus new House, 29, 203n11; proposal to avoid, 132–34, 137, 141, 183–84, 244nn55,56; stalemate in, 78–80, 81–82, 222–23n15, 223nn17,29,30, 241n12; from three candidates, 123–24, 240n8; Twelfth Amendment on, 23, 25, 74–75, 201n59, 202n66, 221–22n2; from two candidates, 123, 240n7; unavailable candidate dilemma of, 146–47, 248n7
Hughes, Charles Evans, 88
Humphrey, Hubert, 125, 202n65

Illinois, 108, 164, 254–55n9
independent candidates. See third-party candidates
"inhabitancy" limitation, 4–5, 14, 157–58, 159, 221n107, 252nn51,55, 252nn56,58
initiative process. See popular initiative
instant runoff election, 139–41, 142–43, 246–47n83
intention, ascribing to multi-member bodies, 106
Irwin, Henry, 229n17

Jackson, Andrew, 28, 211n12
Jackson, Robert, 196–98n23, 234n53, 237n72
Janklow, William, 79, 90–91
Jay, John, 22, 209n89
Jaybird Party, 112
Jefferson, Thomas, 25, 28; on choice of electors from districts, 43, 209n90, 214n25; contingent House selection of, 4, 22–23, 74, 75, 82, 86, 200nn51,54, 201n58, 223–24n30; faithless elector

vote for, 96, 102; on irregular electoral votes, 159, 253n61; in 1796 election, 21–22
Jeffersonian Party, 21–22, 28, 80, 200n48, 223n18
Johnson, Richard M., 99, 230n22
joint meeting on electoral count: "appointment"/disqualification issues of, 154–58, 250–51n39, 251nn43,45, 251nn46,47; with binding uniform law, 120–21, 184; constitutional provision for, 17, 34, 205n40; controversies regarding, 32–33, 34–35, 153–54, 206nn49–52, 250nn36,38, 251n41; date for, 151, 249n26; death of candidate after, 146–47, 248n7; death of candidate before, 118–20, 145, 238n94, 239nn98,100,101, 240nn102,103; divided authority of, with states, 148–50, 248n1; ECA's provisions for, 38–40, 207nn67,70, 207nn72,73; faithless elector votes at, 38–39, 97–98, 120–21, 229n17, 230n21; of incoming Congress, 29, 151, 203n11; popular vote precommitment proposal for, 159–60, 253nn61,62; presiding officer at, 24–25, 27, 29, 202n65; with rival slates of electors, 32–33, 38, 148; survey of pitfalls, 247–48n1; timing issues prior to, 152–53, 249–50n33, 250n34; use of commission, in 1876, 33–34, 192n17, 204–5n34, 205n36

Kennedy, John F., 40–41, 88–89, 209n96, 216–17n57, 245n63
Kentucky, 205n42
Kerry, John, 88, 101, 226n12
Kuroda, Tadahisa, 198n27, 201nn61,62

Leach, Margaret, 225n6
Legislative Conferences, 172
LeMay, Curtis, 39
Lett-Simmons, Barbara, 96, 97, 99, 222n6
Levine, James, 221n108
Levinson, Sanford, 252n58
Liberal Party, 242n18

Lieberman, Joseph, 157
Lincoln, Abraham, 63, 68, 164, 206n57, 219n76, 254–55n9
Llewellyn, Karl, 236n65
Lodge, Henry Cabot, 229n17
Longley, Lawrence, 124, 235n59, 241n12
Louisiana, 31–32, 245n63
Lowell, James Russell, 102–3

MacBride, Roger, 225n6
Madison, James, 15–16, 17, 28, 43, 196n20, 208n87, 213n21, 214n25, 219n74
Maine, 43, 50, 87, 130, 213n20, 240n8
majority vote winner. See nationwide popular vote winner
Marshall, John, 114
Maryland, 78, 114, 168
Massachusetts, 132, 137, 138, 171, 174, 208n87
McAfee, Joy, 218n70
McClellan, George, 204n29
McCulloch v. Maryland (1819), 114, 236n69
McPherson v. Blacker (1892), 50, 130–31, 134, 196–98n23, 245n62
Michener, James, 125, 231–32n32
Michigan, 42–43, 44, 130–31, 206n49
Miles, Samuel, 96, 102
Minnesota, 87, 88, 129, 166, 224n38, 225n6, 226n12, 238n91
minority votes, 60–61, 62, 219n73
minor party candidates. See third-party candidates
Mississippi, 206n50, 234n57
Missouri, 66, 166, 205n42
Monroe, James, 28, 228–29n6
Montana, 169, 256n21
Moore, Michael, 207n67
Morris, Gouvernor, 16

Nader, Ralph, 127–28, 142, 225n5, 242n17
National Association of Secretaries of State, 173
"national bonus" plan for nationwide popular vote winner, 49–50, 212n15
National Conference of Commissioners on Uniform State Laws (NCCUSL), 117–18, 238n91
nationwide popular vote for president: ABA Commission's proposal on, 54, 56–57, 215nn41,43; Compact Clause and, 170–73, 256–57n29; contingent legislation approach to, 173–75; with forty percent plurality, 67–68; geographic campaign strategies in, 62–63, 166–68, 219nn73,74; historical resistance to, 12–13, 15–16, 55–56, 194n1, 196nn18,20; nonconstitutional approach to, 10–11, 161–62, 185; popular initiative as means to, 170; and presidential power, 64–65, 220n86; reformist focus on, 7–8, 48–49, 194n30; with runoff provision, 68–71, 221n99; selecting state electors by, 165–69, 255n15, 256n22; state-based evaluations of, 162–64, 254nn5,8; third-party disincentives in, 63–64; timing problems of, 175; vote counting concerns in, 65–66, 175–76, 220n90; voter eligibility issues in, 176–78, 257n44
nationwide popular vote winner: electoral victory's relation to, 3, 57–58, 191–92n8, 216n54; "national bonus" plan for, 49–50, 212n15; in 1960 election, 40–41; as plausible House choice, 79, 222–23n15; predictions of, in 2000 election, 100, 231n28; problems in determining, 174–76; proposed state pledges for, 165–69, 255n15, 256n22. See also nationwide popular vote for president
Nebraska, 43, 50, 130, 213n20, 240n8
Nevada, 66, 87, 88
New Hampshire, 66, 67, 88, 127, 132, 242n17
New Jersey, 12
New Mexico, 67, 87, 97, 230–31n25
New York, 155, 209n89, 255n16
Nineteenth Amendment, 31, 193n21
Nixon, Richard, 39, 40–41, 89, 125, 225n6, 229n17, 231–32n32

North Carolina, 38–39, 93, 97–98, 230n21, 235–36n60, 245n58, 251n44

Northeast Bancorp, Inc. v. Board of Governors of the Federal Reserve System, 171, 256–57n29

Ohio, 40, 88, 124, 129–30, 168, 207n67

Oklahoma, 229n17

108th Congress, 78–79, 80

Oregon, 164, 166; in 1876 election, 32, 153–54, 203–4n26, 205n36, 250nn36,38,39

originalism: and elector discretion, 106–9, 233–34n52, 234n53, 235–36n60; explanation of, 105–6; origin of term, 233n49

Owens, Bill, 215n33

Padden, Mike, 225n6

Peirce, Neal R., 124, 202n5, 235n59, 241n12

Pennsylvania, 87, 88, 226n10

"the people" (expression), 16, 196n18

Peoples Party, 242n18

Perot, H. Ross, 4, 86–87, 126–27, 222n13

Pinckney, Charles Cotesworth, 22, 25, 86, 208n87

Plumer, Samuel, 228–29n6

political parties: electors' ties to, 20–22, 23–24, 44–45, 186, 200n45, 201nn61,62; geographic balance concerns of, 25–26, 158, 252n56; and House selection process, 77, 80; interstate coordination by, 138; in nationwide popular vote scenario, 167–68; in originalist approach, 107–8; pledge requirements of, 95–96, 104, 232–33n43; reform inertia of, 180; unavailable candidates, 145–46, 248n3. *See also* third-party candidates; two-party system

Polsby, Nelson, x

popular initiative: on proportionality, in Colorado, 51–52, 130, 170, 212–13n18, 214nn30,31,32, 215n33; on term limits, 170

Posner, Richard, 245n69

president: as above factions, 18, 59–60, 198n30; constitutional qualifications for, 34; line of succession for, 81; with nationwide popular vote mandate, 64–65, 220n86; term of, 29, 150. *See also* presidential candidates

presidential candidates: coattail effects of, 167–68; "co-inhabitancy" limitation in elector votes for, 4–5, 14, 157–58, 221n107, 252nn51,56; death/disability of, before electoral count, 118–20, 145, 238n94, 239nn98,100,101, 240nn102,103; death/disability of, before term begins, 146–47, 248n7; regional primaries for, 172–73; search for elector defections on behalf of, 100–102, 231nn26,30,31; separate balloting for, 4, 23, 24, 201–2n63, 202n64; in third-party bargaining scenarios, 123–24, 125, 141–42, 241n13

president pro tempore of the Senate, 81

Progressive Party, 126, 242nn18,19

proportionality proposals, 49, 50, 51–53, 130, 170, 212–13n18, 213n19, 214nn28,30, 214nn31,32, 215n33

Puerto Ricans, 177

racial discrimination, 30, 203n14; white primary use for, 111–13

Ray v. Blair (1952), 104, 115, 196–98n23, 232–33n43, 238n93

Reagan, Ronald, 225n6

Reform Party, 87, 126

regional primaries, 172–73

Rehnquist, William, 3, 4, 136, 200n51, 201n59, 203–4n26, 221–22n2

Republican Party: in 1876 election, 31, 32; in Michigan districting dispute, 42–43; in 1948 election, 124, 241n12; in 108th Congress, 80; Whig Party's displacement by, 242nn18,20

Rhode Island, 22, 195n11, 205n41, 251n44

Richardson v. Ramirez (1974), 139n22

Robb, Richie, 97, 229nn8,9

Roosevelt, Franklin D., 89

Roosevelt, Theodore, 119, 126

Rosenthal, Albert, 78–79, 216–17n57, 236n70
Ross, Tara, 58, 60–61, 199nn38,42, 217n59, 218n71, 219n74, 223n17
runoff elections: in ABA Commission's proposal, 54, 67–68, 139–40; in Georgia election code, 132; instant type of, 140–41, 246–47n83; opposition to, 142–43, 221n99; in two-party system, 68–71, 220n95

safe harbor provision of ECA, 37–38, 151–53, 207n64, 245n58, 249–50n33, 250n34
Scalia, Antonin, 136, 233n46, 237n72
Senate Report (1874), 14–15, 82, 195n14
senatorial "bonus" of electors, 50–51, 52, 162
September 11, 232n38
Seventeenth Amendment, 53, 164, 192–93n19
Sherman, James S., 119, 248n2
short ballots, 2, 108, 191n5, 235–36n60
Siegel, Stephen A., 207n64, 251n41
slaves, 12, 13, 30, 203n14
Socialist Party, 126
South Carolina, 31–32, 219n75, 239n101
speaker of the House, 81
Speta, Jim, x
states: allocation of House seats to, 30, 55, 93, 203n12, 215n45, 228n36; challenges to electoral votes of, 38–39, 207n67; "co-inhabitancy" limitation of elector votes, 4–5, 14, 157–58, 159, 221n107, 252nn51,55, 252nn56,58; contingent designation of electors proposal for, 132–34, 173–75, 183–84, 244nn55,56; discretion of, in elector selection, 43, 130–32, 134–35, 165, 208n86, 243n41, 244n44, 245nn58,59, 245nn62,63, 255n14; discretion of, on voter eligibility, 30–31, 56–57, 176–78; divided authority regarding electors, with Congress, 148–50, 248n11; election dispute resolution by, 36–38, 206n57, 207nn62,64; electoral college delega-

tions of, 90, 226n19, 227n20; elector pledge requirements of, 95–96, 97, 98, 104, 110–11, 115, 230n21, 232–33n43, 236nn68,69,70; elector selection methods in, 2, 13–14, 41–43, 191n5, 195n7, 208n81; House delegations of, 78–80, 222–23n15, 223nn17,18; least populous, in House presidential selection, 76–77; most populous, in 2000 census, 165–66, 255nn15,16; nationwide popular vote perspectives of, 162–64, 254nn5,8; nationwide popular-winner pledge proposal for, 165–69, 256n22; partisan leanings in, 63, 219n75; as plausible swing states, 87–88, 266nn10,11; relevance of Compact Clause in elector selection, 170–73, 256–57n29; rival governments in, 34, 205nn41,42; "state action" criteria in, 112; two-Senator electoral vote "bonus" of, 50–51, 162; uniform laws in, 117–18, 238n91
States' Rights (Dixiecrat) Party, 122, 124, 240n3
Story, Joseph, 196–98n23
strategic voting, 69–71, 128, 140–41
Sutherland, George, 233n49
swing states: plausible examples of, 87–88, 226nn10,11; in popular-vote pledge scenario, 166–67

Taft, William Howard, 126
Tennessee, 66, 87, 119, 239n98, 243n41
Terminiello v. City of Chicago (1949), 237n72
term limits, 169–70, 256n23
Terry v. Adams (1953), 111–12
Texas, 5, 157, 166, 168, 245n58, 252n51, 255n16; white primary cases, 111–13
third-party candidates: ballot access of, 129–30; in bargaining scenarios, 123–24, 125, 141–42, 241n13; geographic campaign strategies of, 63–64, 241–42n16; in House presidential selection, 71–72, 77, 123–24, 222n13, 240n8; and influence on election results, 10, 86–87, 126–28, 225n5, 242n17;

policies disfavoring, 128–29; political influence of, 127, 242nn18,19,20; proposed reassignment of votes for, 133–34, 137, 139, 183–84; in runoff scenarios, 69–71

Thomas, Clarence, 136

Thurmond, Strom, 64, 122, 124, 241–42n16

Tilden, Samuel, 31, 32, 88, 103, 154, 250n38

Truman, Harry, 124, 242n17

Twelfth Amendment, 26, 47; constitutionality of fractionated electoral votes, 214n28; and 1800 election, 4, 74, 201n58; on elector discretion, 104–5; House selection trigger in, 94, 224–25n1; problems unaddressed by, 27; separate-balloting provision of, 23, 24, 80–81, 195n11, 201–2n63, 202n64; three-candidate provision of, 23, 25, 74, 123, 146, 201n59, 202n66, 221–22n2; on vice-presidential qualifications, 205n45

Twentieth Amendment: "acting" president provision of, 80, 119, 146, 147, 223n29, 239n100, 248n7; presidential line of succession in, 81; term provisions of, 29, 150, 151, 203n11

Twenty-First Amendment, 211n8

Twenty-second Joint Rule, 33, 38

Twenty-Third Amendment, 31, 47, 78, 90, 110–11, 162

Twenty-Fourth Amendment, 31, 131, 203n18, 244n44

Twenty-Fifth Amendment, 240n102

Twenty-Sixth Amendment, 31

two-party system: close electoral contests in, 87–89, 226n16; historical dominance of, 86–87, 225nn3,5; House selection procedures in, 77–78, 221nn107,108, 222n11; policies favoring, 128–29; in runoff election scenario, 68–71; Supreme Court rulings on, 129–30; third-party impact on, 127–28, 242nn18,19,20

uniform law forbidding elector discretion: organizational help with, 117–18,

238n91; possible obstacle to, 238n92; provisions of, 118, 119–21, 182–83, 184, 238nn93,94, 240n103

U.S. Congress: bicameralism of, 13, 55–56; divided authority over electoral college, with states, 148–50, 248n11; electoral college dates set by, 150–51, 249nn21,26; electoral reform after 2000 election, 7, 193n27, 194n28; elector faithfulness in District of Columbia, 110, 236n68; framers' competing views on, 17–18, 198n29; incoming, at joint meeting, 29, 151, 203n11; and joint meeting challenges, 38–39, 207n67; joint meeting presiding officer, 24–25, 202n65; resignation from, by acting president, 81; spending authority of, 117, 238n90; term of, 29, 151, 203nn9,11; on untimely elector choice, 135–36, 246nn70,71; vote requirement for constitutional amendments, 8. *See also* House of Representatives; U.S. Senate

U.S. Constitution: Compact Clause of, 170–71, 174, 256–57n29; contingent selection procedures in, 19–20, 82, 198n33, 199nn34,37, 199nn38,39; on elector discretion, 14–15, 195nn11,12,14; on elector ineligibility, 32, 153, 203–4n26, 250n36; on elector meetings, 17, 35, 95, 198n27; on federal spending authority, 117, 238n90; five-candidate provision of, 23, 74, 201n59; on House allocation of seats, 93, 228n36; on joint meeting, 17, 34, 205n40; on presidential qualifications, 34; and sanctions, 159–60, 253n62; on selection of U.S. Senators, 164; tenure/ term provisions in, 29, 202n6; on time/manner of choosing electors, 13–14, 135; vice-presidential provisions in, 14, 205n45; on voter eligibility, 6–7, 192–93n19, 257n44. *See also* constitutional language

U.S. Senate: contingent vice-presidential selection in, 19–20, 23, 72, 80–81, 199n39, 221nn106,107, 228n40; and

1836 election, 99, 230n23; history of selection of senators, 164–65, 192–93n19, 254–55n9; resignation from, by acting president, 81; vote requirement for constitutional amendments, 8

U.S. Supreme Court: Compact Clause rulings by, 170–71, 174, 256–57n29; on congressional redistricting, 92; on congressional term limits, 256n23; on 1892 Michigan elector districts, 43, 44, 208n86; as electoral commission members, 33, 204–5n34; on elector discretion, 196–98n23; on pledge requirements, 104, 110, 232–33n43; on state discretion for elector selection, 130–32, 134–35, 245n62; timing of rulings by, 115; on two-party system, 129–30; 2000 election decision of, 134–35, 136–37, 151–52, 155, 180–81, 246n78, 249n29; unprecedented election role of, 5–6, 192nn16,17; white primary cases before, 111–13

Utah, 91, 93

Van Buren, Martin, 99

Van Rensselaer, Stephen, 202n5

vice president: as acting president, 81, 147, 223n29, 241n12; contingent procedures to select, 19–20, 23, 72, 80–81, 199nn38,39, 221nn106,107, 228n40; duties/qualifications for, 14, 205n45; at joint counting meeting, 24–25, 27, 29, 202n65; term cycle of, 29. *See also* vice-presidential candidates

vice-presidential candidates: "co-inhabitancy" limitation of elector votes, 4–5, 14, 157–58, 221n107, 252nn51,55,56; death/disability of, before election, 145–46, 248nn2,3; and deceased/disabled president-elect, 146–47, 248nn6,7; and deceased/disabled presidential candidate, 119–20, 239n100, 240nn102,103; elector faithlessness to, in 1836, 98–99, 230nn22,23; separate balloting for, 4, 23, 24, 201–2n63, 202n64

Virginia, 12, 43, 78, 99, 205n42, 225n6, 230nn22,23

voters: eligibility of, in nationwide popular vote context, 176–78; limitations on disenfranchisement of, 6–7, 30–31, 56–57, 193nn21,22, 203n18, 216n50; living abroad, 177, 257n44; and political parties, 138; popular vote turnout of, 163, 172; qualifications, and constitution, 6, 192–93n19, 257n44; secondary preferences of, 139–40; strategic voting by, 69–71, 128, 140–41

Wallace, George, 39, 64, 122, 125, 231–32n32, 241n13

Wallace, Henry, 64, 241–42n16, 242n17

Warren, Earl, 241n12

Washington, George, 18, 21

West Virginia, 66, 97, 205n42, 225n6, 229n9

Whig Party, 242nn18,20

white primary cases, 111–13

Williams v. Rhodes (1968), 196–98n23

Wilmerding, Lucius, 198n29, 201nn58,62

Wilson, James, 13, 16, 20

Wilson, Woodrow, 88, 126

winner-take-all elector selection: background on, 43–44, 208nn87,88, 209n90; in counting controversies, 147–48, 220n90; as federalizing, 59, 209n93; as reform disincentive, 50–51; states advantaged by, 162, 172, 254n5; states without, 43

Wirt, William, 122

Wisconsin, 35, 88, 119, 154–55, 159, 166, 239n98

Witcover, Jules, 201–2n63

"wrong winner" problem, 3, 48–49, 52, 102, 211n12, 232n38

Wyoming, 256n21

Yoo, Professor, 246n70

Young, Ernest A., 252n58

Youngstown Sheet & Tube Co. v. Sawyer (1952), 234n53